IMAGES
of America

ROCKDALE

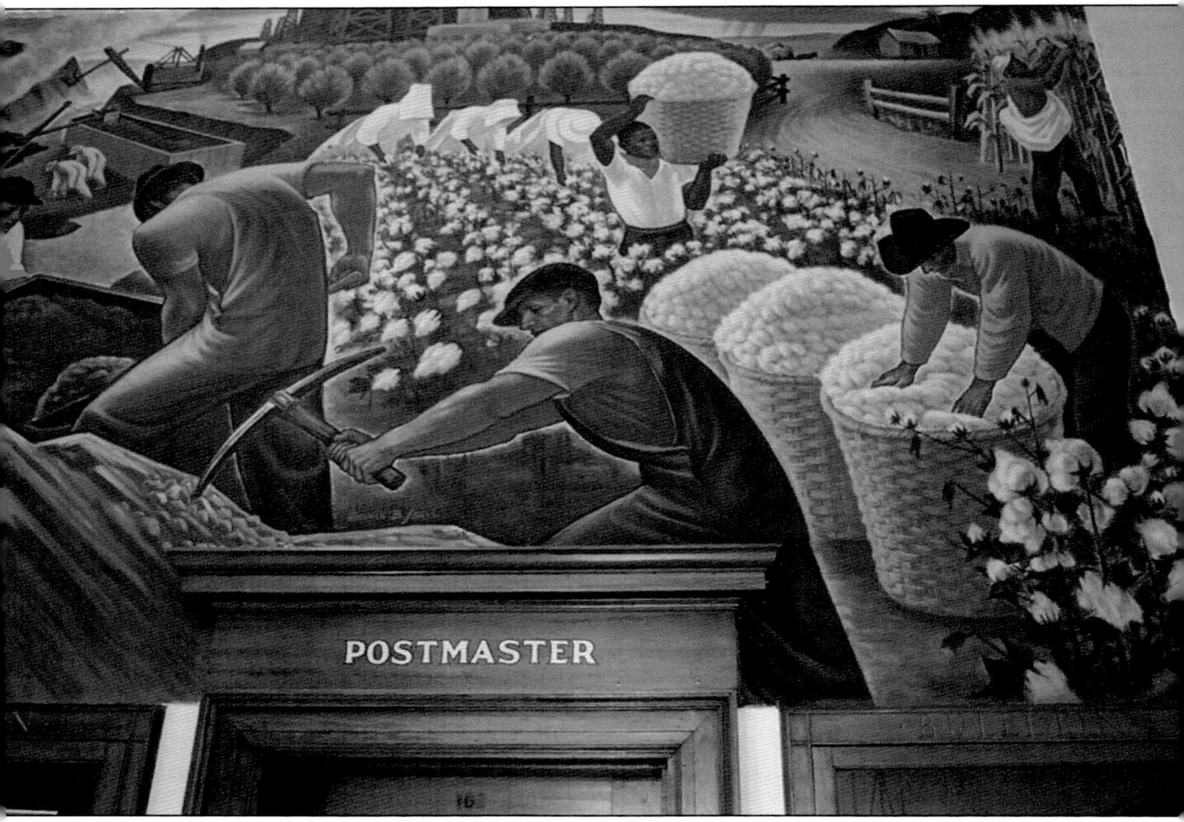

Soon after the Rockdale Post Office was built in 1939, well-known artist Maxwell B. Starr painted this mural reflecting activities in the county. The painting depicts cotton picking, corn harvesting, lignite mining, orchards, and oil wells. The mural is still there today and still reflective of the energy that is so much a part of the Rockdale scene. The only thing missing from the mural is the enthusiasm for history its present-day citizens possess. (Photograph courtesy of the author.)

On the Cover: Rockdale native Dr. Wesley Bert Henry made this photograph of his uncle Buck Henry's garage. Dr. Henry and his wife now reside in Richardson, Texas. (Photograph courtesy of Bert Henry.)

IMAGES
of America

ROCKDALE

Dr. Lucile Estell

ARCADIA
PUBLISHING

ISBN 978-0-7385-8506-2

Published by Arcadia Publishing
Charleston, South Carolina

Printed in the United States of America

Library of Congress Control Number: 2012932566

For all general information, please contact Arcadia Publishing:
Telephone 843-853-2070
Fax 843-853-0044
E-mail sales@arcadiapublishing.com
For customer service and orders:
Toll-Free 1-888-313-2665

Visit us on the Internet at www.arcadiapublishing.com

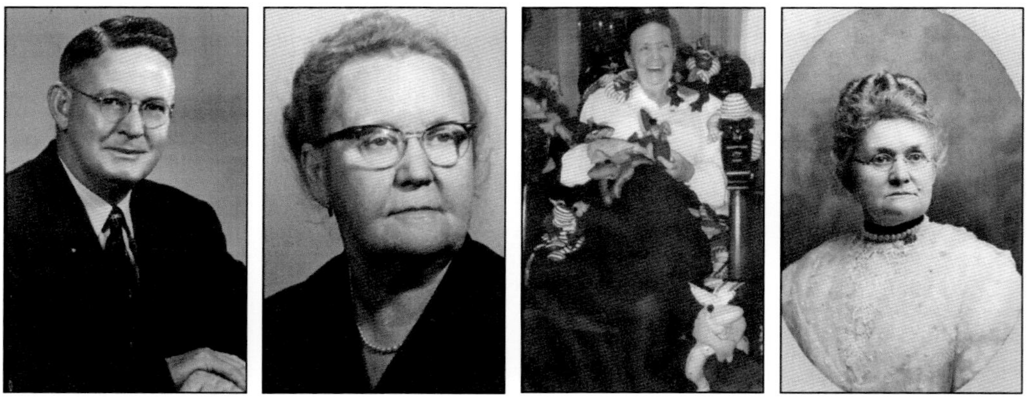

This book is dedicated to my family, from left to right, Hugh Estell and Lucile Poole Estell, Mary Elizabeth "Betty" Estell Harris, and most of all, my Granny, Dora Orr Poole, who gave to me the priceless gift of the love of history.

Contents

Acknowledgments		6
Introduction		7
1.	First, There Was the Land	9
2.	Then Came the People	17
3.	The Railroad Births a Town	25
4.	Black Gold from Beneath the Earth	41
5.	Rockdale Grows and Grows	51
6.	George Sessions Perry	63
7.	School Bells Ring	71
8.	And the Church Bells Chime	79
9.	Ramblin' 'Round Rockdale	87
Bibliography		127

ACKNOWLEDGMENTS

Locating original photographs of Rockdale is an awesome task. There is no one repository for these, so one must seek and search. Some photographs are filed safely away by the Milam County Historical Museum located in Cameron. Curator Charles King helped with finding and scanning these. Dr. Bert Henry, a Rockdale native now living in Richardson, Texas, provided many photographs, including the one used on the cover. His cousins David Henry of Mineral Wells and Ann Henry of Austin also provided priceless photographs. Patricia Vogel McKee generously shared her photographs related to the Vogel Mines, which were a large part of Rockdale history. Train enthusiast Bert Dockall shared many of his photographs related to trains. Historian and master craftsman Gary Jackson shared many photographs, as did local historian Robert Edwards. Dr. Joseph Loewenstein provided valuable photographs of his family's early business endeavors in Rockdale. Local historian and lifelong Rockdale resident Joy Graham shared photographs and other information about this little town we love so well. Other longtime residents, including Tommy Coffield and Eugenia Newton and sisters Doris Seelig and Ruth Storey provided photographs. Rockdale native Charles Robison shared some of his collection of Rockdale photographs. And, last but not least, Peggy and Bill Cooke, publishers emeritus of our wonderful *Rockdale Reporter*, provided photographs and assistance in many ways. Many of the photographs were scanned by an employee of the *Rockdale Reporter*, Shannon Wharton.

Chapter six of this book was written by Dr. Garna Christian, a professor at the University of Houston–Downtown. He is also the author of a book about the life of George Sessions Perry.

INTRODUCTION

In *Milam County: Birthplace of a Region*, author Marion Travis writes, "No place like the original Milam County and Land District, once pristine and beautiful will ever appear again." Looking from a vantage point more than 100 years down the road, this statement appears to be true. This is the story of Milam County and one of its communities, Rockdale. First, there was the land, rich and varied, breathtaking in its beauty and in its great expanses of forests and fertile soil. And then came the people. They came with valor and courage, bringing to the new land a stability previously present. First, there were the Native Americans, some 25 or 30 tribes of them, making their homes and working out an existence on this fertile land. They were joined by Europeans, primarily French and Spanish, looking for a land with cities of gold. Then came those seeking a new land on which to own property and begin a new life. Among the many important things that they brought with them were their memories and their dreams, the two of which combined to transform the pristine land into communities of homes and families. One such community is Rockdale, near where Highway 79 and Highway 77 intersect on a sprawling Texas prairie.

Rockdale was established as a railroad town in 1874. The International & Great Northern Railroad was forging southward in an effort to accommodate travelers anxious to leave behind the destruction brought on by the great war that divided this nation. The railroad donated the land for a cemetery and helped in other ways to establish the town. People were drawn to Rockdale and the land around it. Many of the early settlers who came had an agrarian background. Ethnic origins were varied, but a large number of them were German, Czech, or Wendish. Evidence of that influence still exists today, seen in the wonderfully maintained farms and ranches in the area around Rockdale.

Rockdale and the surrounding communities sit atop one of the largest deposits of lignite in the world. In the late 1800s and early 1900s, mining took on an important role in the area. This role grew in 1954, when the Aluminum Company of America (Alcoa) came to Milam County and located six miles from Rockdale. The plant operated at this site until 2008, and the footprint left by the industry will be forever present.

The future of Rockdale is impacted by several changes, especially the closing of the Alcoa operation and the decline of farming and ranching. Another important impact on the future began in 2004 when the El Camino Real de los Tejas National Historic Trail was authorized by the US government. The trail crosses Milam County and thus focuses attention on sites of high potential interest in the area. Development of the trail is almost certain to affect the economy of Rockdale and the entire county.

It is the intent of this book to tell the story of Rockdale and its people, and in doing so, pay tribute to those who made Rockdale the delightful place to live that it is today. Many things have changed, but there is a strong sense of place here. Many basic values abandoned in other parts of our nation are still present here. The American flag still commands respect, and most people go to church on Sunday. People are still interested in their neighbors, sitting on front porches, and bringing in covered dishes when there is death or illness in the family. As the old slogan says, Rockdale continues to be "Regal Rockdale in Matchless Milam County" to those who love it.

For the past 137 years, the lovely little town of Rockdale has stood as a symbol of strength and ingenuity, a gem gracing the Texas landscape with strength and integrity. Its geographic history goes back much further, as archeologists assure us that the land has been inhabited for more than 10,000 years. My own family goes back only four generations in Rockdale, having relocated here from Mississippi after the Civil War. We have been here in the good times and the bad. As we review history here, we see the threads on hard work, honesty, and integrity running through it. Even in hard times, we see promising signs for the future as the El Camino Real de los Tejas emerges and shares with us all the glorious heritage which made it a nationally recognized trail.

I wrote this book in order to record for the seventh generation of our family and others like them the heritage that is theirs. As a teacher, I am charged, along with many others, with preserving this heritage because this is who we are, this is what we believe, and it is a key to our survival as a nation.

It is my fervent wish that this history does justice to those who lived it. Unfortunately, our photographs of Rockdale are not well-preserved, nor are they readily available from all sources. I hope that this opens our eyes to that fact and that we remedy it.

I love Rockdale, Texas, and I hope that this publication will strengthen it and make it a better place to live.

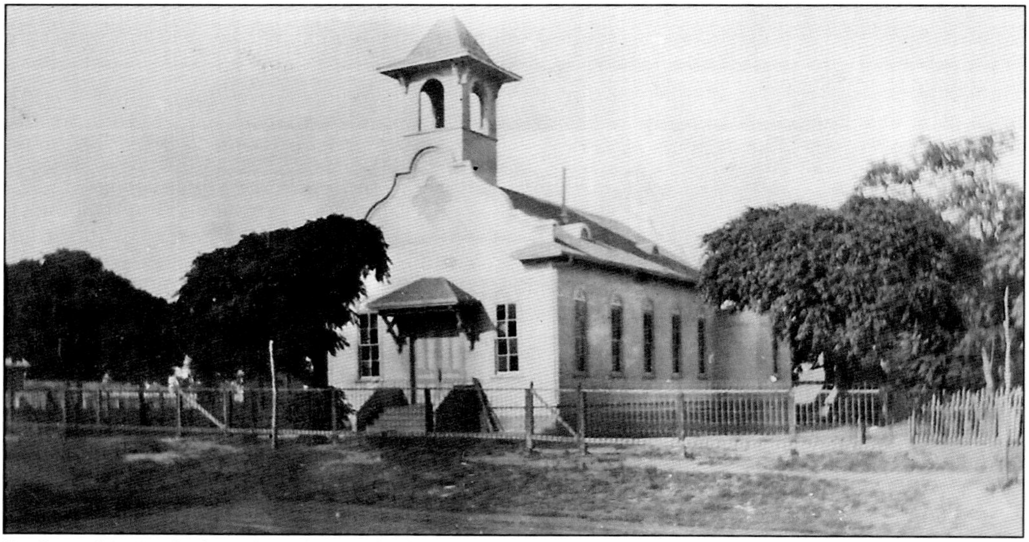

St. Joseph's Catholic Church was built in 1912. After it was no longer in use by the Catholic Church, it was used for a time as a Pentecostal church. Next, it belonged to several different parties who purchased it to use as a church or perhaps as an investment. At one point during that time, it was called Love Tabernacle, a name still used by many today. It is now the property of Joan and Dan Ratliff, owners of Rainbow Courts. Plans are to restore it and make it an integral part of the lovely historic Rainbow Courts, for use in weddings and on other special occasions. In 1995, it was listed by the Texas Historical Commission as one of the Ten Most Endangered Sites in Texas. Its historical significance was recognized by the Texas Legislature in a resolution sponsored by the late Dan Kubiak, a resident of Rockdale. (Photograph courtesy of Joan and Dan Ratliff.)

One

First, There Was the Land

Rockdale is located very near the center of Milam County. The present county covers 1,019 square miles, but Milam County was formerly a much larger tract of land, extending northward and comprising approximately one-sixth of the land area of Texas. Robert Leftwich first received a grant from the Mexican government, permitting him to bring colonists to the area. Leadership of the effort to colonize was given to Sterling Clack Robertson in 1827, but the contract was suspended in 1830 because he had made no progress toward colonization. The contract then went to Stephen F. Austin and Samuel May Williams, but again little progress was made toward colonization, and the contract went back to Robertson. Actual settlement began in what was then the municipality of Viesca, later changed to the municipality of Milam. The area was renamed Milam County in honor of Benjamin Rush Milam in 1835. As settlement progressed, 15 counties were carved from the original grant, and in 1835, the boundaries still observed today were set.

Milam County, from which Rockdale emerged as a city in 1874, was a land of fertile soils and abundant water. The southern and eastern portions of the county are in the post oak savannah region and the northern and western region lie in the blackland prairie. The Brazos, San Gabriel, and Little Rivers are the major rivers through the county. Humans have inhabited this area for at least 10,000 years because of the fertile land and ample water. These resources attracted settlers, not only to labor on the railroad, but also to work in agricultural pursuits and mining.

Rockdale was officially founded in 1874, but settlers moved into the area in 1873. By January 1874, the terminus of the International & Great Northern Railroad was established in Rockdale. It was a bustling frontier town, described thusly in the *Galveston News* on February 9, 1874:

> "It is in the heart of one of the best agricultural districts in Texas. The town already contains twenty to thirty houses, and is rapidly growing. Being the present terminus of this immense road, situated in a most healthy and convenient locality . . . what is to prevent Rockdale from becoming one of the most important points in the interior? Rockdale is destined to become the great shipping point for Texas stock."

The railroad purchased 400 acres of land from the William Allen Survey, a town of 35 blocks was laid out, and the stage was set. The history of Rockdale had begun.

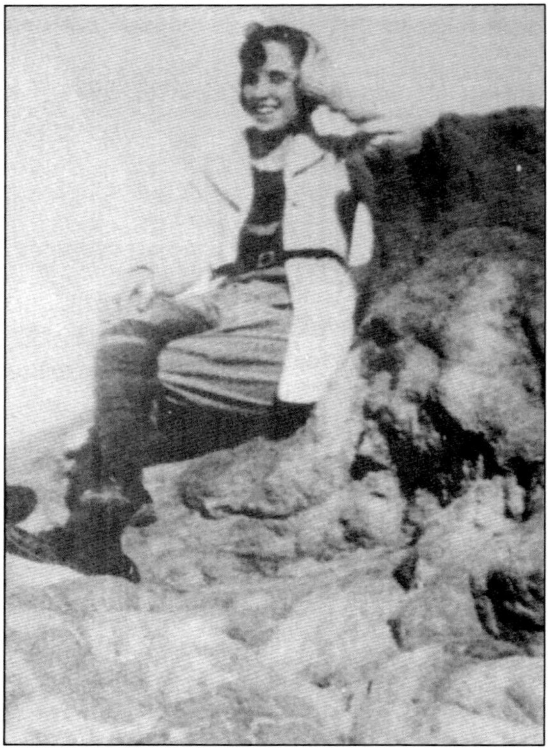

On February 4, 1874, the first passenger train left Hearne headed for the newly created town of Rockdale. It was on this day that the town was named by Mrs. B.F. Ackerman, whose husband had sold much of the land for Rockdale. The railroad had requested that Ackerman name the town. As Mr. and Mrs. Ackerman rode through the countryside, she noticed a large rock on a sandy prairie just north of town. This brought to her the idea of Rockdale as the name of the new town, and Rockdale it became. (Photograph courtesy of *Rockdale Reporter*.)

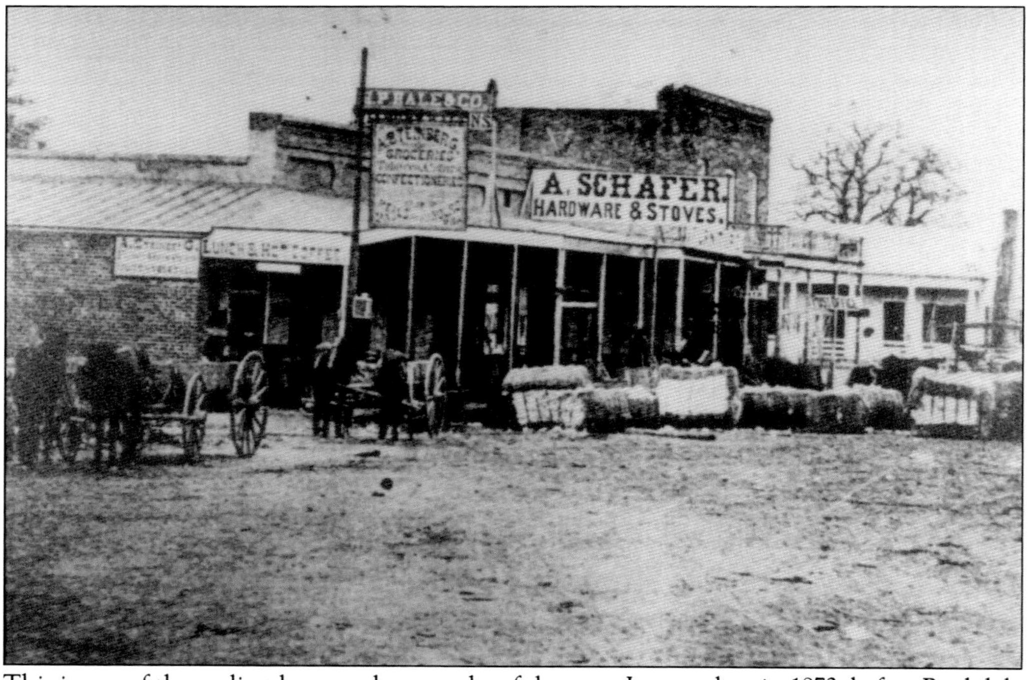

This is one of the earliest known photographs of the area. It was taken in 1873, before Rockdale was officially a town. Many people had already arrived, ready to cast their fortunes with the emerging community. (Photograph courtesy of Milam County Historical Museum.)

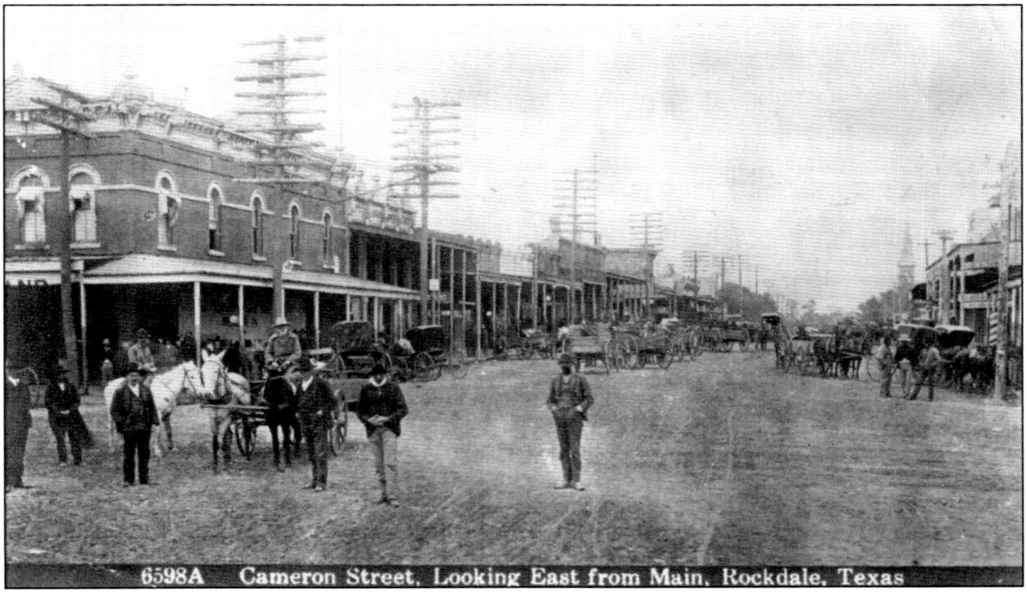

A large amount of horse and wagon traffic clogs up Cameron Avenue in 1908. (Photograph courtesy of *Rockdale Reporter*.)

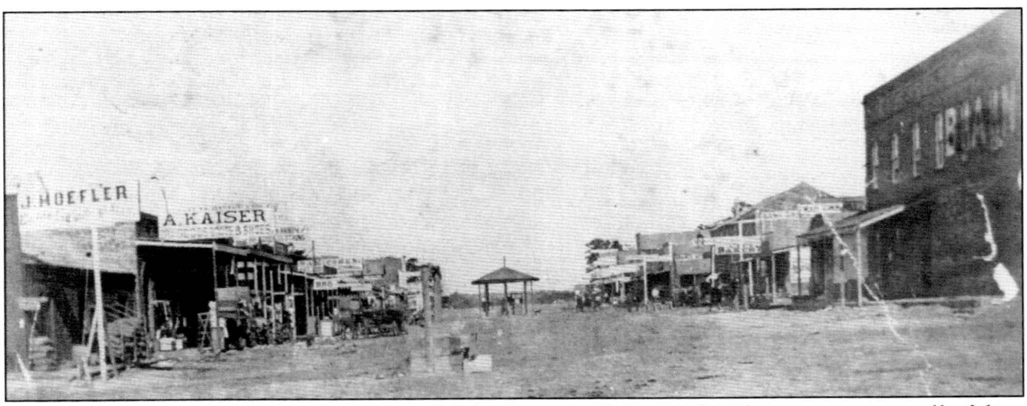

By the early 1920s, the young city of Rockdale showed solid growth. The streets were still of dirt, but there was a horse-drawn watering truck to keep things more pleasant. The intersection also sported a drinking fountain. (Photograph courtesy of *Rockdale Reporter*.)

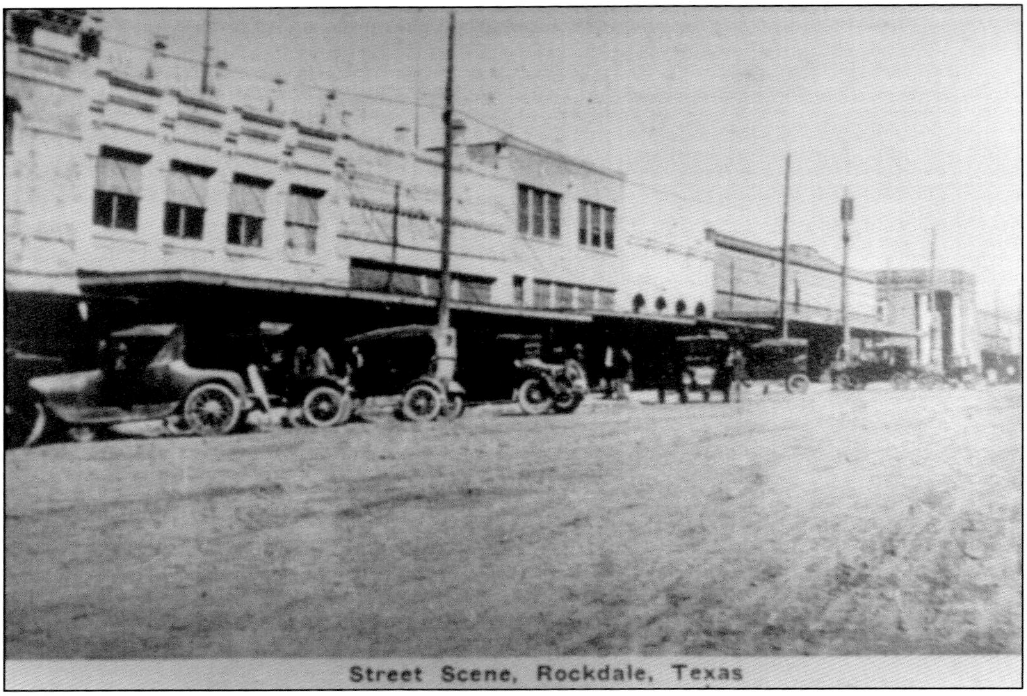

The automobile had arrived in Rockdale by the time this photograph was taken. The First State Bank is on the right. (Photograph courtesy of Milam County Historical Museum.)

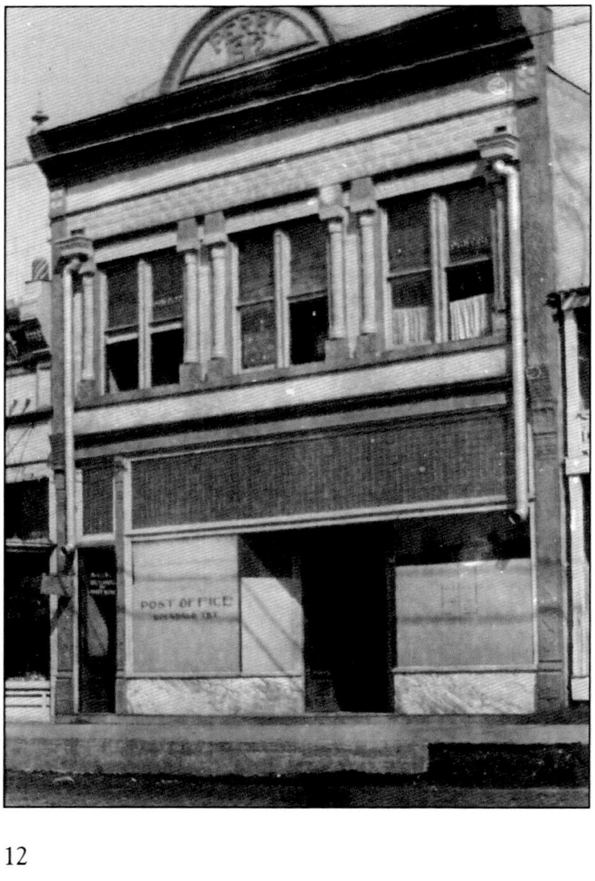

The Perry Building, on Cameron Street, served a number of other purposes until it burned to the ground. At this time, it was home to the Rockdale Post Office. (Photograph courtesy of Gary Jackson.)

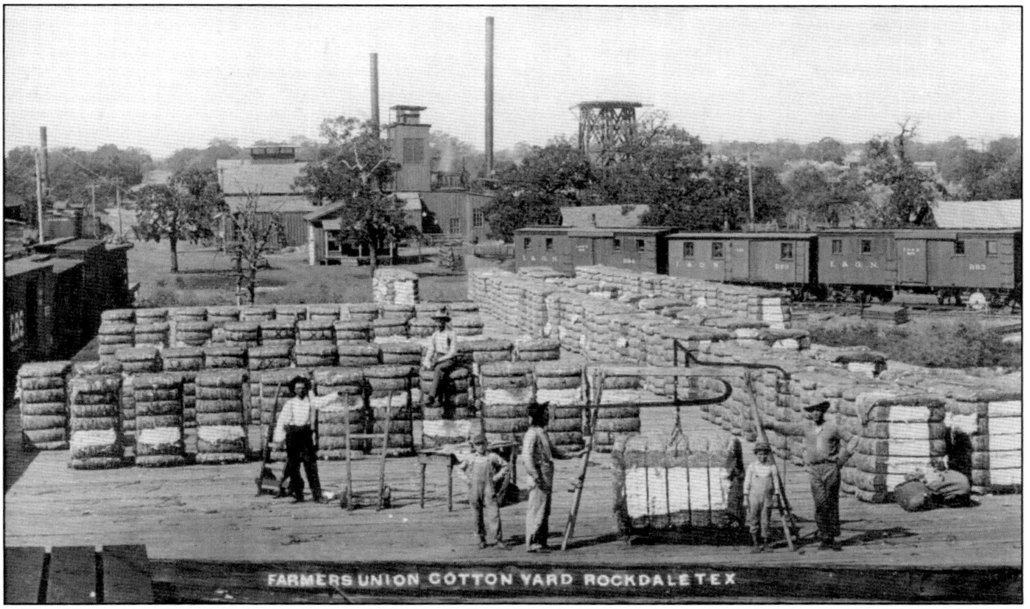

The busy Farmers Union Cotton Yard shows the importance of cotton to Rockdale's early citizens. (Photograph courtesy of *Rockdale Reporter*.)

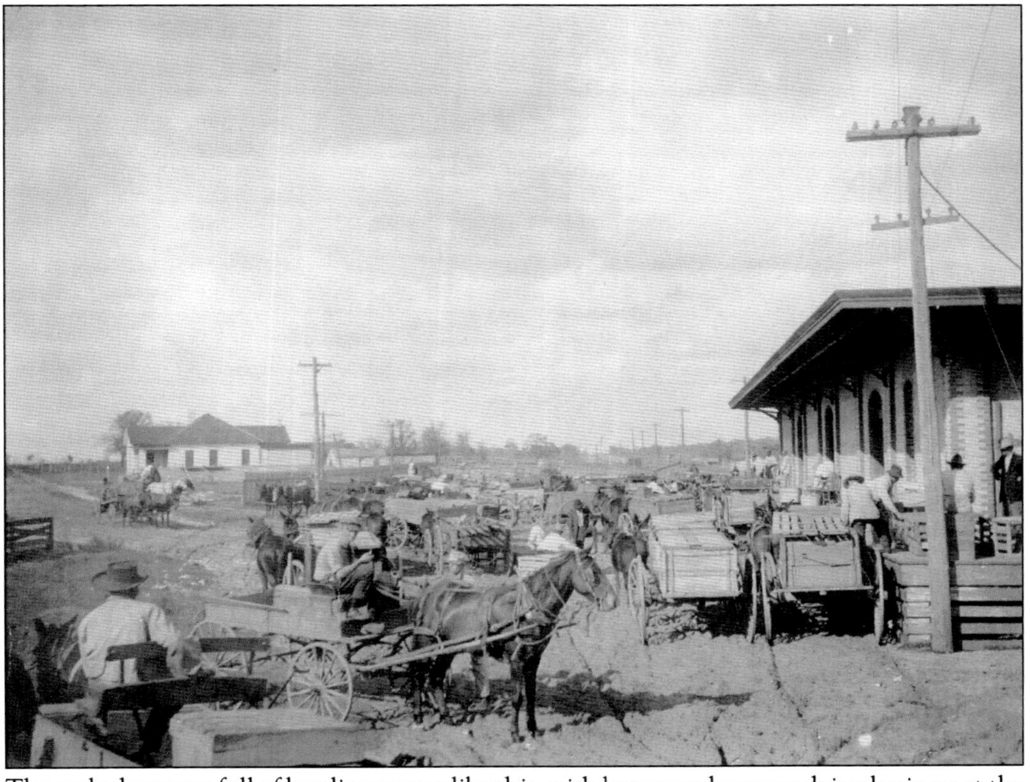

The early days were full of bustling scenes like this, with horses and wagons doing business at the San Antonio and Aransas Pass Railway depot. (Photograph courtesy of *Rockdale Reporter*.)

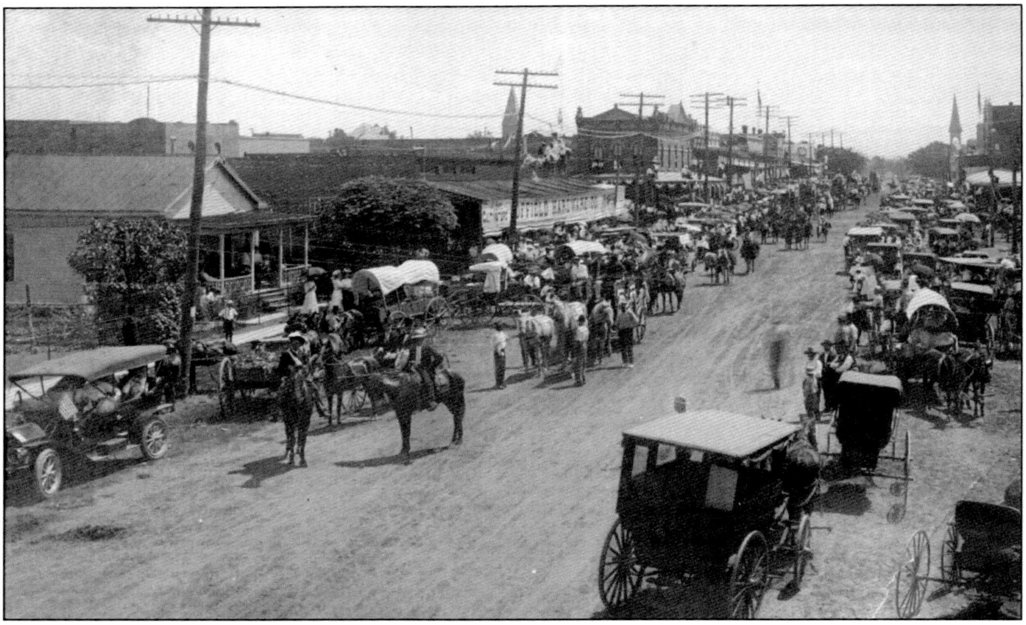

The citizens of Rockdale prepare for a parade, most likely the 1908 Rockdale Fair. Note the large number of people and horses lining this wide street. (Photograph courtesy of *Rockdale Reporter.*)

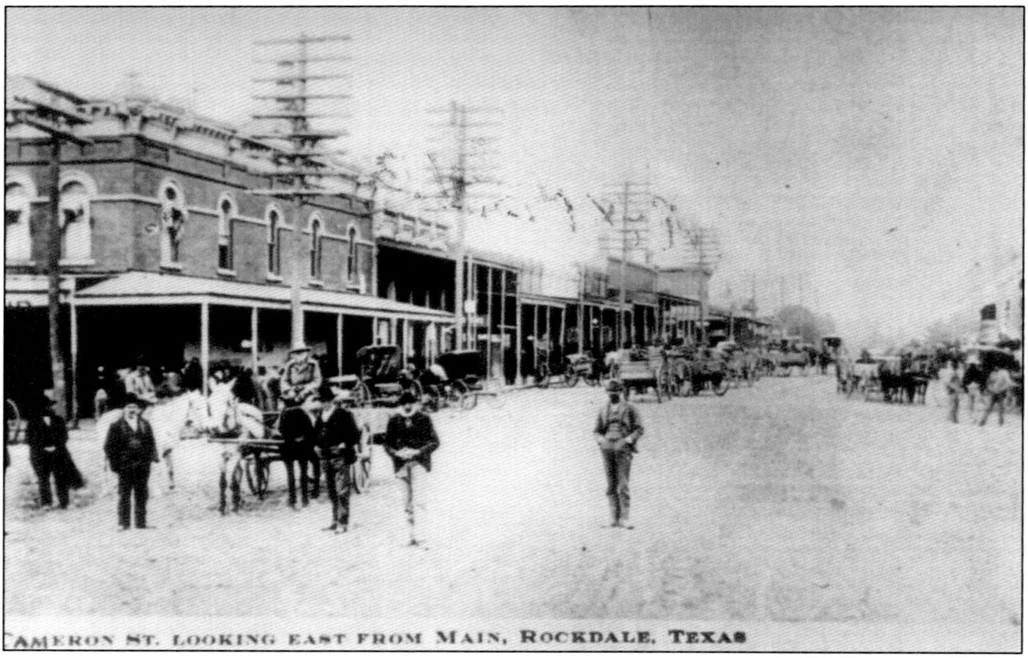

The corner of Cameron and Main Streets were the center of everything in the early days. (Photograph courtesy of Milam County Historical Museum.)

In 1880, John Mundine of Lexington built a three-story building across the street from the International & Great Northern Passenger depot. The hotel opened in 1881 under the supervision of Dr. and Mrs. W.A. Brooks. It was destroyed by fire on June 8, 1888, and 12 people lost their lives. (Photograph courtesy of *Rockdale Reporter.*)

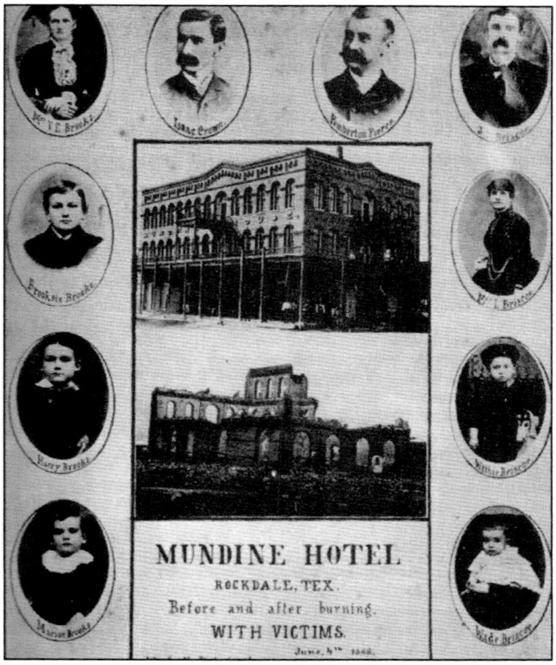

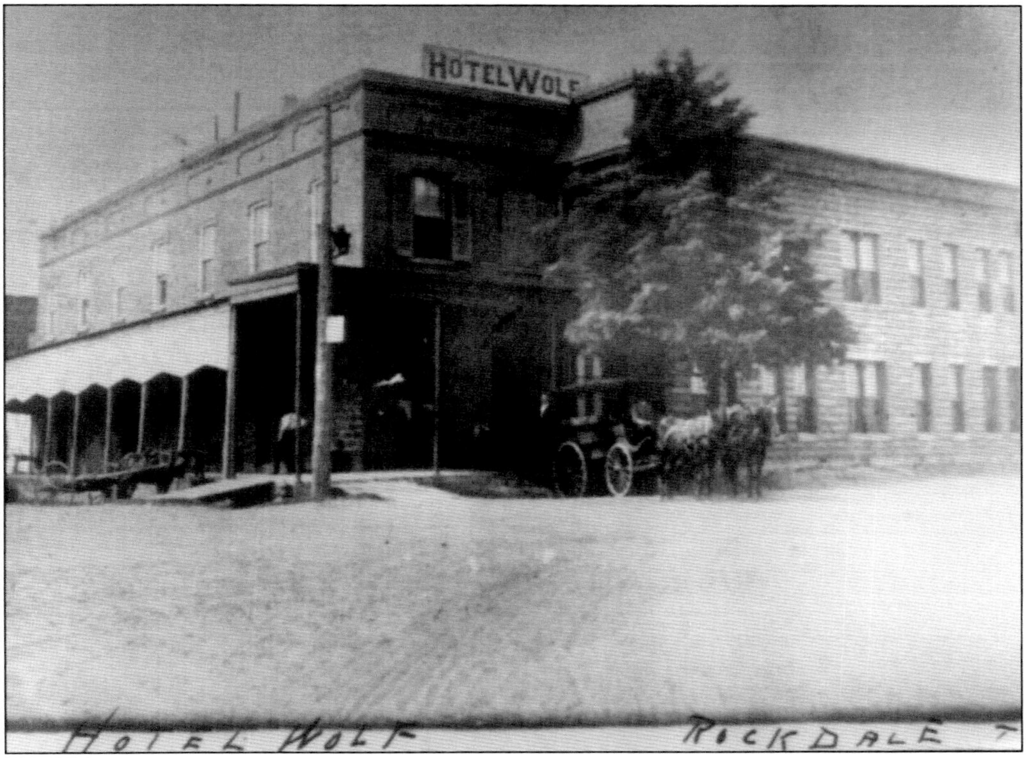

The Wolf Hotel was located at the corner of Main and Milam Streets, directly across the street from the Mundine Hotel. Before becoming a hotel, the building housed a bank. It is now the site of Wolf Park. (Photograph courtesy of Milam County Historical Museum.)

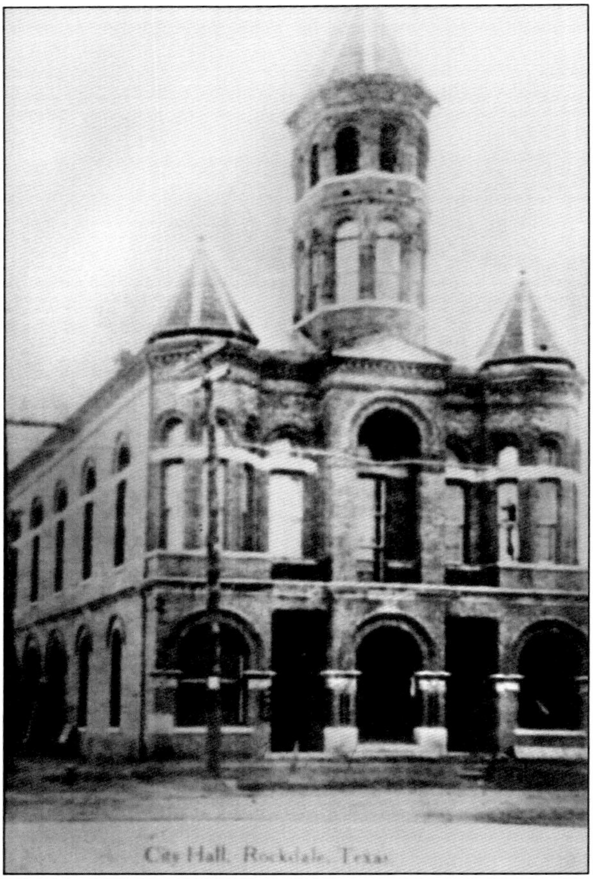

According to its cornerstone, Rockdale City Hall was completed in 1895. However, a Sanborn map dated 1896 indicates that the inside was still incomplete. The top portion of this structure has been removed, and the building now houses the Rockdale Police Department. (Photograph courtesy of Milam County Historical Museum.)

This early photograph of Fair Park shows the interior of the racetrack. Note the pond in the background. (Photograph courtesy of *Rockdale Reporter.*)

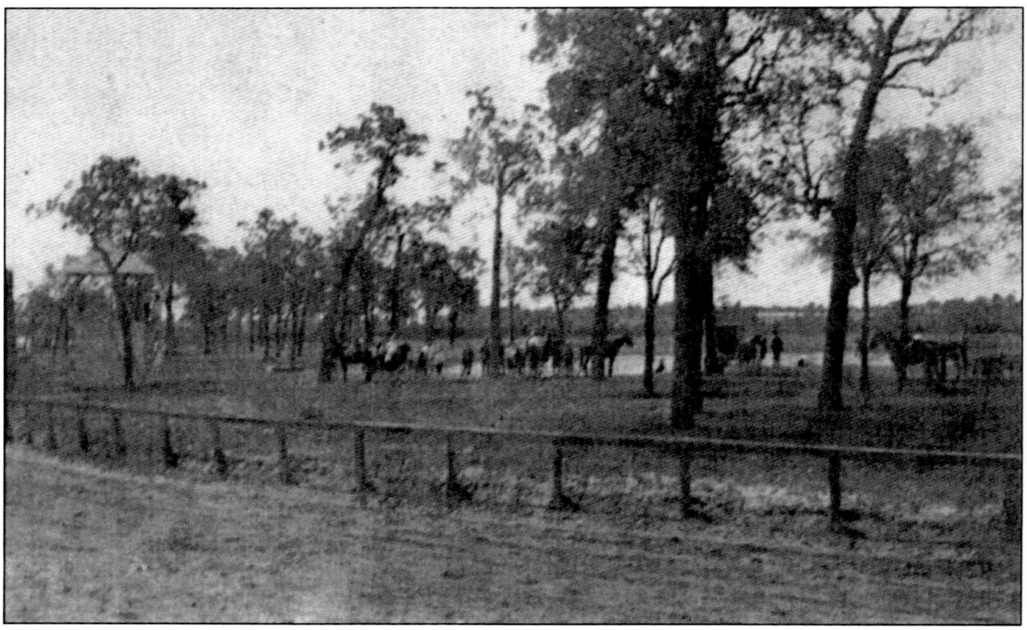

Two

Then Came the People

The land on which Rockdale now lies shows evidence of human habitation for at least 10,000 years. Through the years, people were drawn to Rockdale because of its fertile soil and ample supply of water. They were attracted by the railroad with its promise of thriving industry and by what they called black gold, the lignite beneath the earth. Others sought to rebuild their lives after the Civil War and took the opportunity to take advantage of the many resources here.

A number of people had already settled in Milam County before Rockdale was established. Many of these were Czechs and Germans who had come, many of them directly from Europe, to take advantage of the fertile land and pleasant climate. The landscape today features perfectly manicured farms and ranches, many of which are still in the family of their first inhabitants. Rockdale was incorporated in 1878. By 1884, there were 1,700 residents. The town was developing, with five churches, two schools, two steam gristmill cotton gins, a 250-seat opera house, a private bank, and a weekly newspaper.

On December 23, 1873, Benjamin and Joseph Loewenstein, originally from Prussia, opened B. Loewenstein and Bros. Their initial inventory was valued at about $300. It had been brought to the new town by an ox team.

As newcomers arrived in 1873, they were greeted by a photographer, John Scott, who had a tent studio to welcome them. Solon Joynes weighed and shipped the first bale of cotton in 1874. Hale and Company, of Hearne, established a mercantile business with E.M. Scarborough as a clerk, which became Scarborough and Hicks. Isaac Jaolonick, representing Snow and Wilmerding, of Galveston, opened the Rockdale Bank, the first bank in the county.

In addition to the Czechs and Germans who had settled in Milam County, there were a number of Jews. In 1880, the Jewish community established a burial ground, which is recognized by the Texas Historical Commission as a historic cemetery.

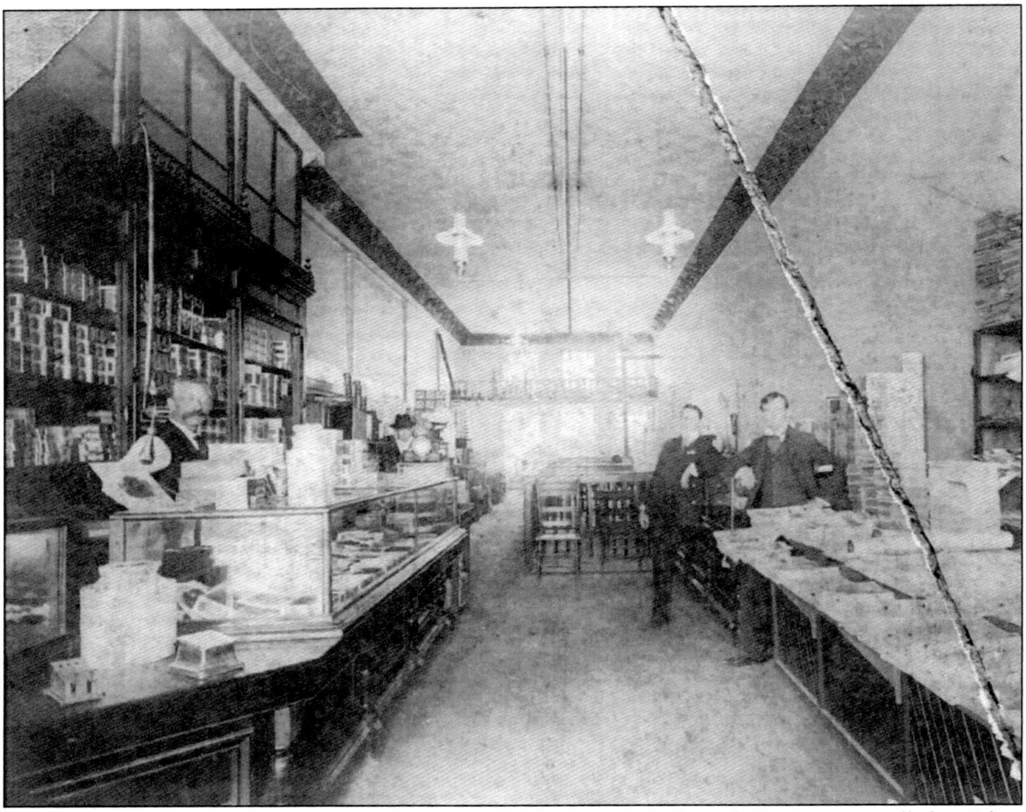

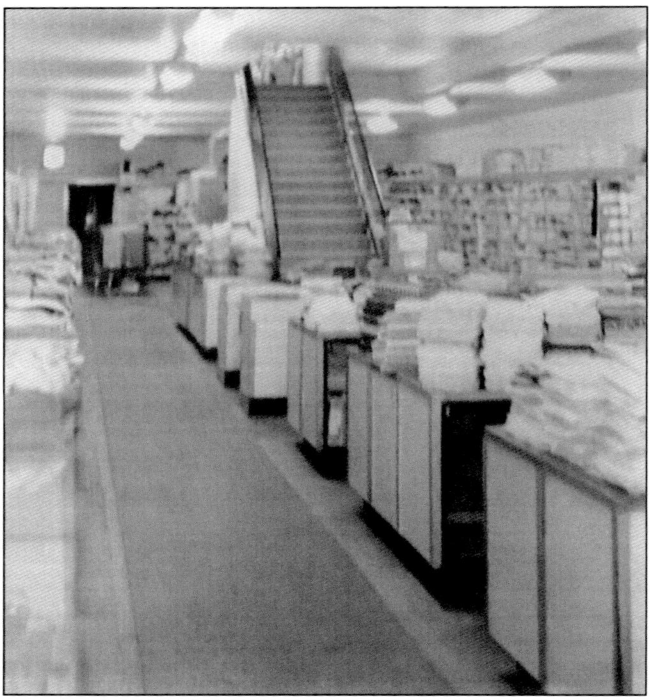

Joseph Loewenstein (left, with Prussian moustache) is seen inside the store he started with his brother, Benjamin, around 1895. The brothers arrived in Rockdale from Washington County, most likely from New Ulm, and founded the business on Christmas Eve 1873. (Photograph courtesy of Joseph Loewenstein, MD, Midland, Texas.)

Loewenstein's store is seen here in the 1930s, when the business was run by Lena Howse Loewenstein, the widow of Ben Loewenstein Jr. (Photograph courtesy of Joseph Loewenstein, MD, Midland, Texas.)

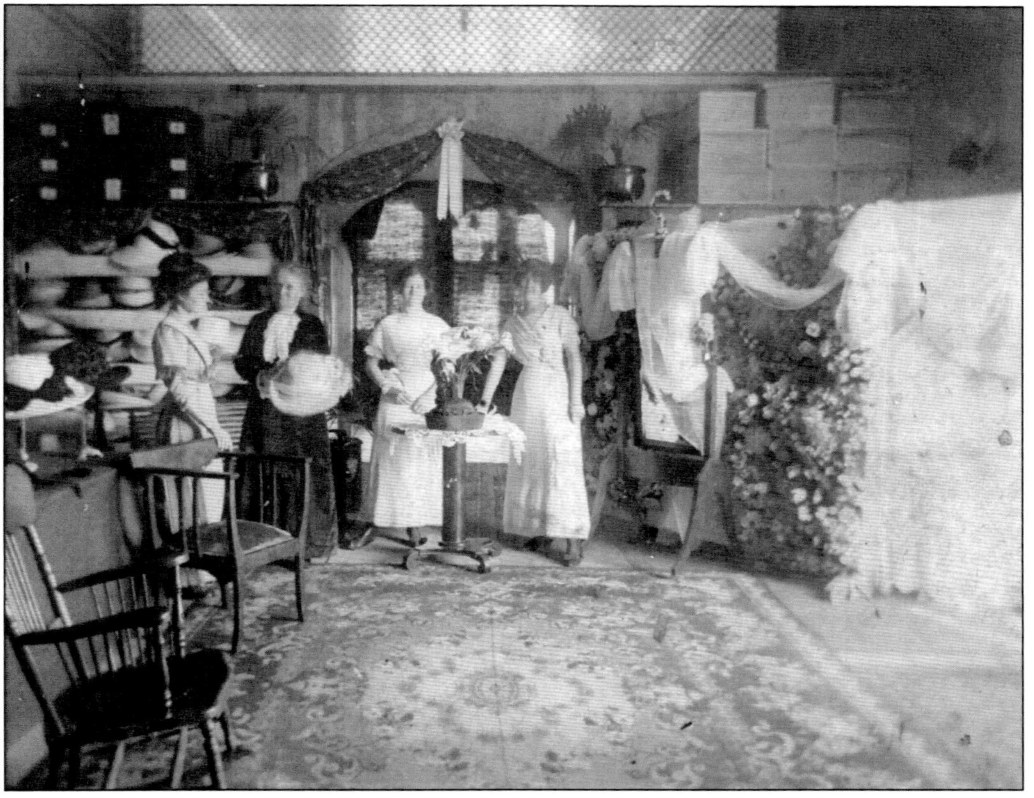

Dora Orr Poole (second from left) opened a millinery store in Rockdale in 1886. The business operated for 50 years before closing its doors in 1936. She also operated two other millinery stores, in Mumford and in Lott. (Photograph courtesy of the author.)

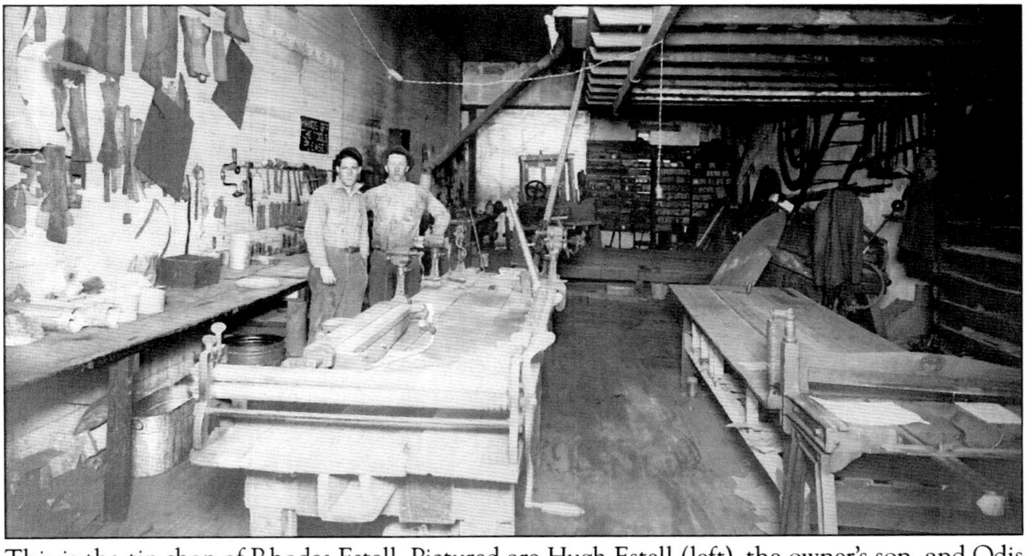

This is the tin shop of Rhodes Estell. Pictured are Hugh Estell (left), the owner's son, and Odis Muston, an employee. Among their most visible products were the cisterns used throughout the countryside. Most of these have now disappeared (Photograph courtesy of the author.)

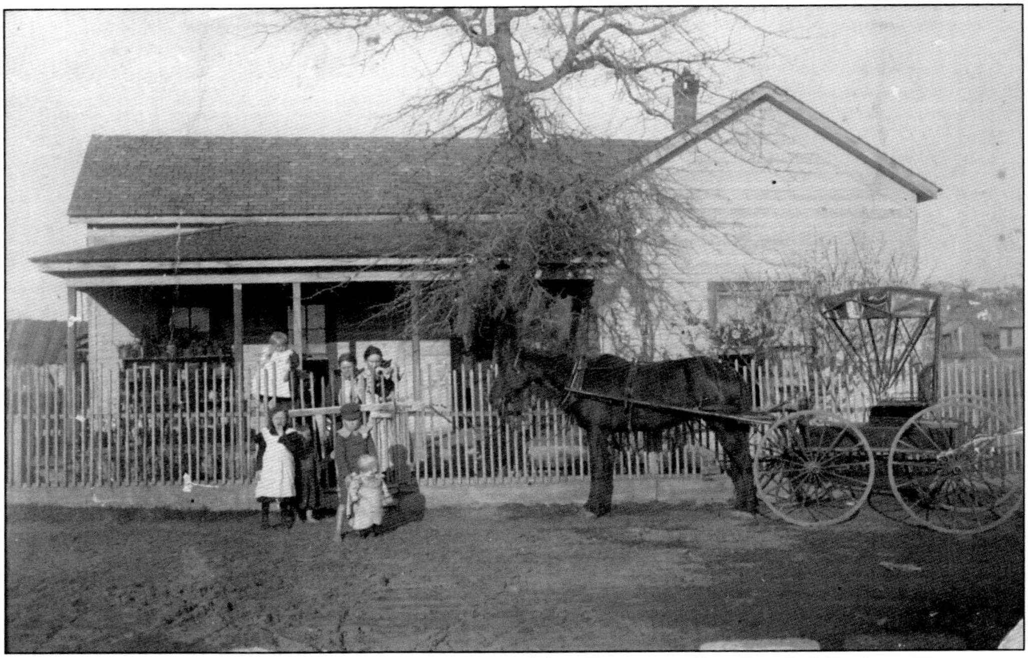

Valentine Barry Orr and Martha Jackson Mauldin Orr moved to Rockdale from Pontotoc, Mississippi, where Valentine had been a silversmith, in about 1890. Their family is shown here in front of their home at 622 North Scarborough Street. (Photograph courtesy of the author.)

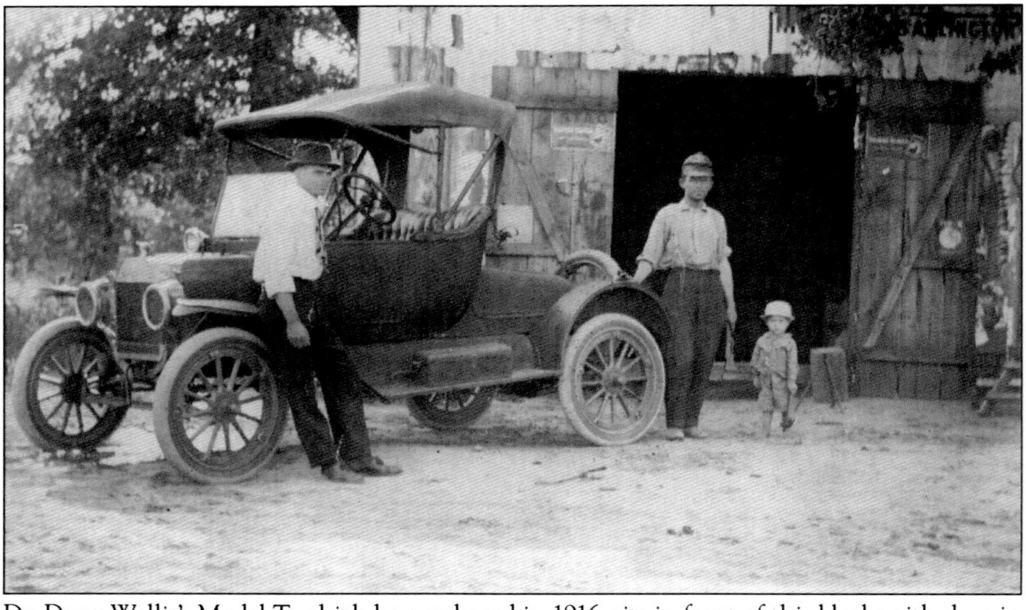

Dr. Dunc Wallis's Model T, which he purchased in 1916, sits in front of this blacksmith shop in Minerva. (Photograph courtesy of Robert Edwards.)

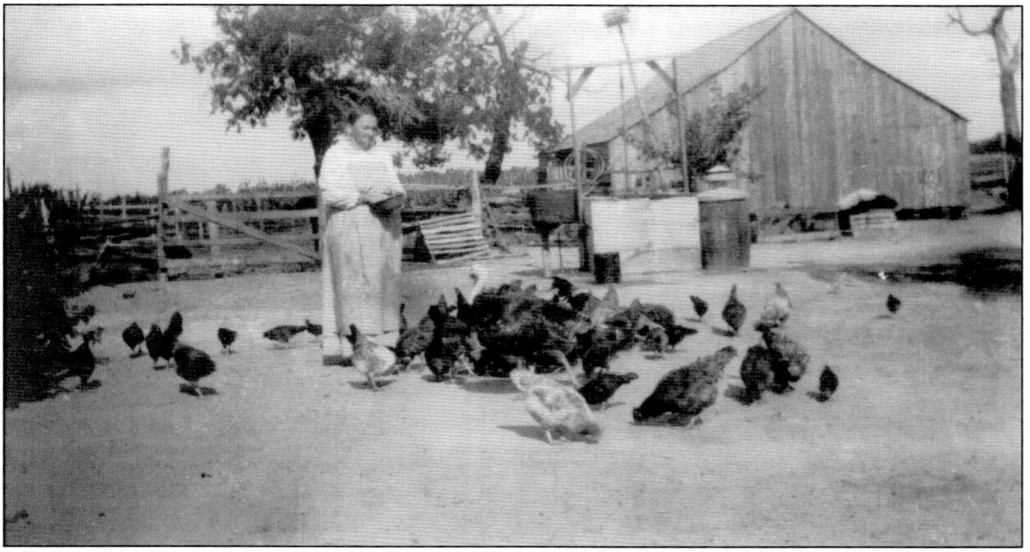

Emma Drecher, seen here feeding her chickens, lived in the Bushdale community. Parasols or umbrellas were often used to shield chickens and turkeys from the hot Texas sun. (Photograph courtesy of Robert Edwards.)

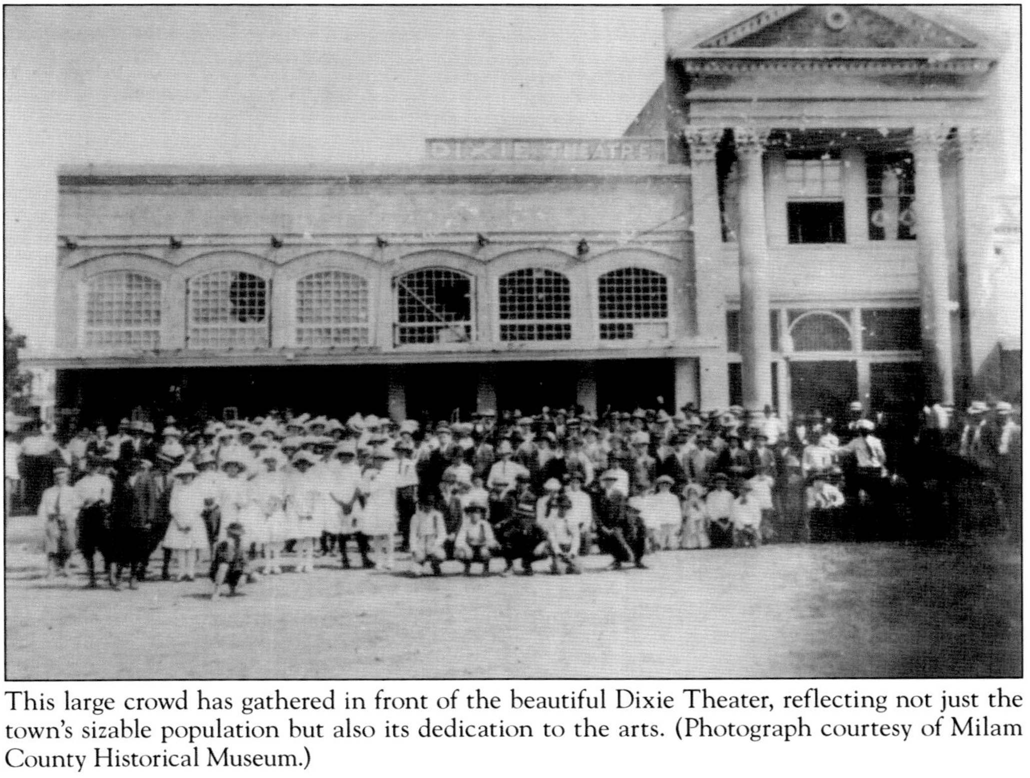

This large crowd has gathered in front of the beautiful Dixie Theater, reflecting not just the town's sizable population but also its dedication to the arts. (Photograph courtesy of Milam County Historical Museum.)

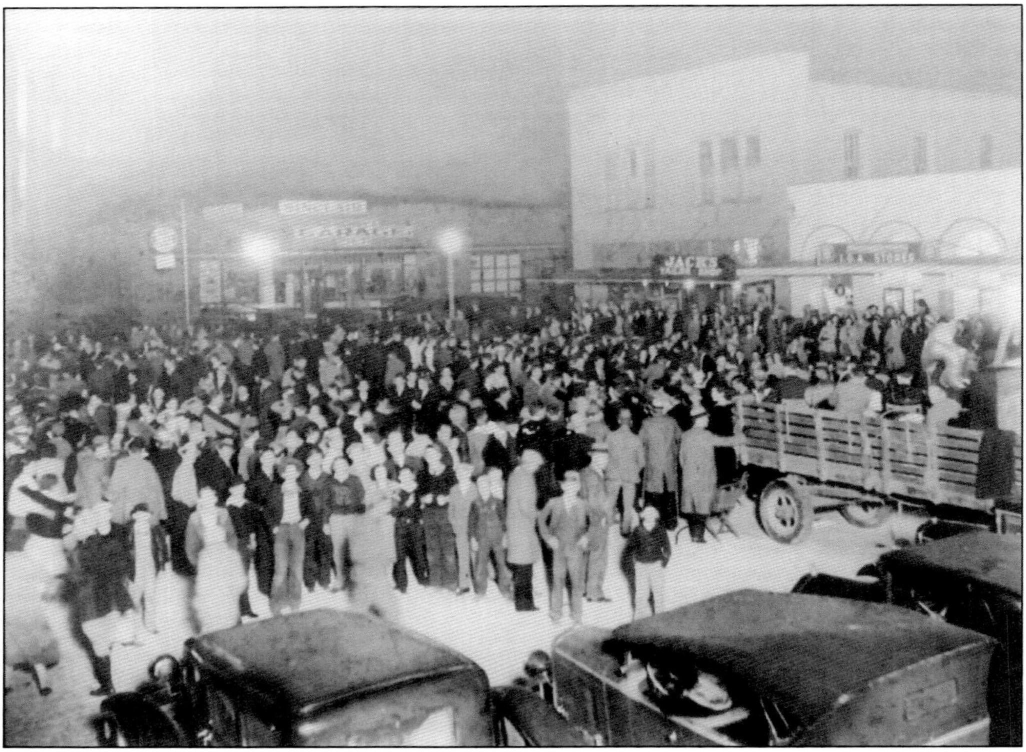

For many years, the name *Backhaus* was connected with the grocery business in Rockdale. When the three Backhaus brothers—John, Gus Jr., and Eddie—went into business together, they put on a huge celebration featuring a live band (upper right, in the truck bed). Coffee was 18¢ a pound and flour was 94¢ for a 48-pound bag. (Photograph courtesy of Ann Henry.)

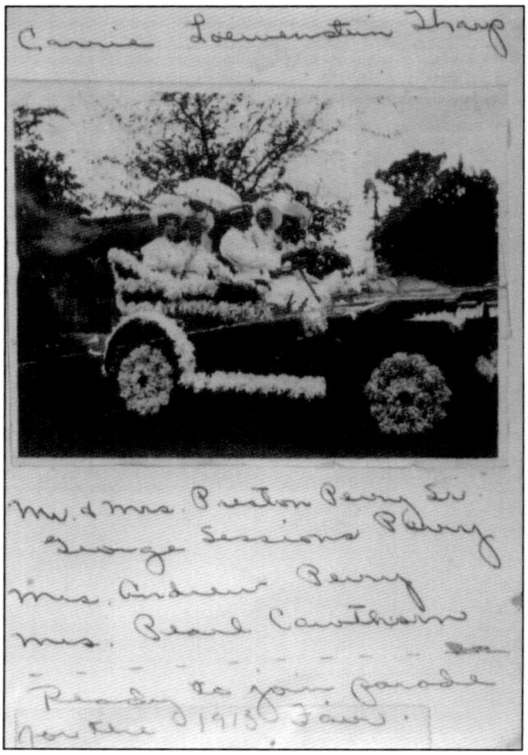

This early vehicle is all decked out for the 1915 fair parade. Riding in the car are Mr. and Mrs. Preston Perry Sr., George Sessions Perry, Mrs. Andrew Perry, Carrie Loewenstein Tharp, Miriam Loewenstein, and an unidentified woman. (Photograph courtesy of Milam County Historical Museum.)

Early citizens in the Pleasant Hill community included, from left to right, Mary Luella Simmons, Mary Ethel Simmons, and Enoch Simmons. (Photograph courtesy of Joy Graham.)

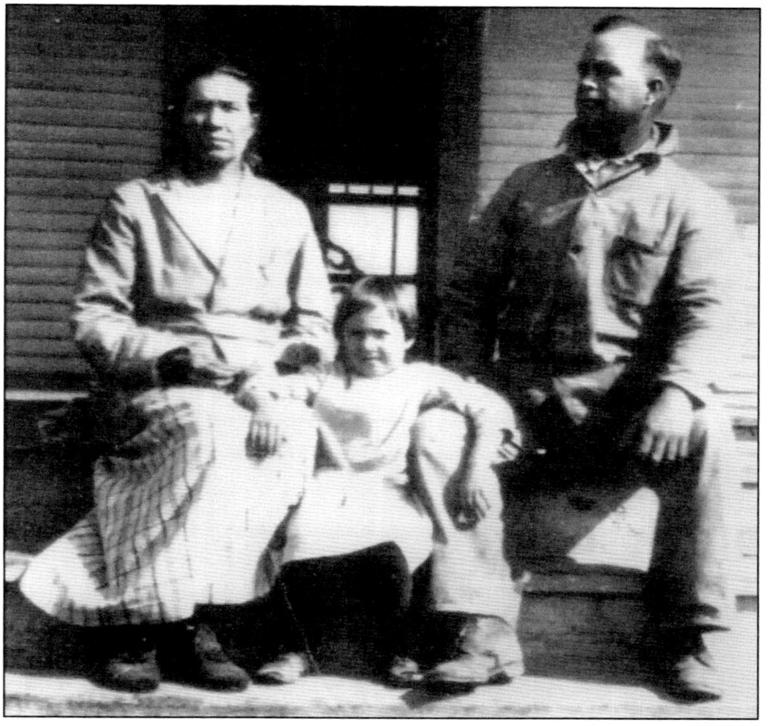

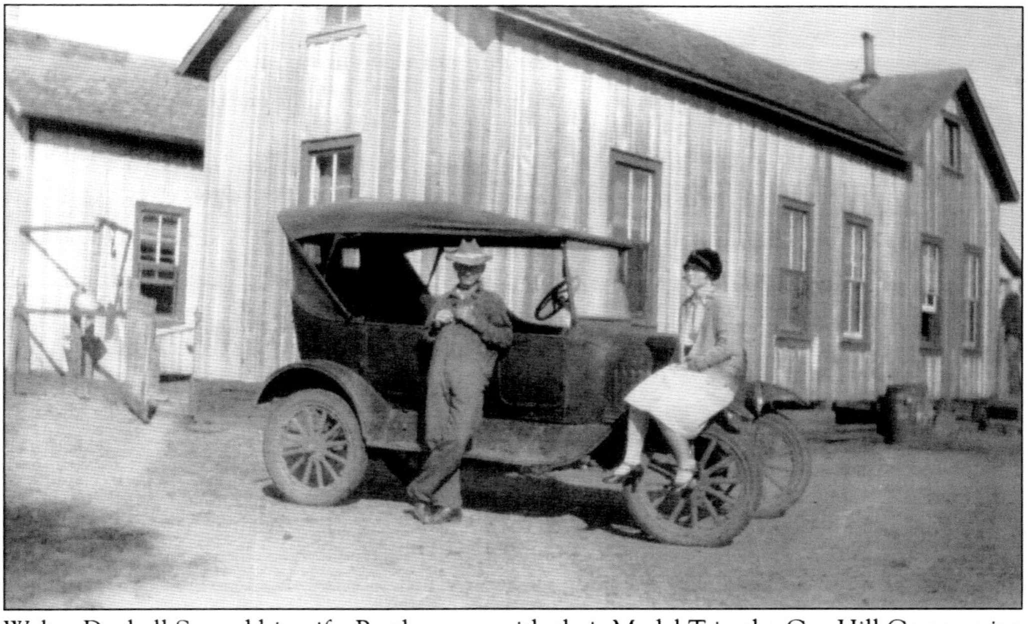

Walter Dockall Sr. and his wife, Bertha, pose with their Model T in the Gay Hill Community. (Photograph courtesy of Robert Edwards.)

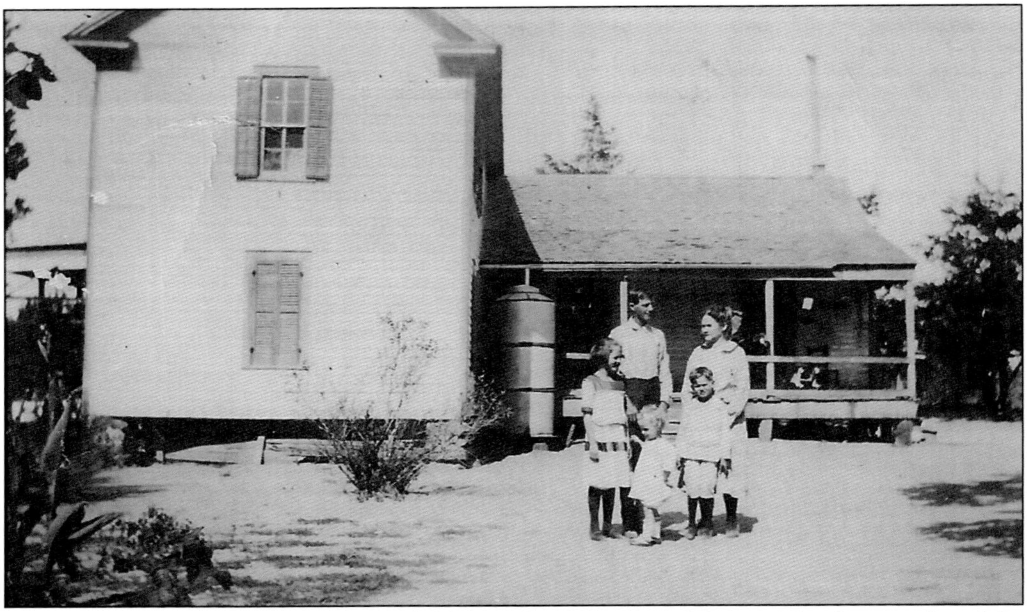

John and Ida Timmerman and their children, Alma, Harry, and Annie Mae, have gathered for this photograph at the Von Gonten home in Bushdale in 1921. Residents of Bushdale played an important role in the Rockdale's history. (Photograph courtesy of Joy Graham.)

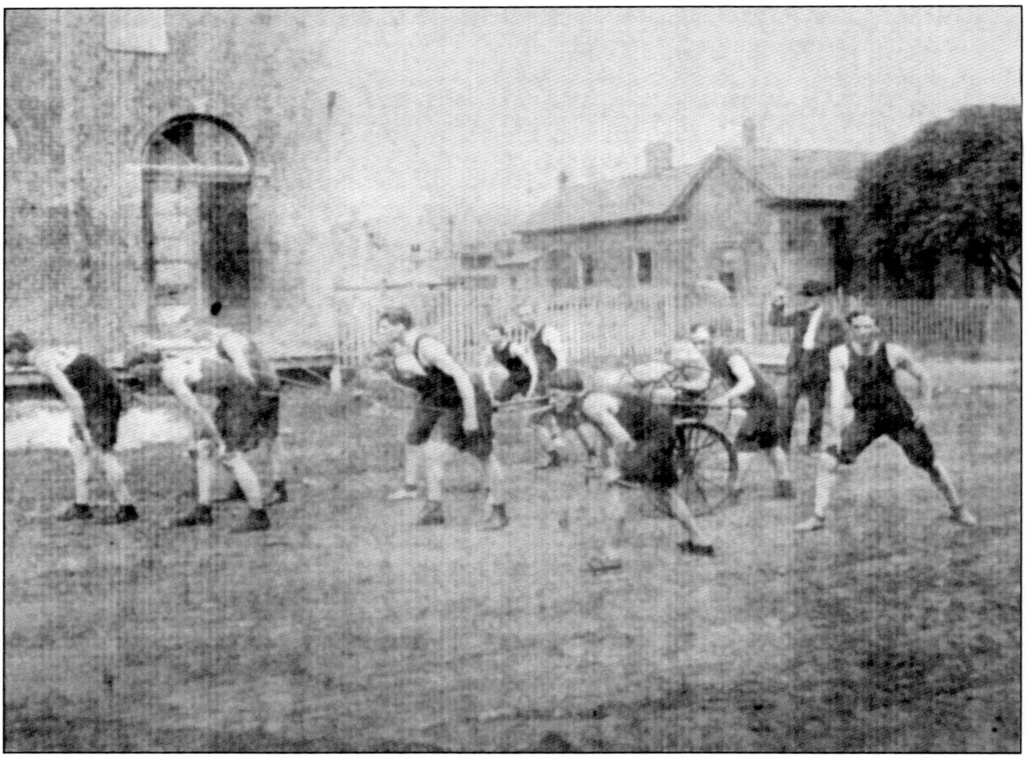

This drill team performs exercises on Burleson Street off Cameron Avenue in 1901. (Photograph courtesy of *Rockdale Reporter.*)

Three

The Railroad Births a Town

Three railroads—the International & Great Northern, the San Antonio and Aransas Pass, and the Rockdale, Sandow & Southern—contributed to the establishment and early history of Rockdale. The International & Great Northern exerted the strongest influence. It began operation in 1874, the same year it helped found and name the town. Growth was somewhat slow, but things began to flourish in 1876 when regulations regarding the sale and development of land became more relaxed and favorable to the railroads.

By 1906, the International & Great Northern Railroad had constructed two buildings, one to handle passengers and one to handle freight. The passenger depot still stands, a continuous reminder of the importance of the railroad in Rockdale's history. It has been restored with complete attention to historical integrity. The iconic depot has been named a Texas historic landmark by the Texas Historical Commission and is listed in the National Register of Historic Places. In 2009, the Texas State Downtown Association named it the best restoration of a historic building in Texas.

In 1884, the San Antonio and Aransas Pass (SAAP) railroad was chartered to connect the two cities. It reached Rockdale in 1892 and operated successfully here until 1959. The SAAP depot still stands and is in use as an office.

The Rockdale, Sandow & Southern was never technically a railroad, nor did it come to Rockdale. The rails, covering a six-mile stretch from Marjorie to Sandow, were served by Old Number 26, which was not a train but rather a refurbished Pierce-Arrow automobile. When Alcoa came to Rockdale, this operation was changed to work in cooperation with Alcoa.

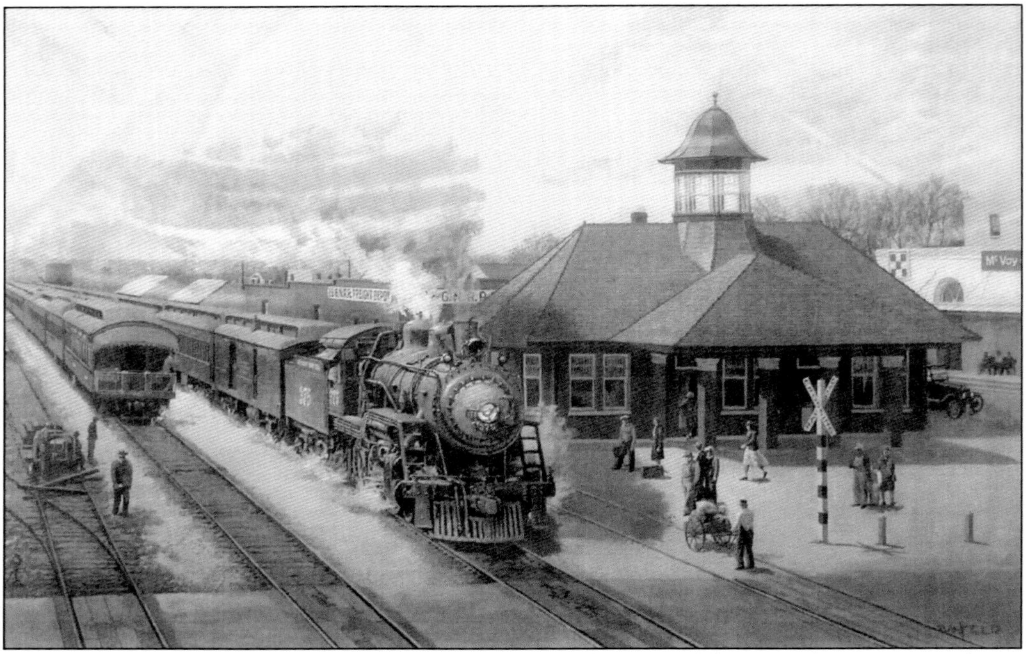

Rockdale's International & Great Northern depot is truly a Rockdale icon. This artist's rendition shows how the depot may have looked on a busy day. (Photograph courtesy of Bert Dockall.)

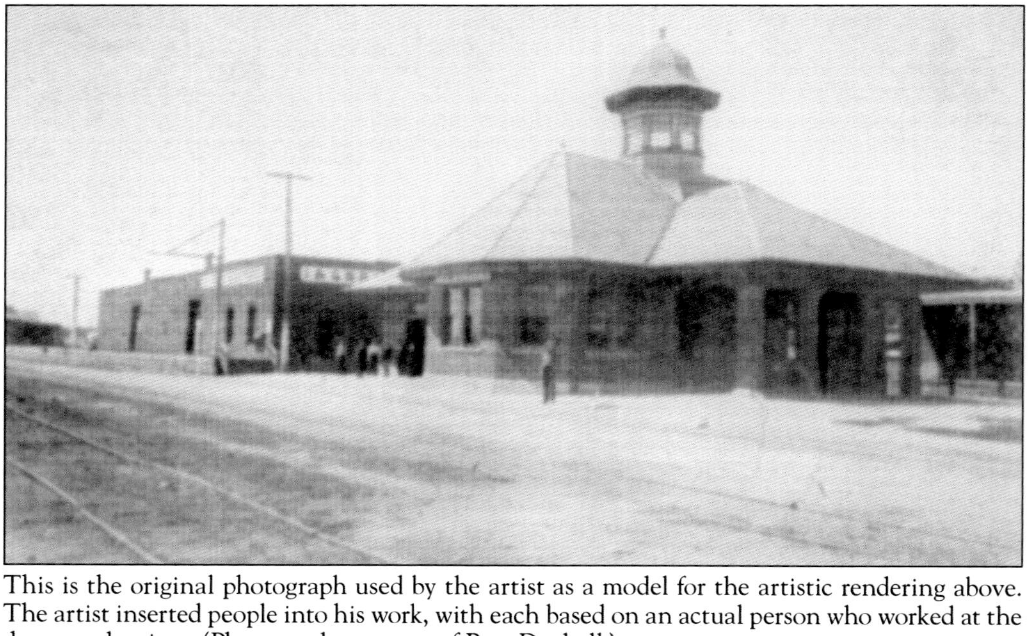

This is the original photograph used by the artist as a model for the artistic rendering above. The artist inserted people into his work, with each based on an actual person who worked at the depot at the time. (Photograph courtesy of Bert Dockall.)

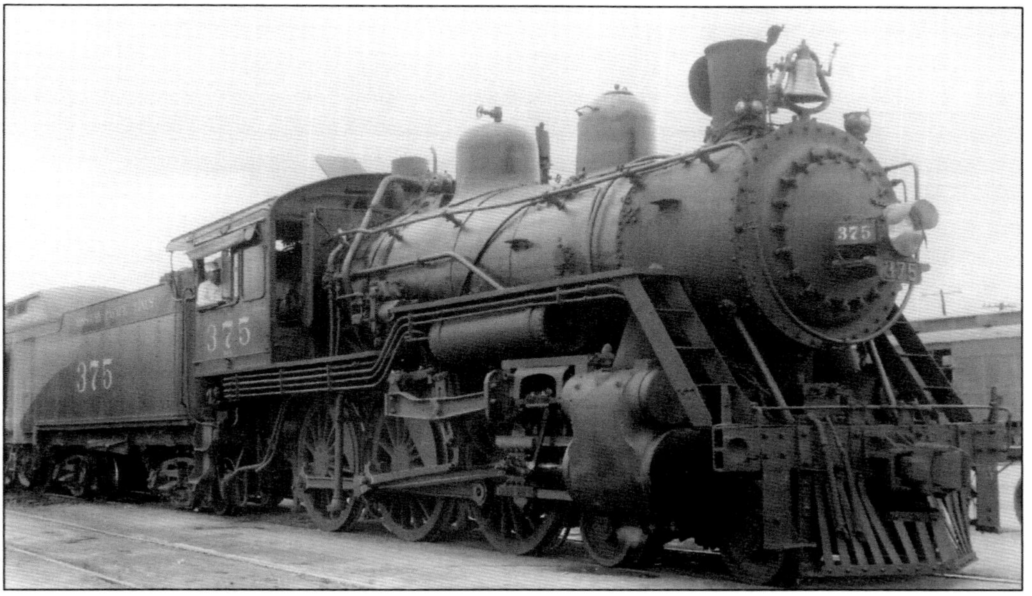

International & Great Northern Steam Engine No. 1705 was used as a model for this painting. (Photograph courtesy of Bert Dockall.)

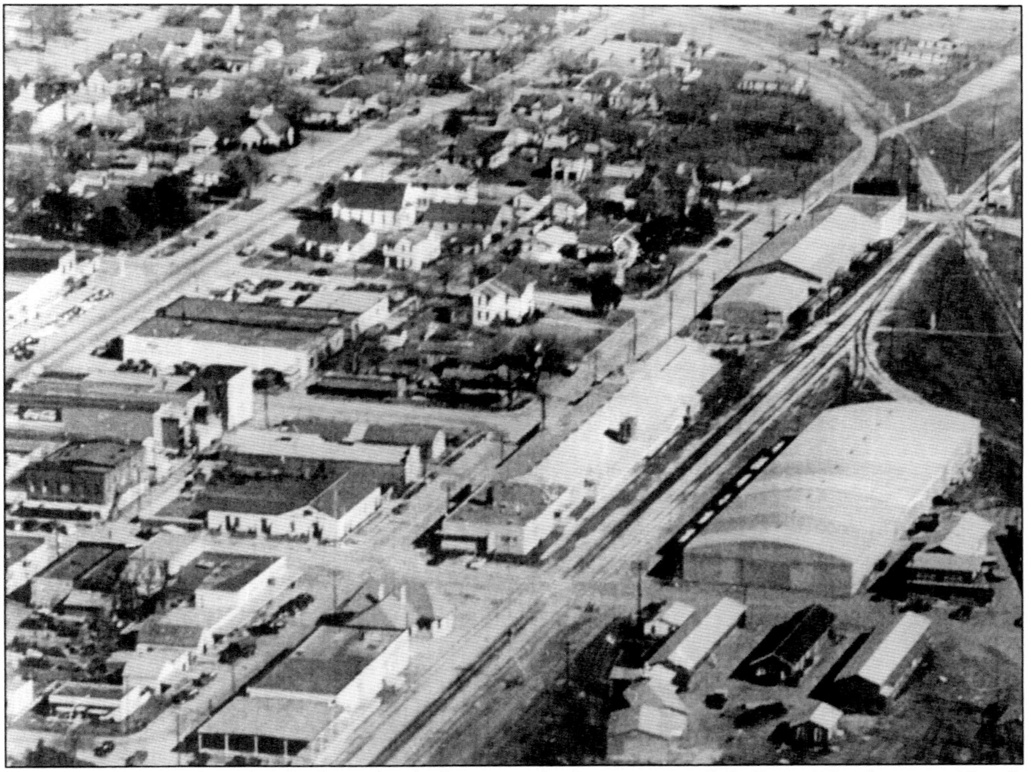
This aerial view of Rockdale shows both depots—the International & Great Northern on North Main Street and the San Antonio and Aransas Pass on East Cameron Street. (Photograph courtesy of Bert Dockall.)

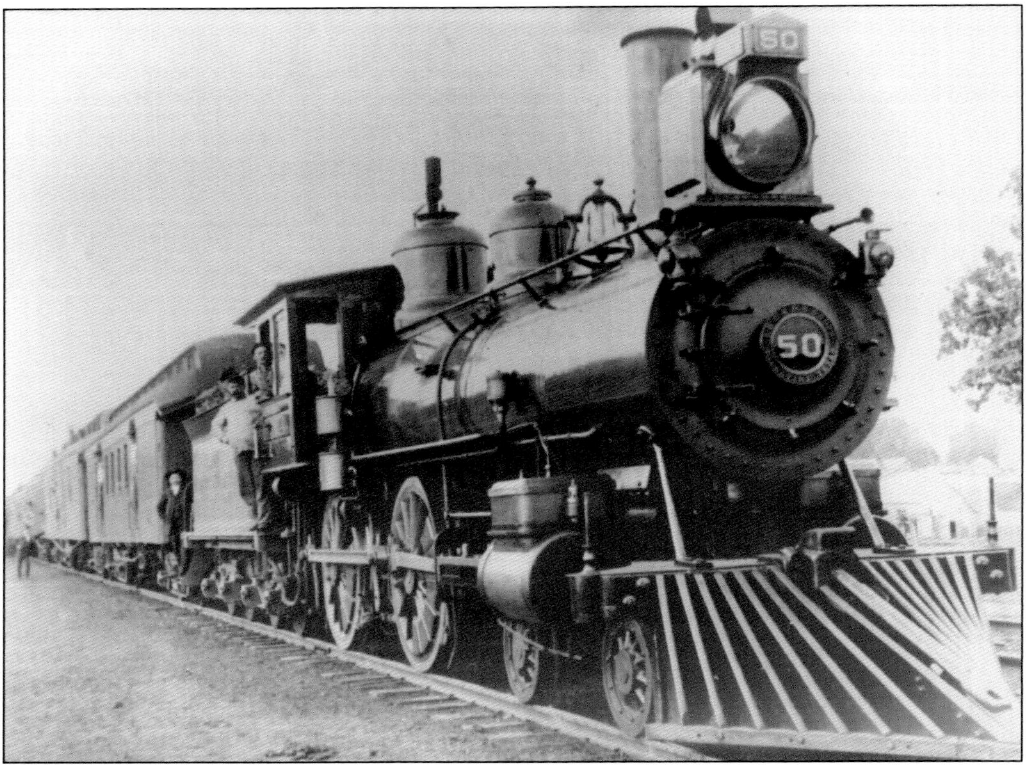

This is International & Great Northern Engine No. 50, which was popular in the 1850s. (Photograph courtesy of Bert Dockall.)

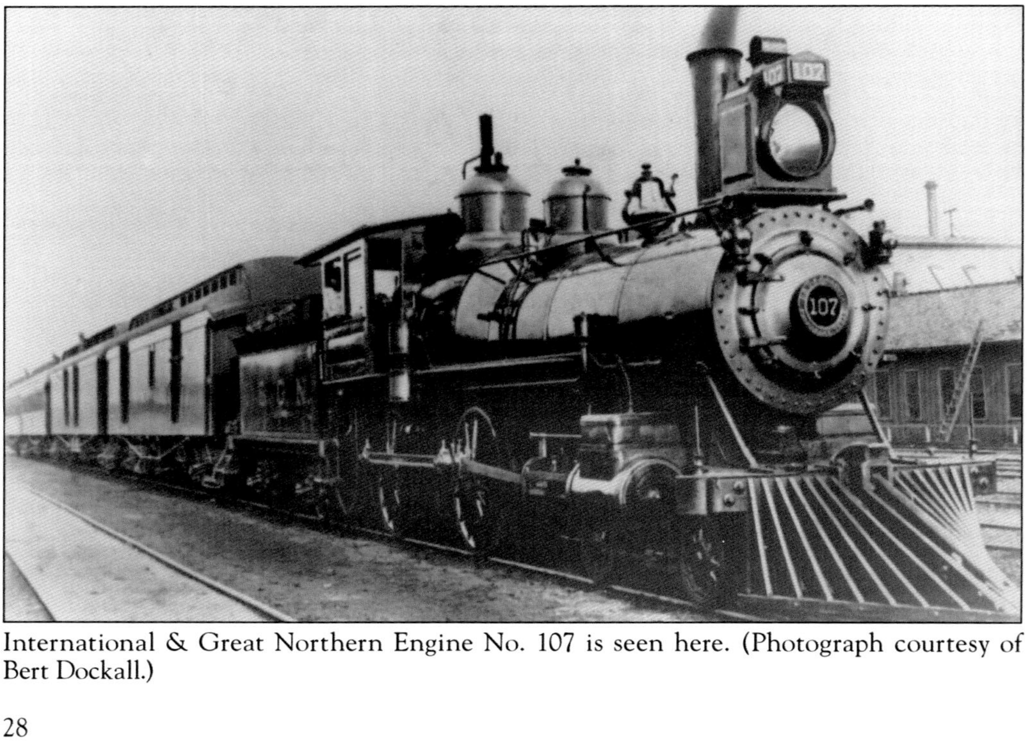

International & Great Northern Engine No. 107 is seen here. (Photograph courtesy of Bert Dockall.)

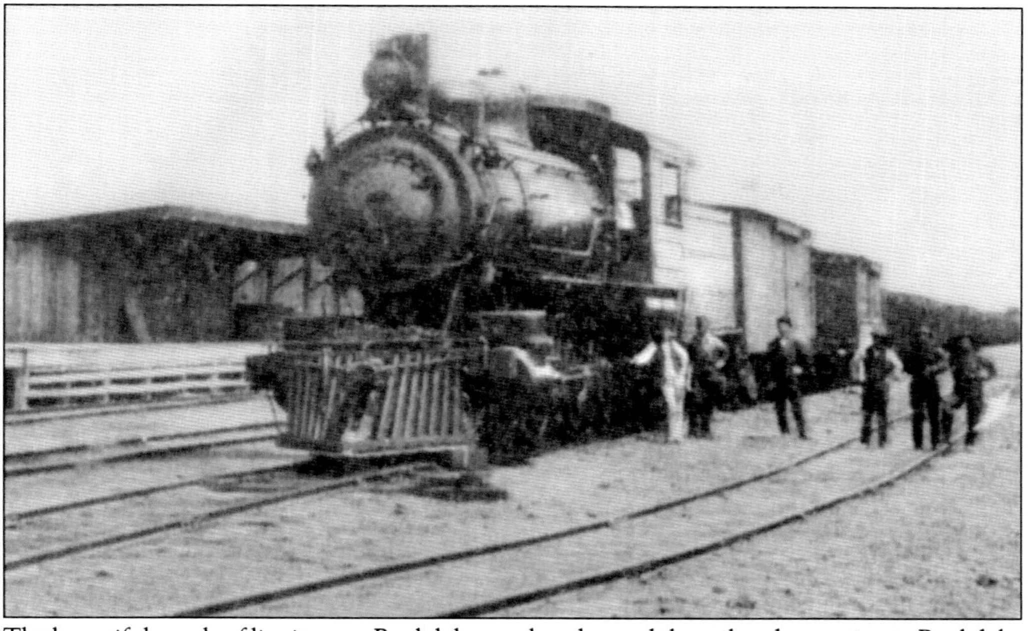

The bountiful supply of lignite near Rockdale greatly enhanced the railroad operation in Rockdale. This International & Great Northern train leaves Rockdale on its daily run. (Photograph courtesy of Bert Dockall.)

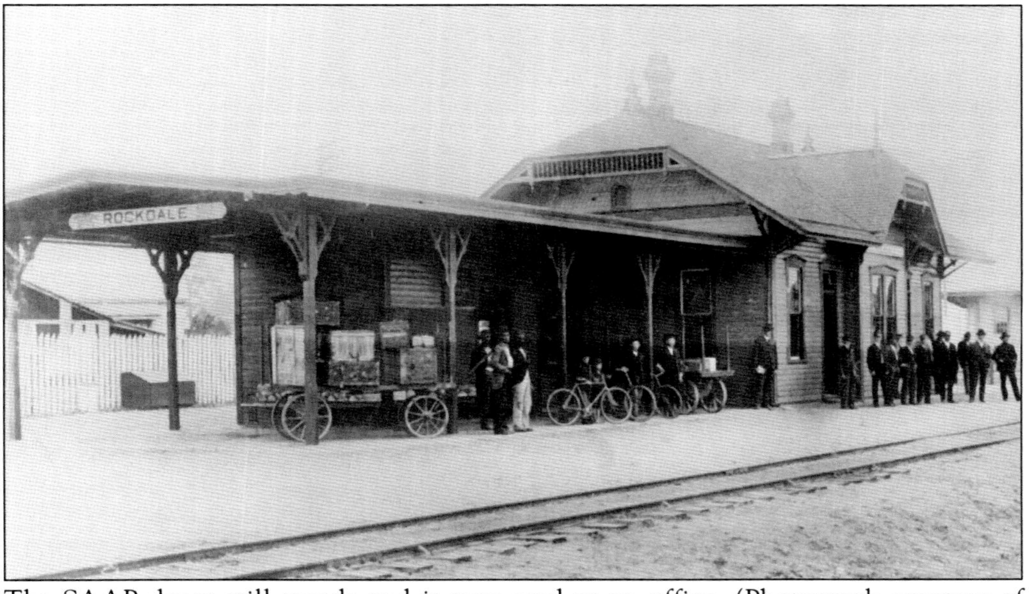

The SAAP depot still stands and is now used as an office. (Photograph courtesy of Bert Dockall.)

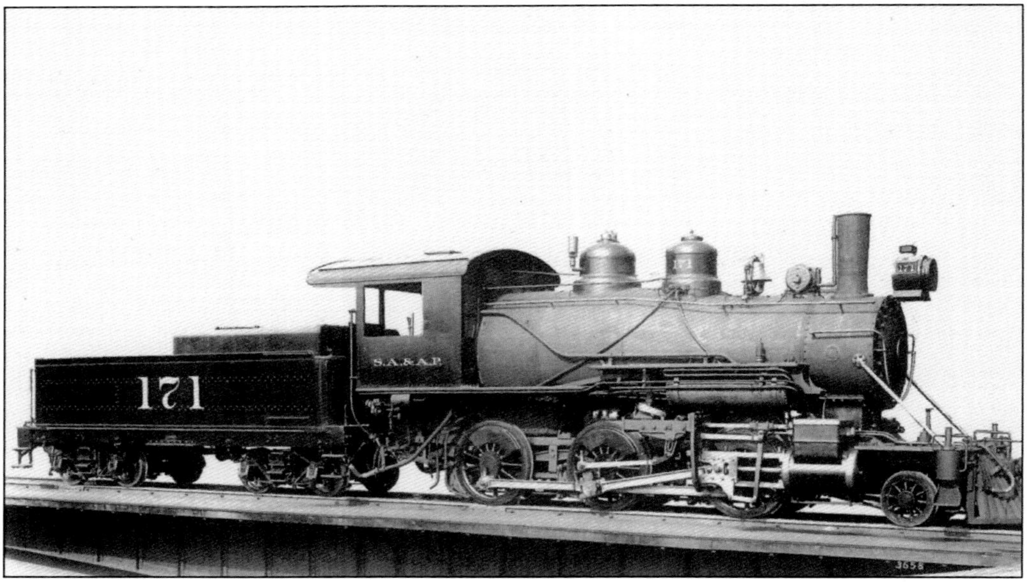

The SAAP railroad was chartered in order to connect San Antonio with Aransas Pass. (Photograph courtesy of Bert Dockall.)

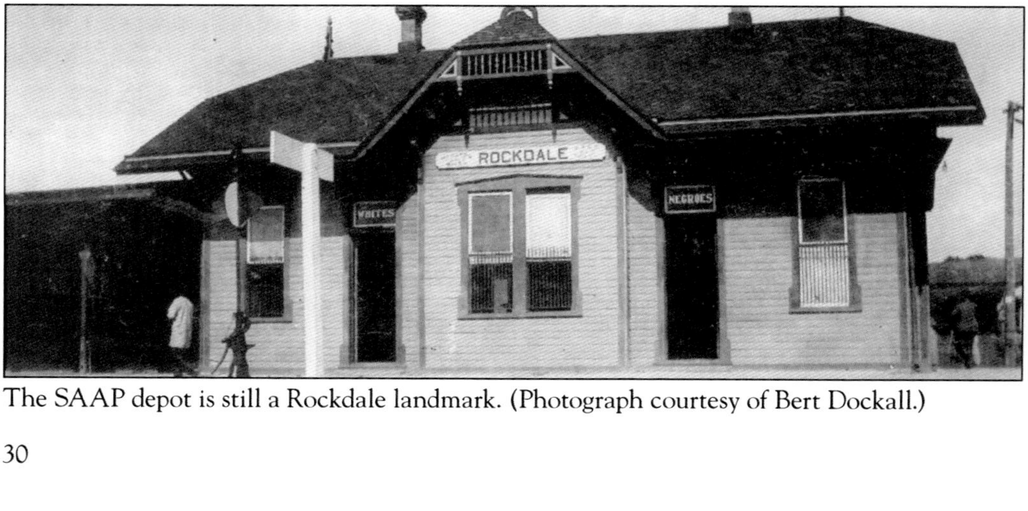

The SAAP depot is still a Rockdale landmark. (Photograph courtesy of Bert Dockall.)

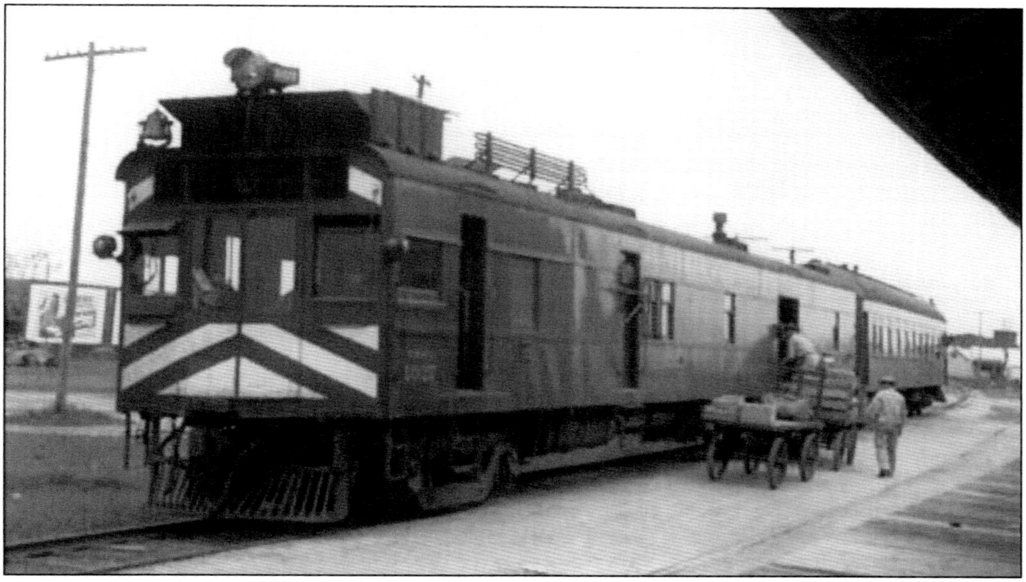

This train belonged to the Texas and New Orleans Railroad. Because of its size, the train was commonly called the "Dinky" and was a popular means of transportation. (Photograph courtesy of Bert Dockall.)

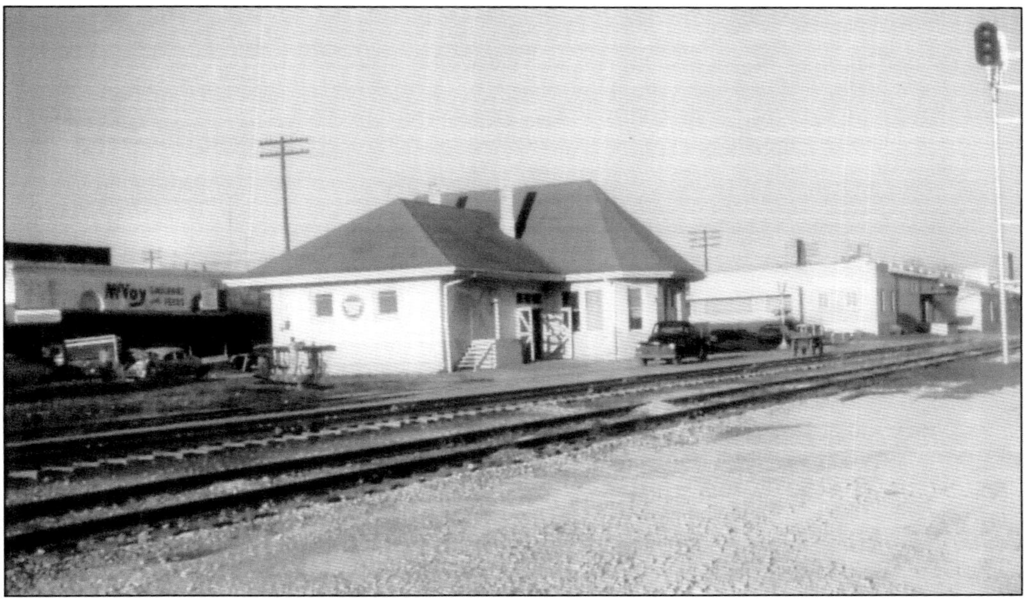

By 1962, the International & Great Northern depot was under the control of the Missouri Pacific Railroad. (Photograph courtesy of Bert Dockall.)

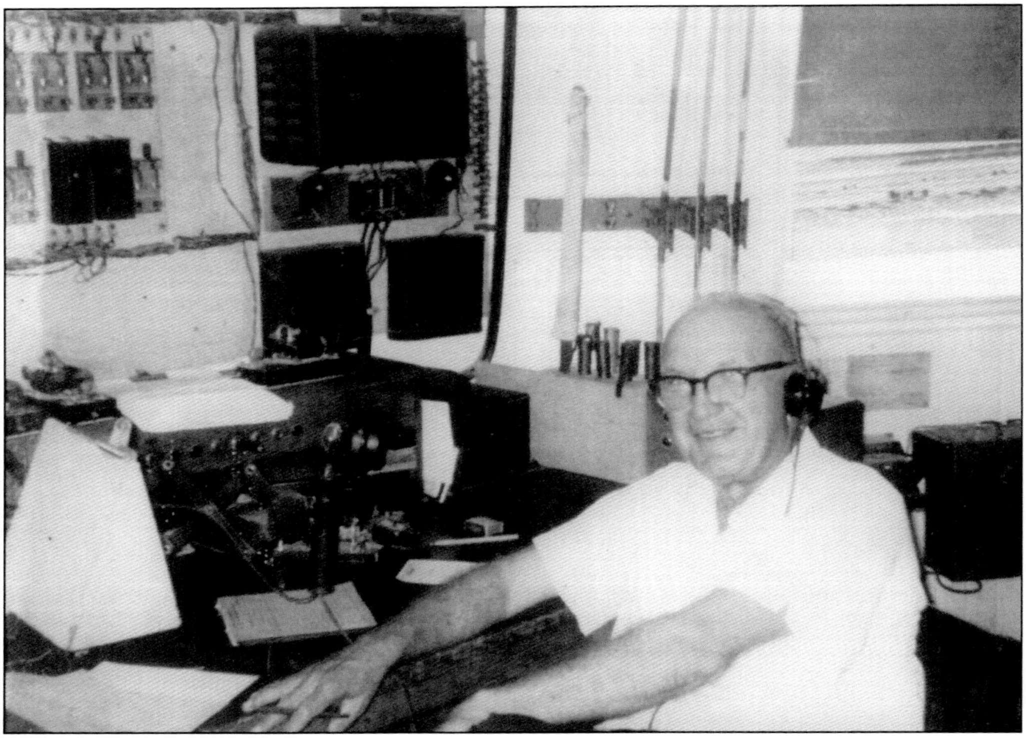

John Brockman, seen here, was the last stationmaster to serve the International & Great Northern Railroad in Rockdale. (Photograph courtesy of Bert Dockall.)

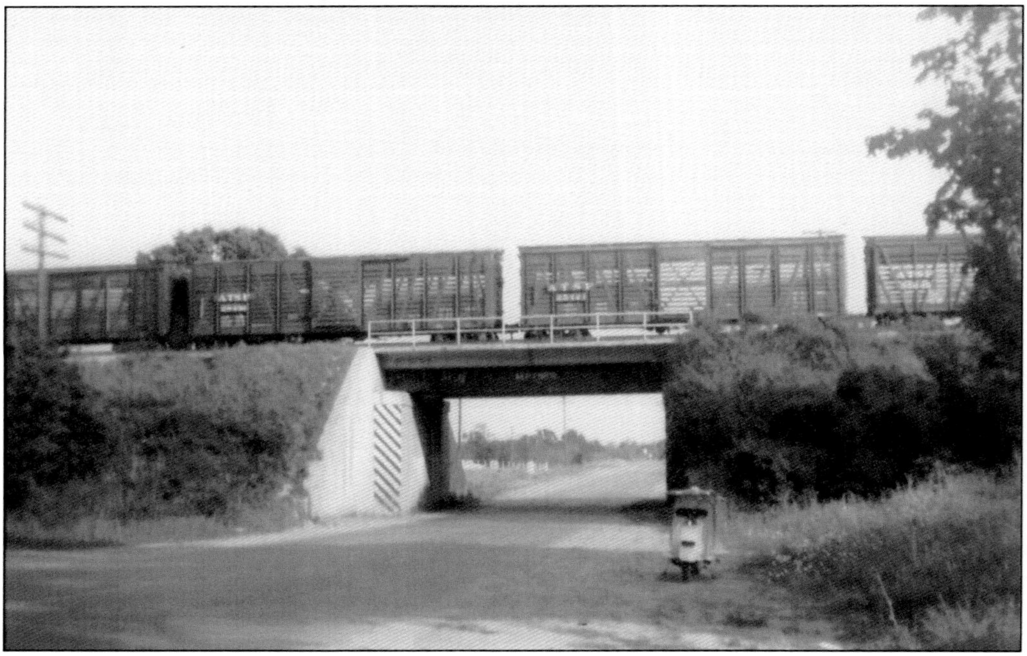

Cattle are hauled to market over the Wilcox Street underpass, which is still in use today. (Photograph courtesy of David Henry.)

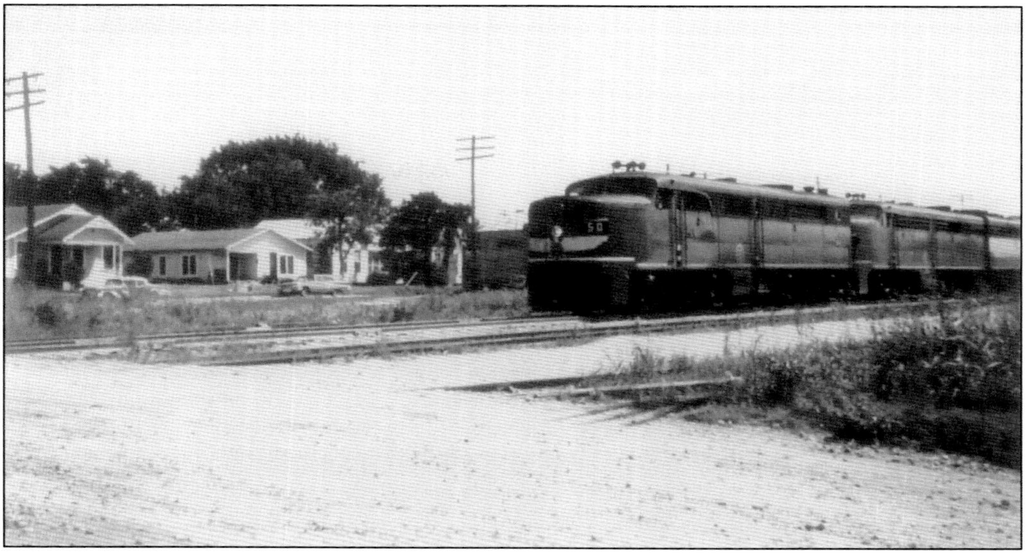

The famous Texas Eagle stopped at the International & Great Northern Depot in 1962. (Photograph courtesy of David Henry.)

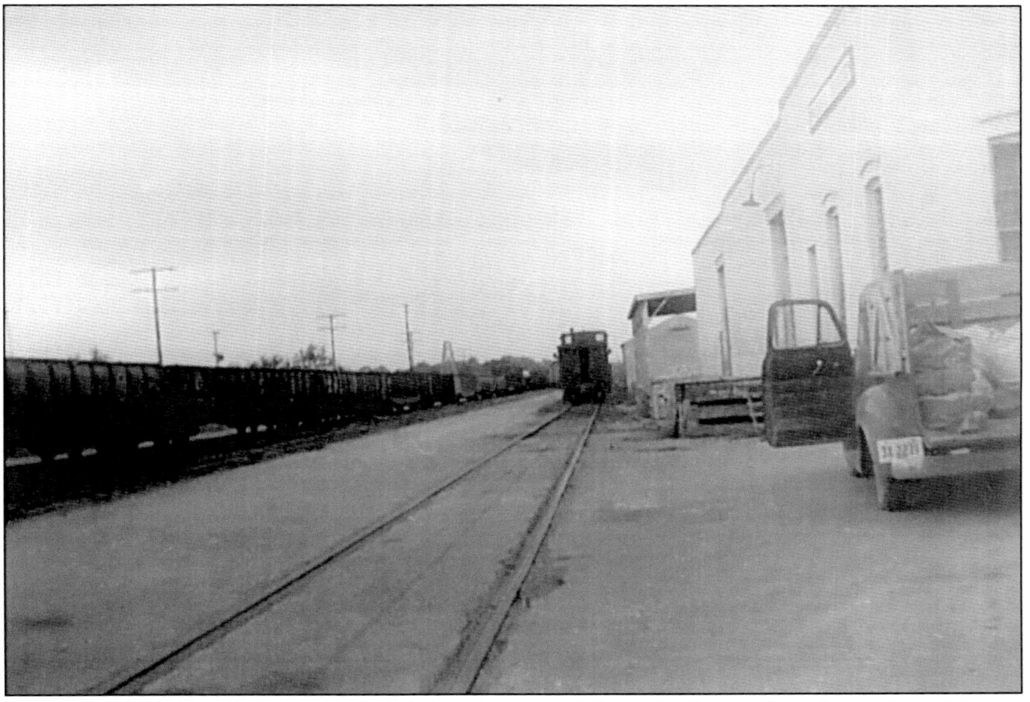

The pickup truck in the lower right of this photograph brought the mail to this train waiting at the station platform in Rockdale. (Photograph courtesy of David Henry.)

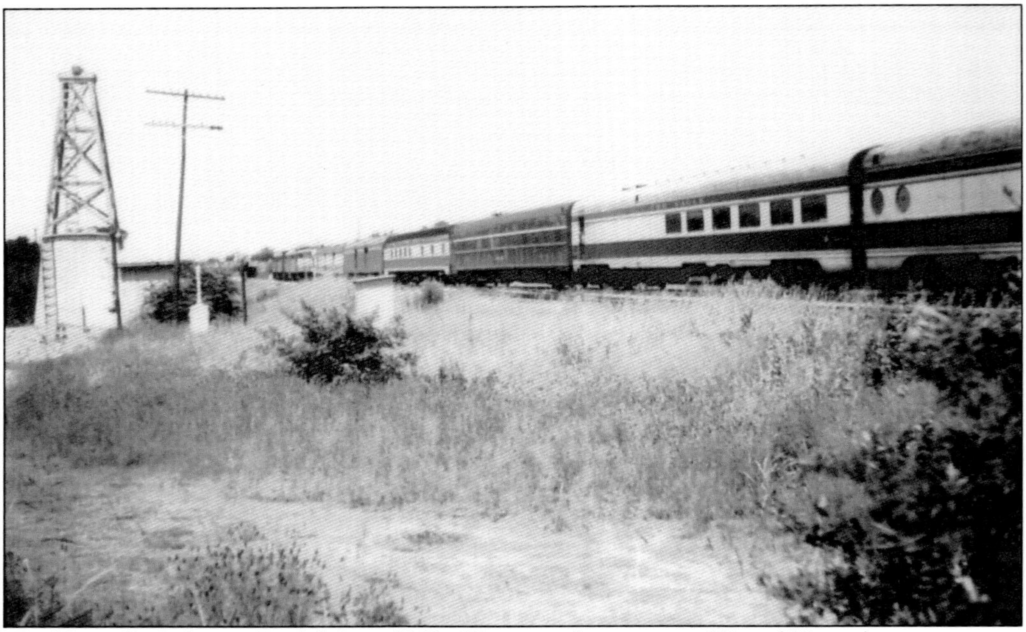

The Texas Eagle leaves Rockdale in 1962. (Photograph courtesy of David Henry.)

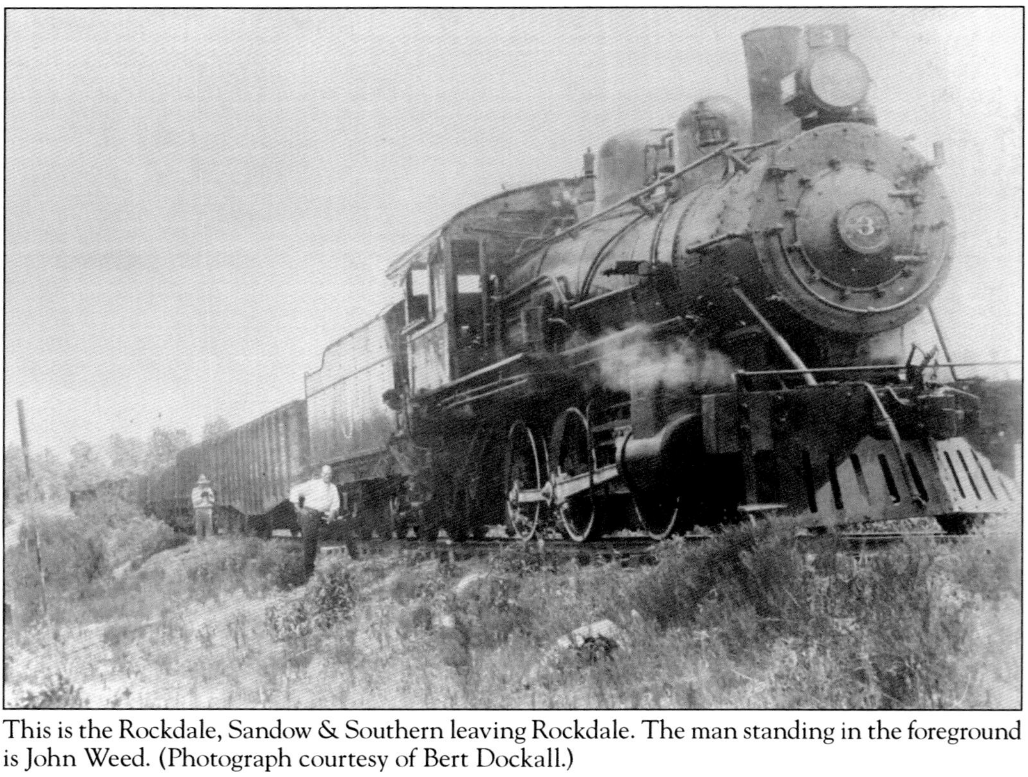

This is the Rockdale, Sandow & Southern leaving Rockdale. The man standing in the foreground is John Weed. (Photograph courtesy of Bert Dockall.)

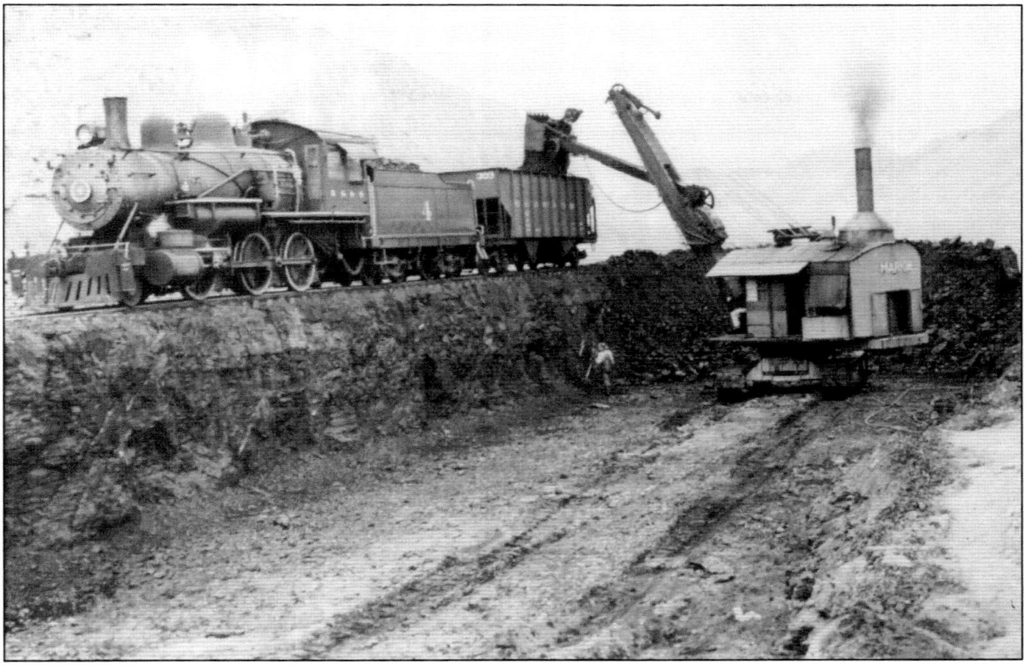

Cars on the Rockdale, Sandow & Southern get filled to the brim with coal. (Photograph courtesy of Bert Dockall.)

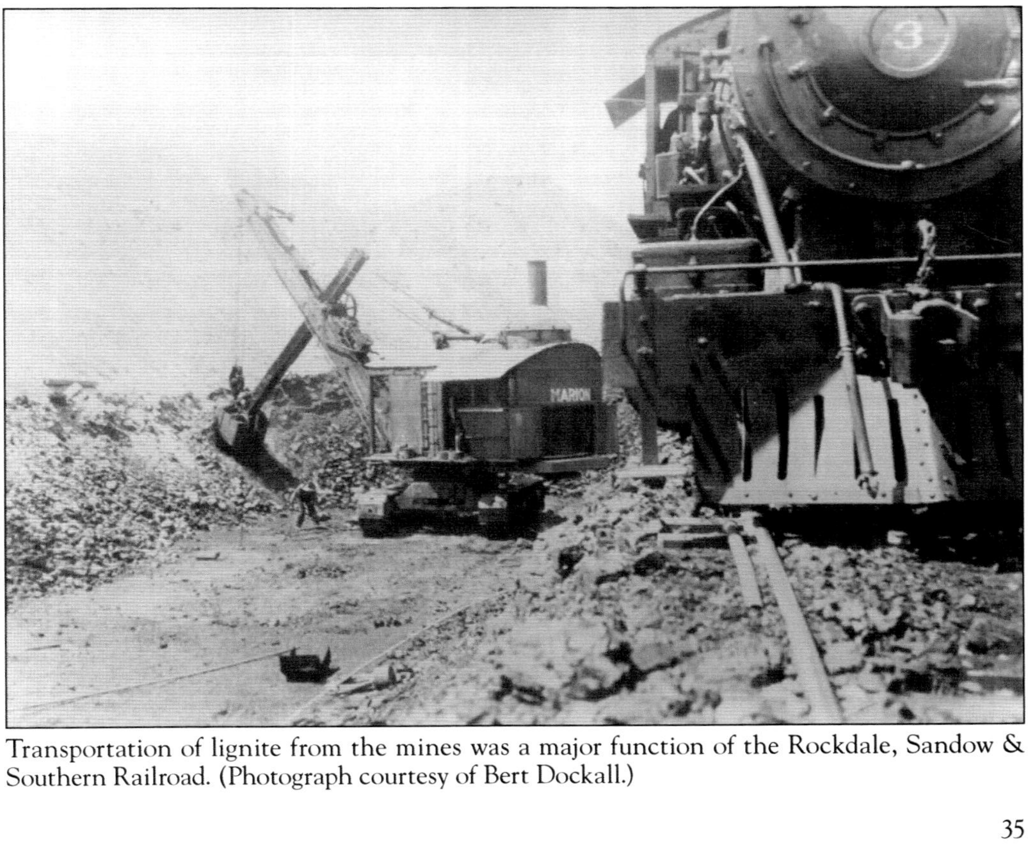

Transportation of lignite from the mines was a major function of the Rockdale, Sandow & Southern Railroad. (Photograph courtesy of Bert Dockall.)

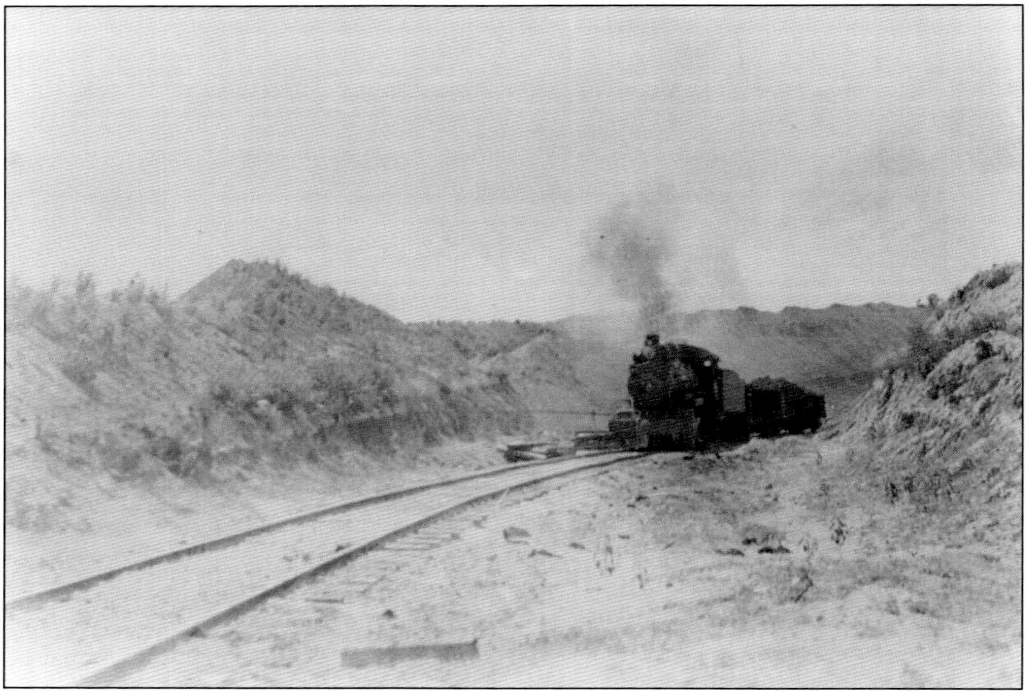

A Rockdale, Sandow & Southern engine pulls a load of coal out of the pit. (Photograph courtesy of Bert Dockall.)

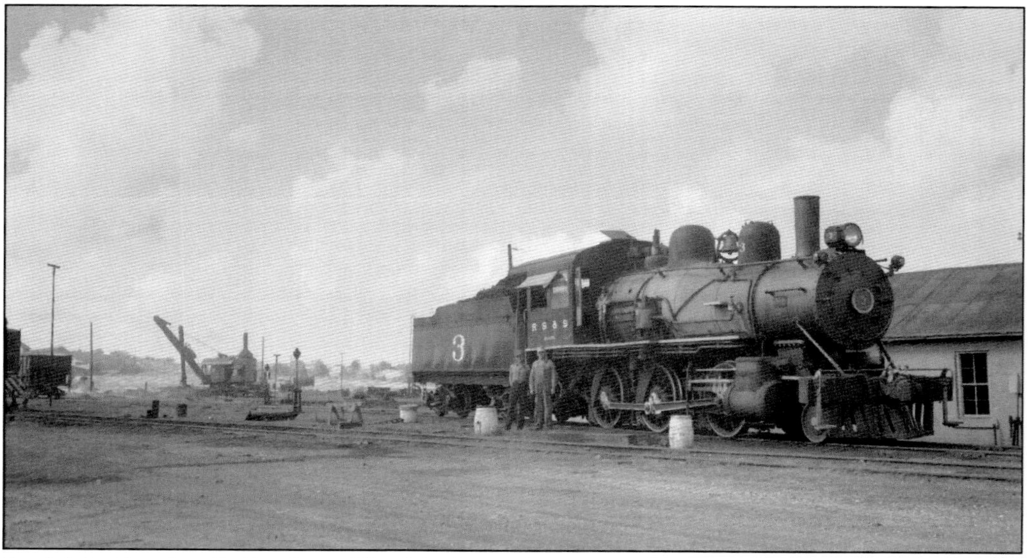

Rockdale, Sandow & Southern No. 3 is shown here near the mines. (Photograph courtesy of Bert Dockall.)

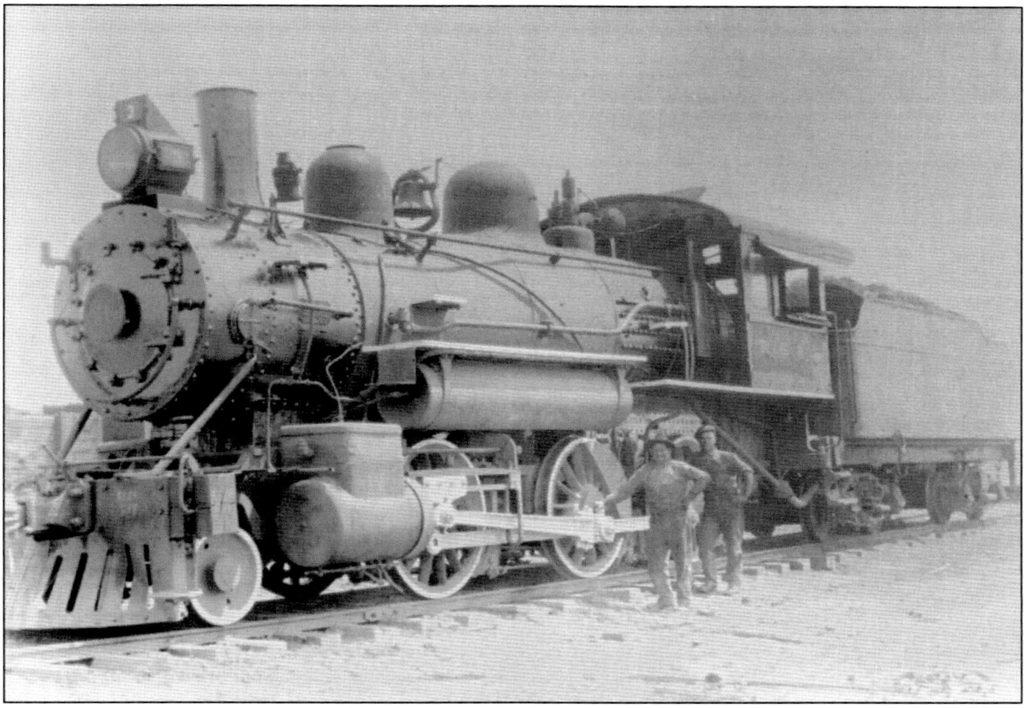

Two unidentified railroad workers pose alongside the Rockdale, Sandow & Southern No. 3. (Photograph courtesy of Bert Dockall.)

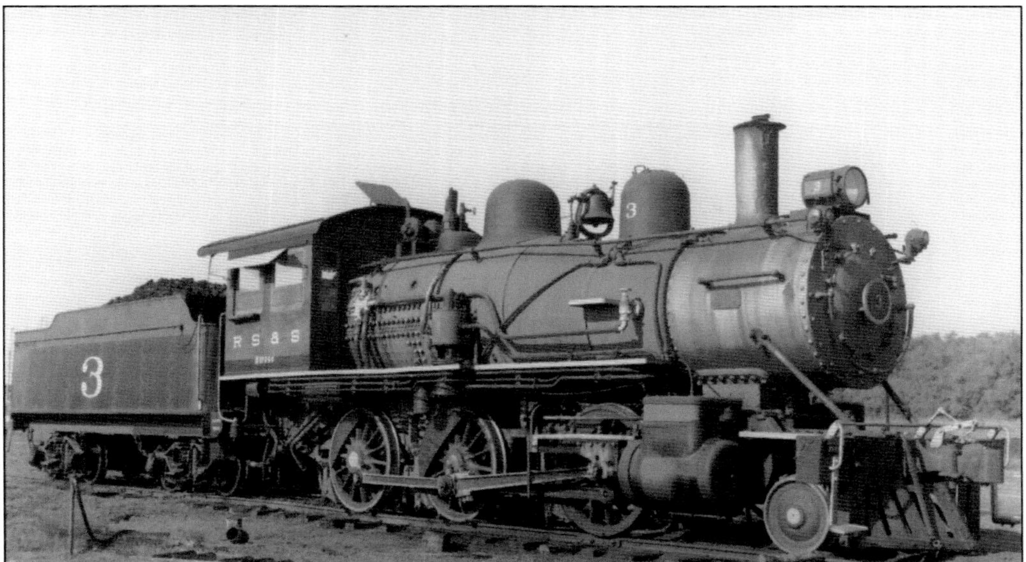

The Rockdale, Sandow & Southern No. 3 brought the victory bell, awarded annually to the winner of the Rockdale/Cameron football game, to town. (Photograph courtesy of Bert Dockall.)

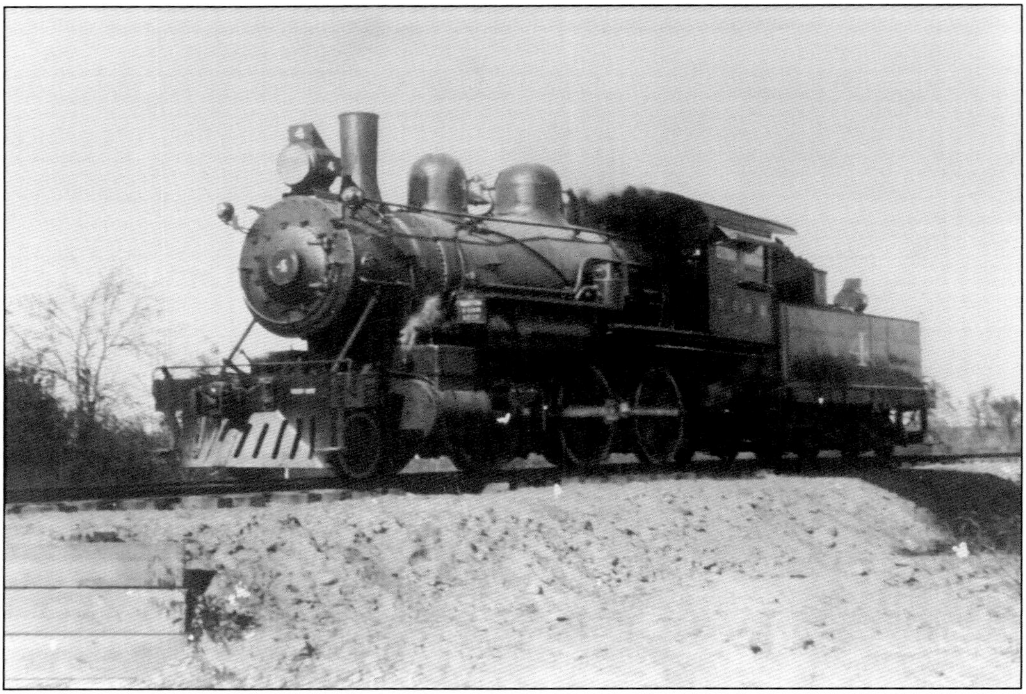

Rockdale, Sandow & Southern No. 5 hauls a load of coal. (Photograph courtesy of Bert Dockall.)

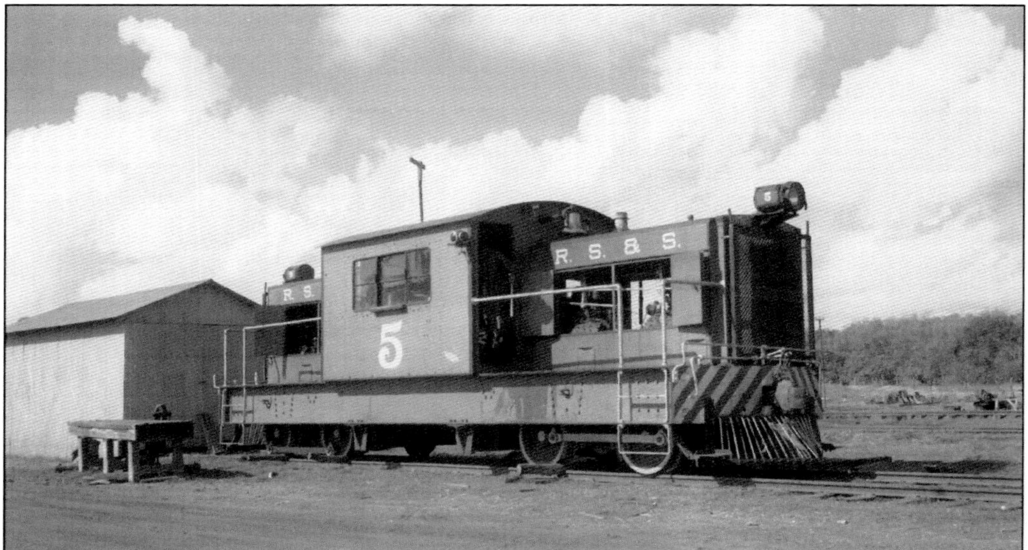

Rockdale, Sandow & Southern No. 5 rests against an equipment shed. (Photograph courtesy of Bert Dockall.)

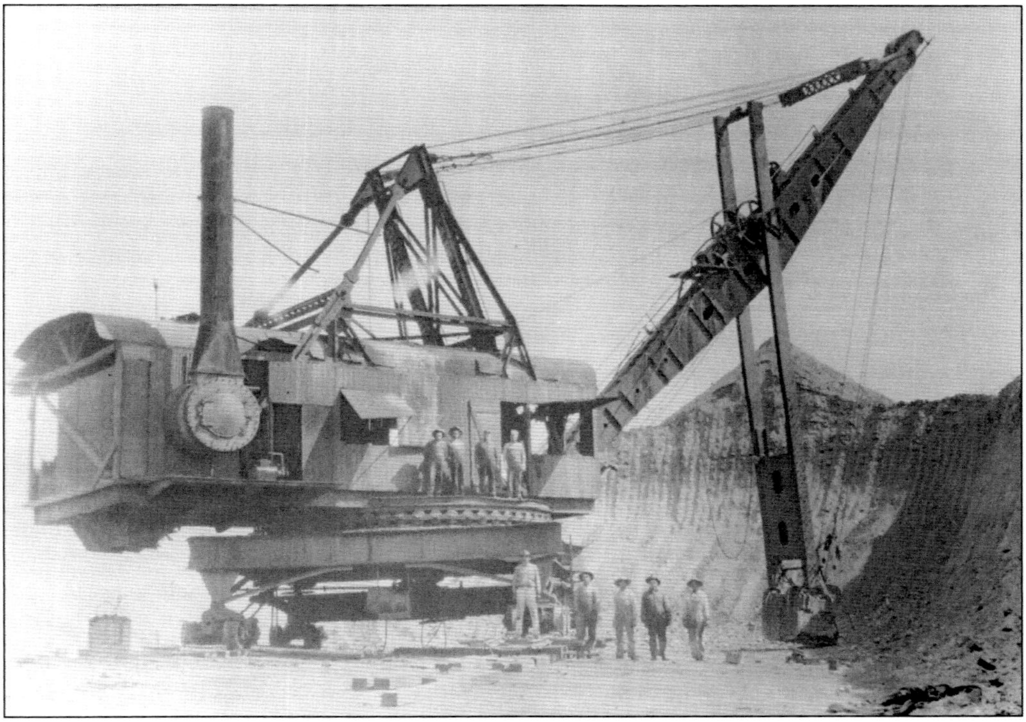

The steam shovel for McAlister Fuel at Sandow worked almost as hard as the men who operated it in the mines. (Photograph courtesy of Bert Dockall.)

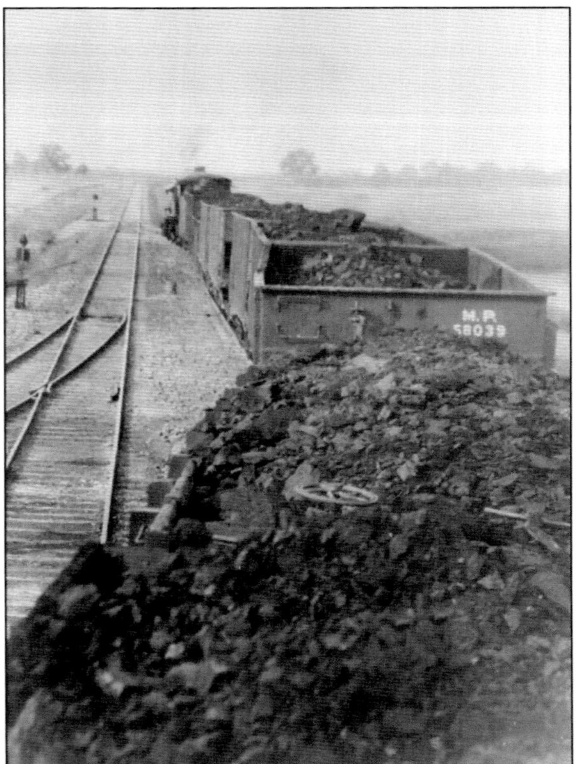

Carloads of coal wait to be weighed at Sandow. (Photograph courtesy of Bert Dockall.)

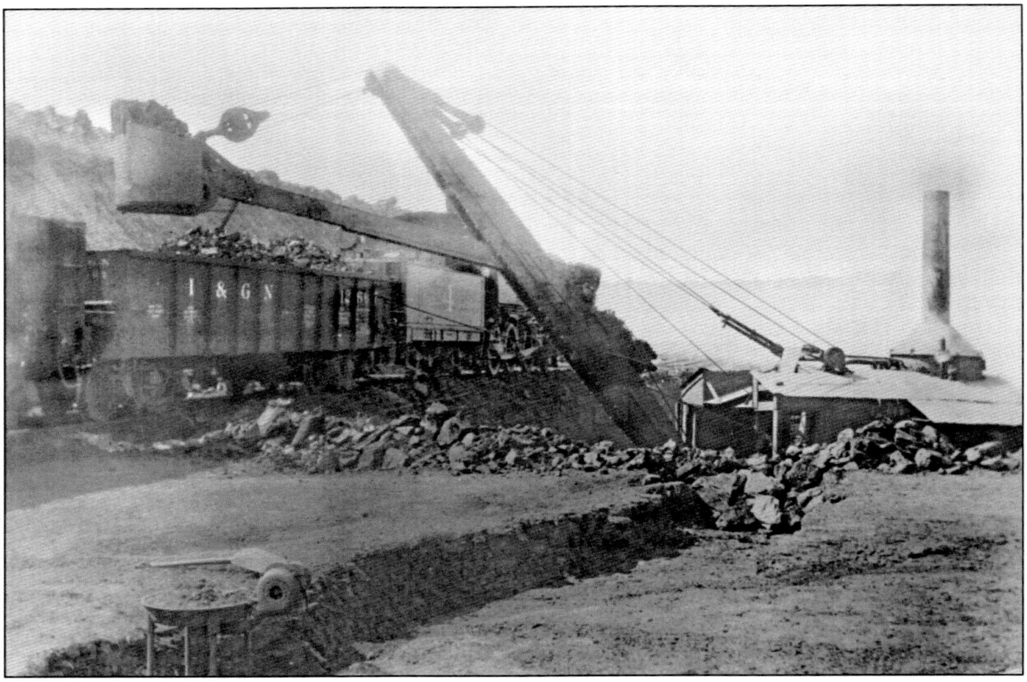

Heavy machinery loads coal from the pit at Sandow. (Photograph courtesy of Bert Dockall.)

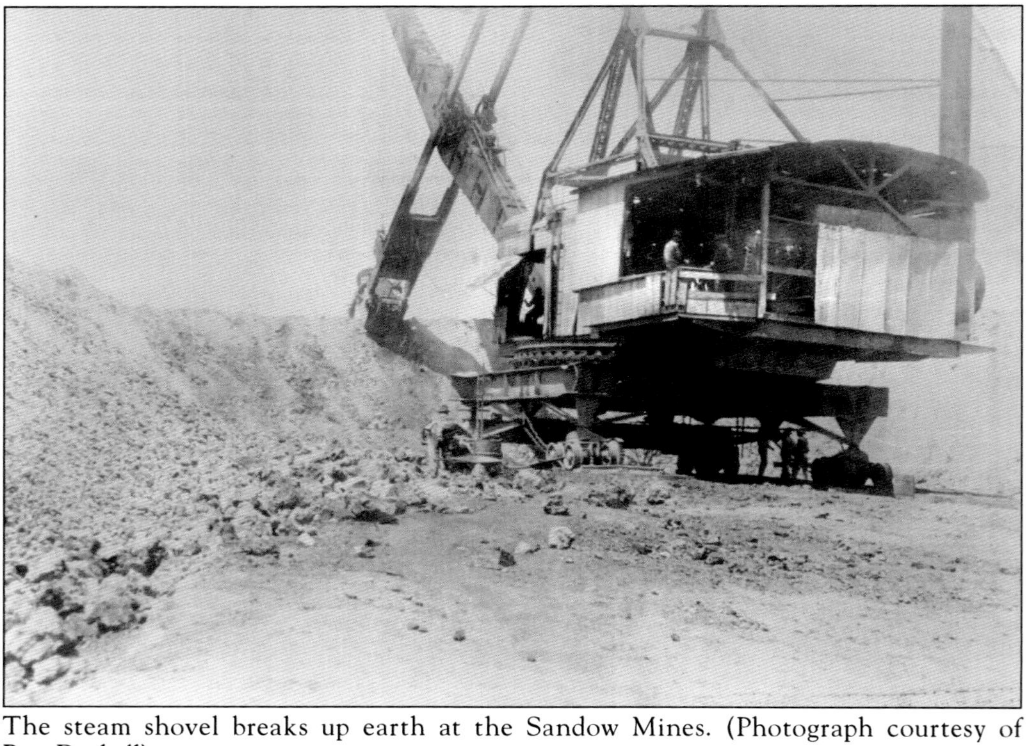
The steam shovel breaks up earth at the Sandow Mines. (Photograph courtesy of Bert Dockall).

Four

Black Gold from Beneath the Earth

Lignite played a major role in the early development of Rockdale. Its presence grew even more important in the 20th century, as the Aluminum Company of America (Alcoa) became a major player in Rockdale's economy.

Hermann F. Vogel immigrated to the United States in 1881 with his wife, Wilhelmine, and their two children, landing first in New York and then traveling by boat to Galveston and overland to Lee County and eventually Milam County. The Vogels purchased 100 acres of land known as the Talbott Ridge community and began farming the land. One day, as Vogel walked about his property, he found coal sticking up from the ground. He had a background in mining from his days in Germany, so he switched from farming to mining. In 1890, he and Gus Lorenz opened the first coal mine in Texas, the Black Diamond Coal Company. Later, there would be the Big Lump, Stribling, Worley, and Swancoat Mines. Other mines on this property included the Dunk Wallace, Witcher, and International Mines. A brick factory was also operated here.

The establishment and operation of this lignite mining operation added yet another dimension to the growth of Rockdale. Camps of Mexican nationals, who were either smuggled in or came on their own seeking work, sprang up near each mine. These settlements grew and soon housed families. It was understood that they would stay in the area or be subject to deportation. A commissary was available for them to purchase necessities.

Vogel died as the result of a fall in the mines, but mining continued until all of the coal was gone from his property. Lignite mining was revived in 1954, when Alcoa took over operation of the Sandow mines and began the production of aluminum in Milam County.

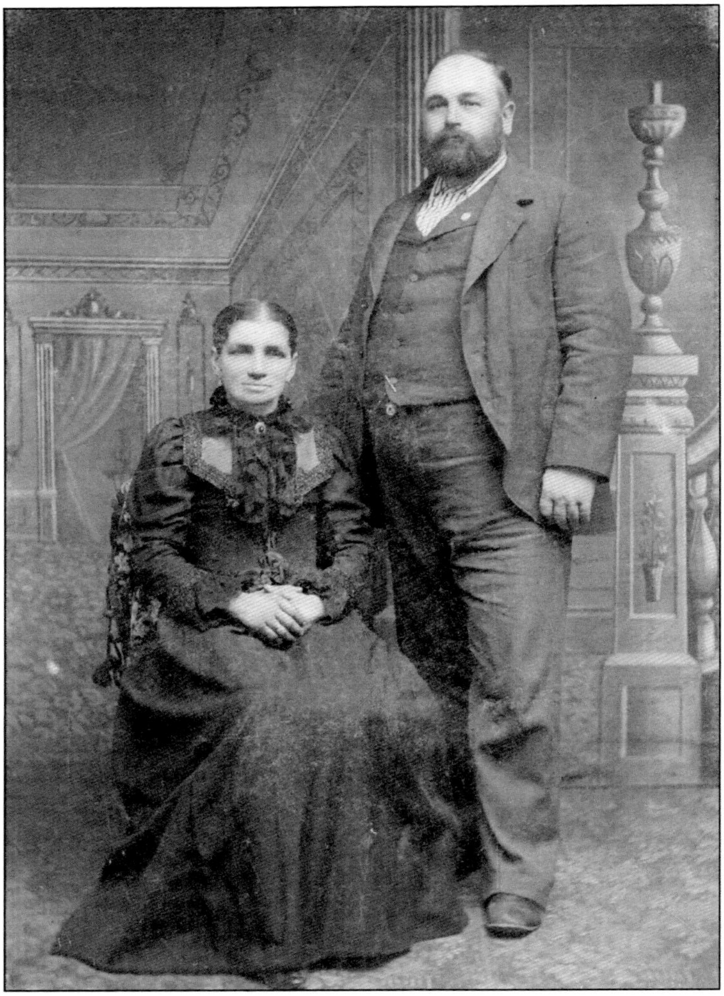

Hermann Frederick and Wilhelmine "Mina" Vogel owned the first mining operation in Texas, the Black Diamond Mine. Unfortunately, Hermann died as the result of a fall down a 45-foot shaft at his mine. (Photograph courtesy of Patricia Whitley McKee.)

The shaft of the first Vogel mine, which began operation in 1890, is seen here. The coal was hoisted by Wyndam machinery. (Photograph courtesy of Patricia Whitley McKee.)

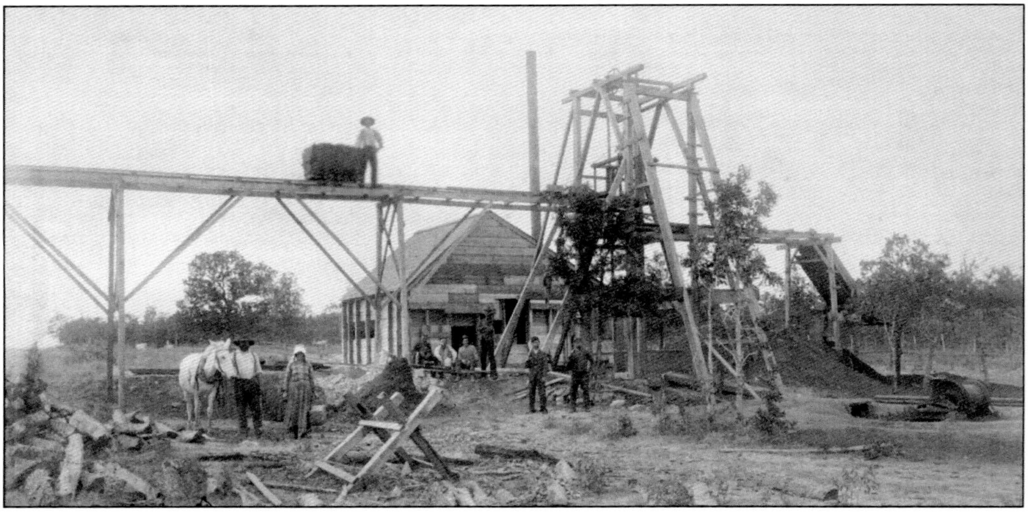

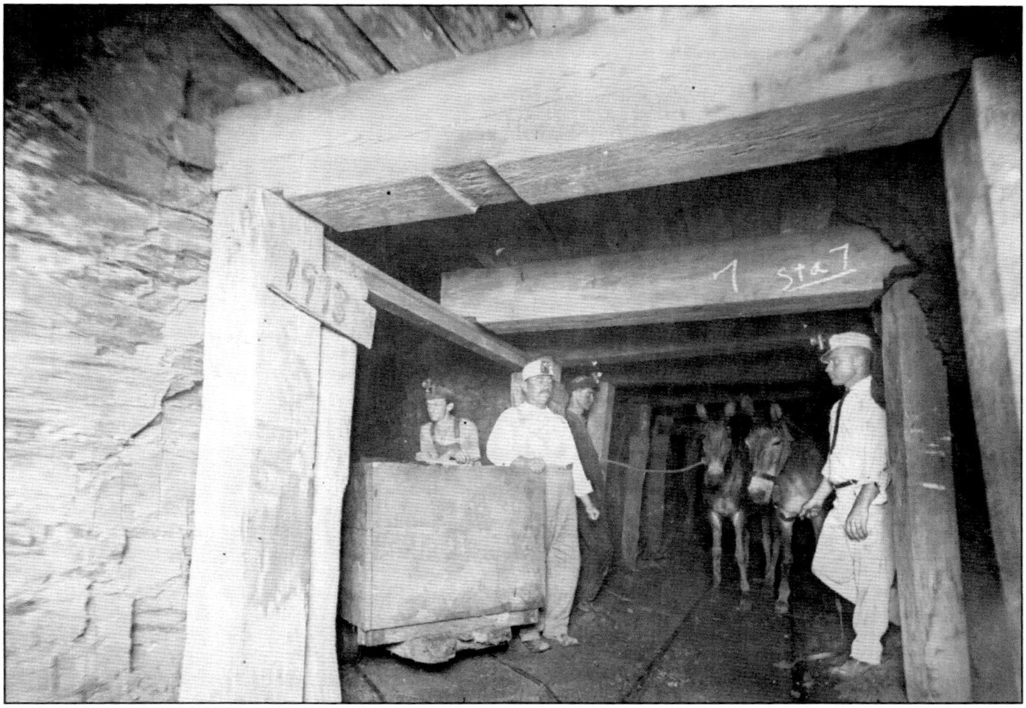

Gustav Vogel (far left) and other miners roll the cart through the interior of the Black Diamond Mine. (Photograph courtesy of Patricia Whitley McKee.)

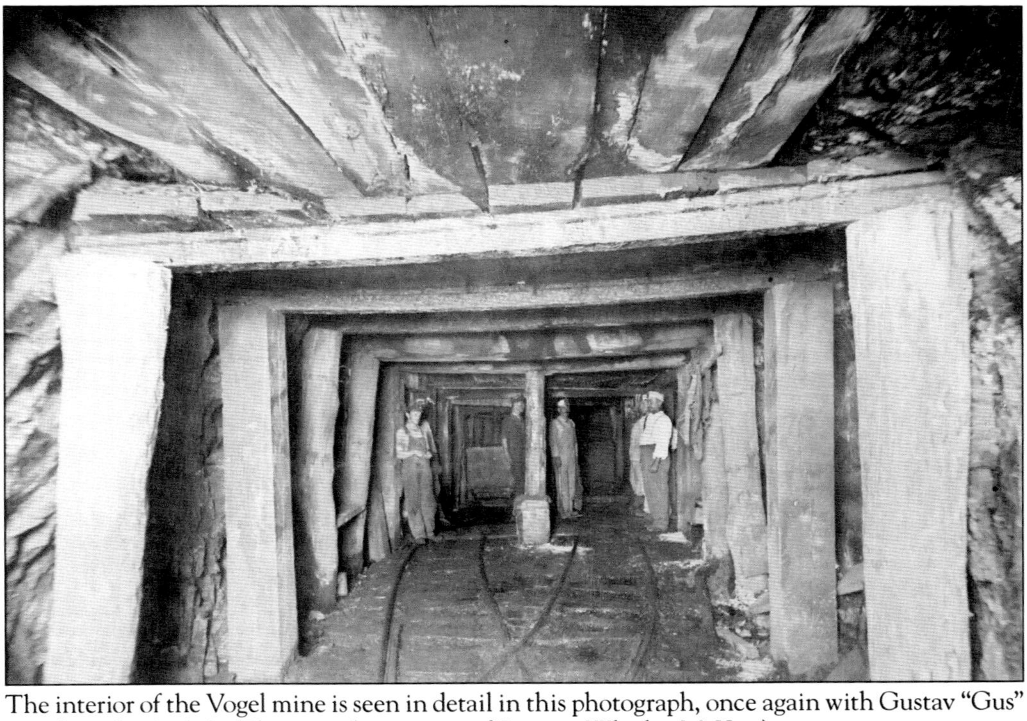

The interior of the Vogel mine is seen in detail in this photograph, once again with Gustav "Gus" Vogel on the far left. (Photograph courtesy of Patricia Whitley McKee.)

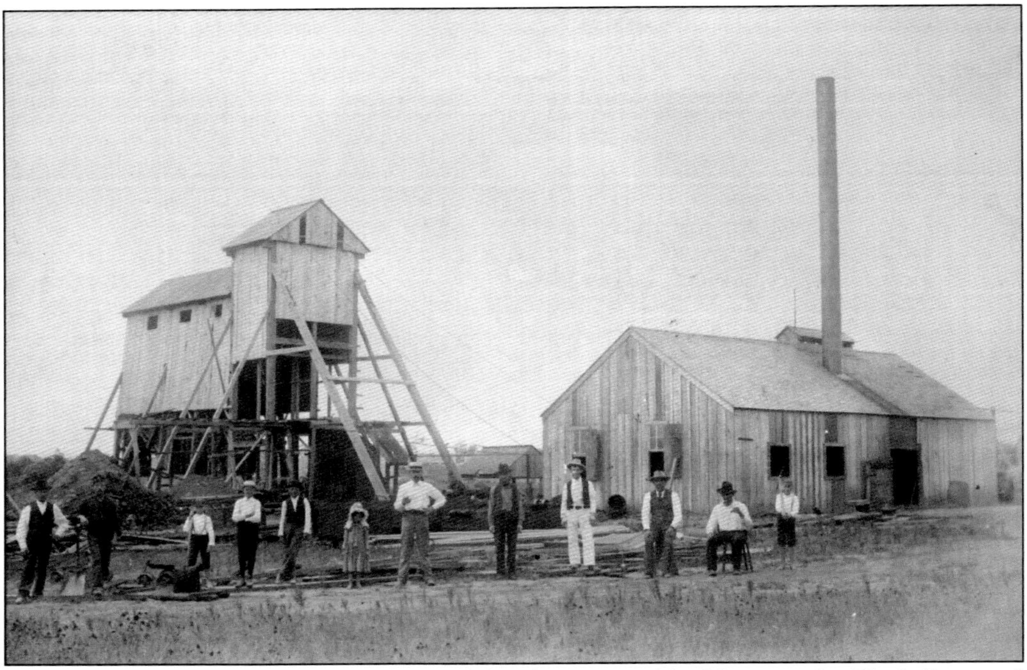

Workers pose for a photograph in front of the aboveground buildings at the Black Diamond Mine in its early days of operation. Gus Vogel is on the far left. (Photograph courtesy of Patricia Whitley McKee.)

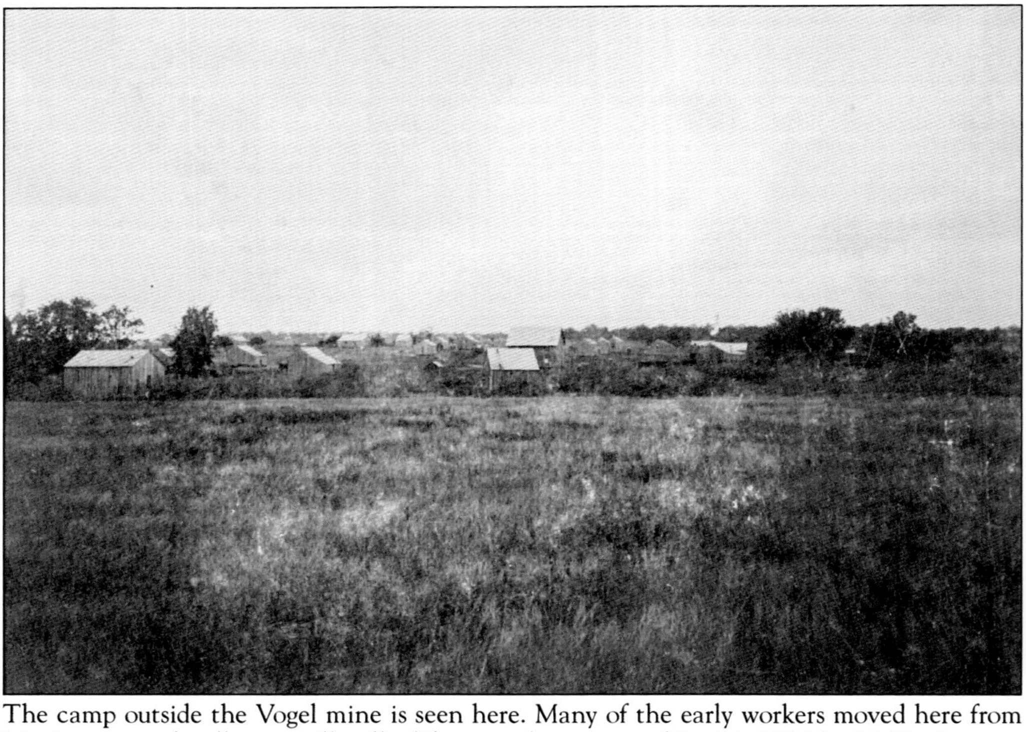

The camp outside the Vogel mine is seen here. Many of the early workers moved here from Mexico—some legally, some illegally. (Photograph courtesy of Patricia Whitley McKee.)

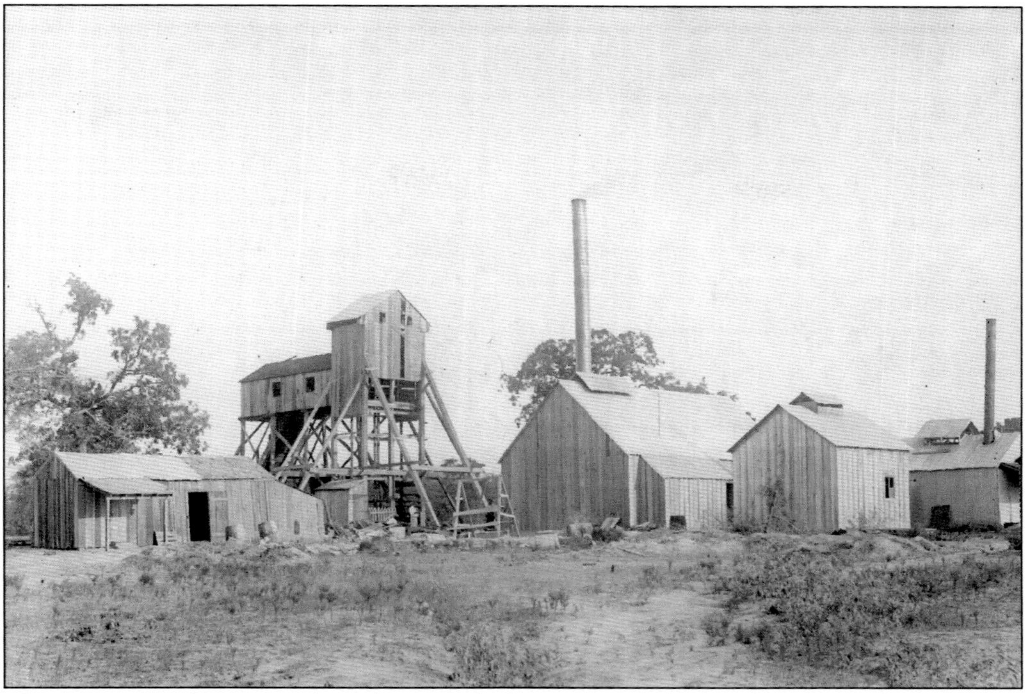

The mine is seen here soon after it began. A boiler once exploded here but thankfully there were no injuries. (Picture courtesy of Patricia Whitley McKee.)

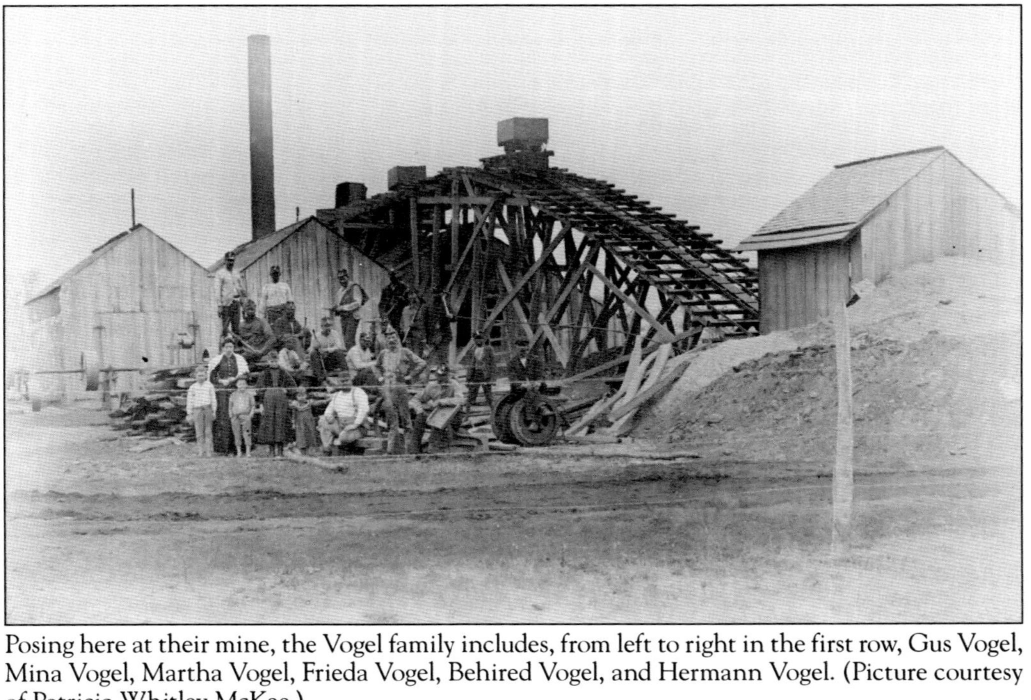

Posing here at their mine, the Vogel family includes, from left to right in the first row, Gus Vogel, Mina Vogel, Martha Vogel, Frieda Vogel, Behired Vogel, and Hermann Vogel. (Picture courtesy of Patricia Whitley McKee.)

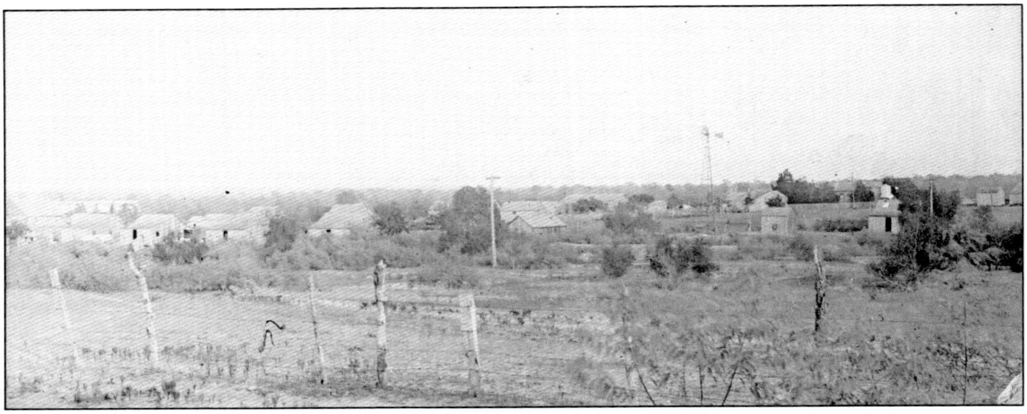

The vastness of the Vogel mining operation is seen here, with Hermann Vogel's home in the distant background. (Photograph courtesy of Patricia Whitley McKee.)

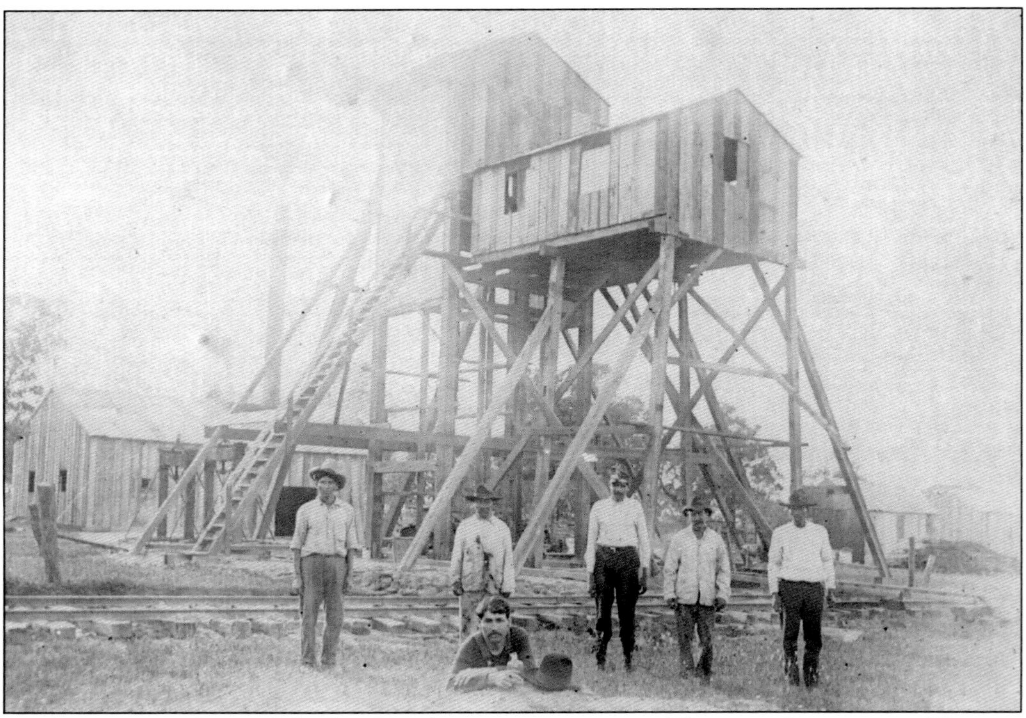

Workers pose in front of the last Vogel mine in operation. (Photograph courtesy of Patricia Whitley McKee.)

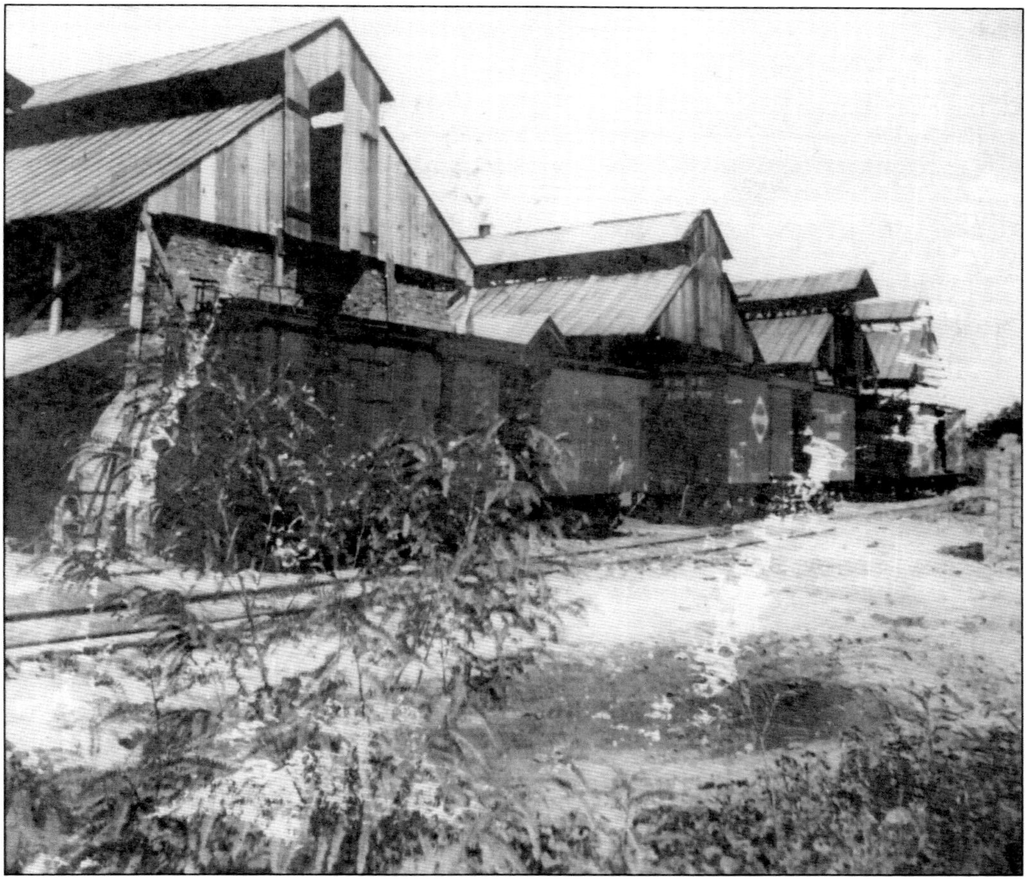

The Lorenz-Vogel brickyard, seen here, was operating in 1918. (Photograph courtesy of Patricia Whitley McKee.)

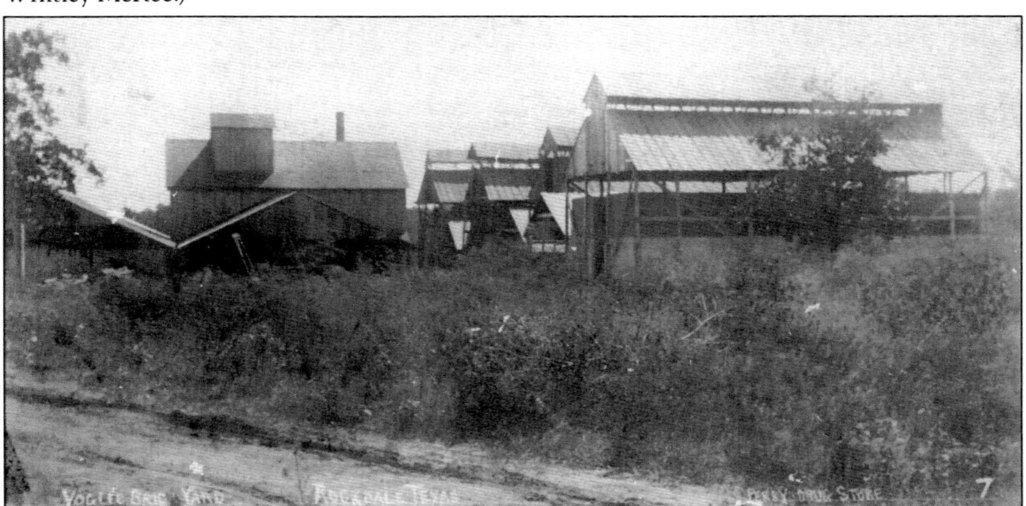

Hermann Vogel stands on the left at the Lorenz-Vogel brickyard. (Photograph courtesy of Patricia Whitley McKee.)

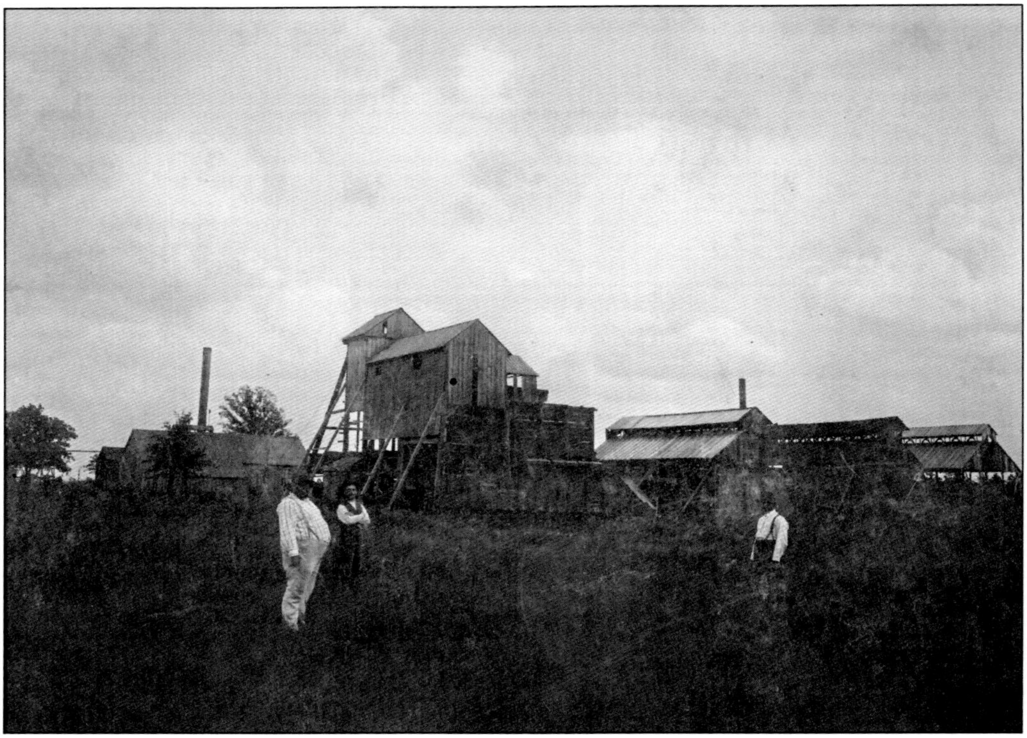

The brickyard in the background, on the site of the Vogel mines, was owned and operated by Gus Lorenz and Hermann Vogel. (Photograph courtesy of Patricia Whitley McKee.)

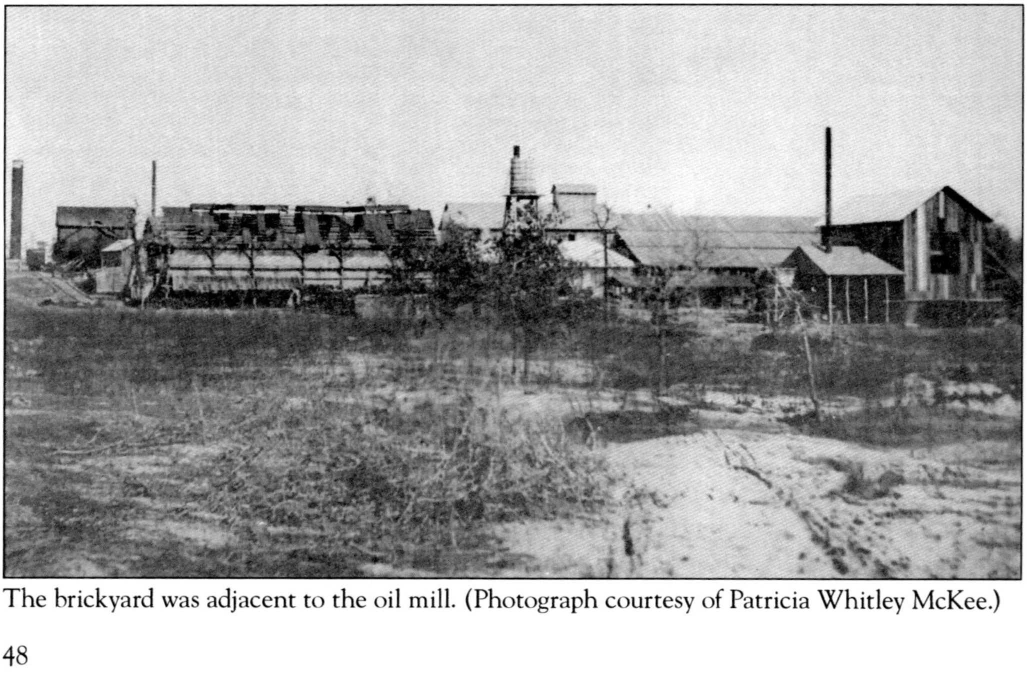

The brickyard was adjacent to the oil mill. (Photograph courtesy of Patricia Whitley McKee.)

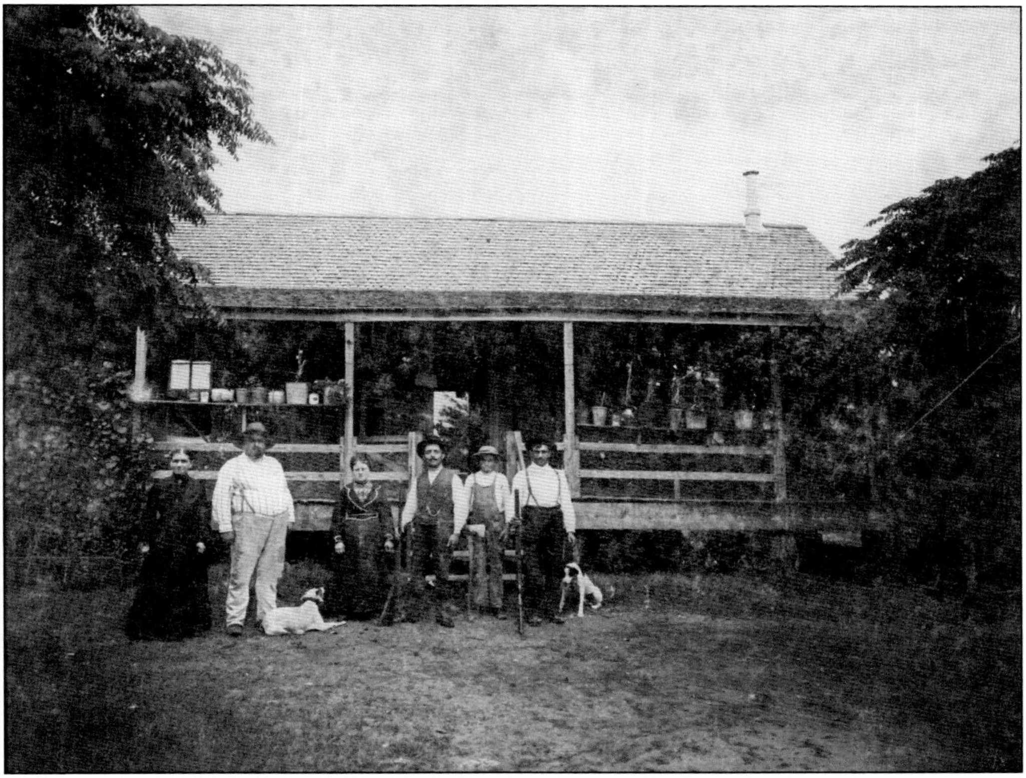

Standing in front of the Vogel home at the mine site are, from left to right, Wilhelmine Frenzel Vogel, Hermann Frederick Vogel, Mrs. Robert Frenzel, Robert Frenzel, Hermann Vogel, and Gus Vogel. The younger Hermann married Anna Schukraft of Rockdale. After Herman's death, Anna opened Vogel's Variety Store, now a part of the building occupied by Patterson Library. The Frenzels were friends of the Vogels. (Photograph courtesy of Patricia Whitley McKee.)

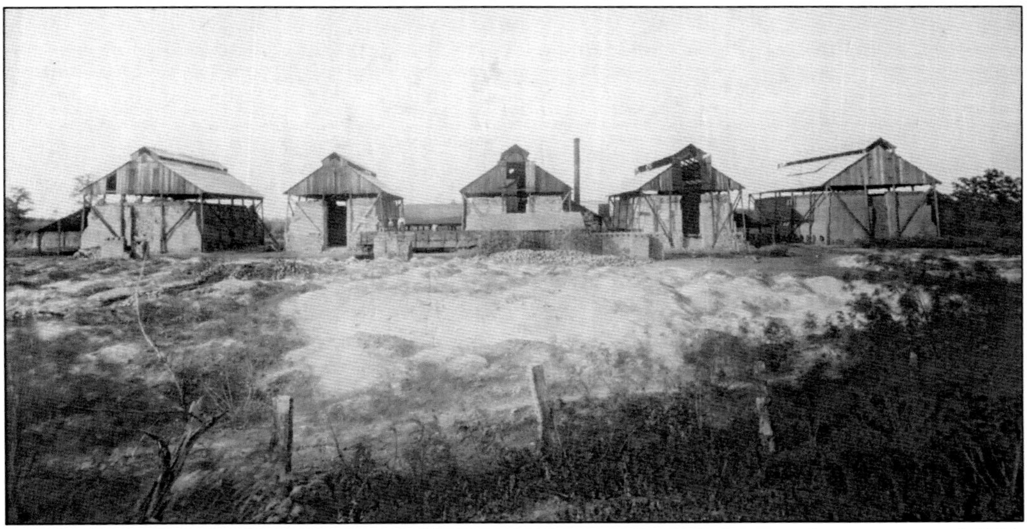

The Vogel-Lorenz brickyard is pictured here on the grounds of the original mine around 1914. (Photograph courtesy of Patricia Whitley McKee.)

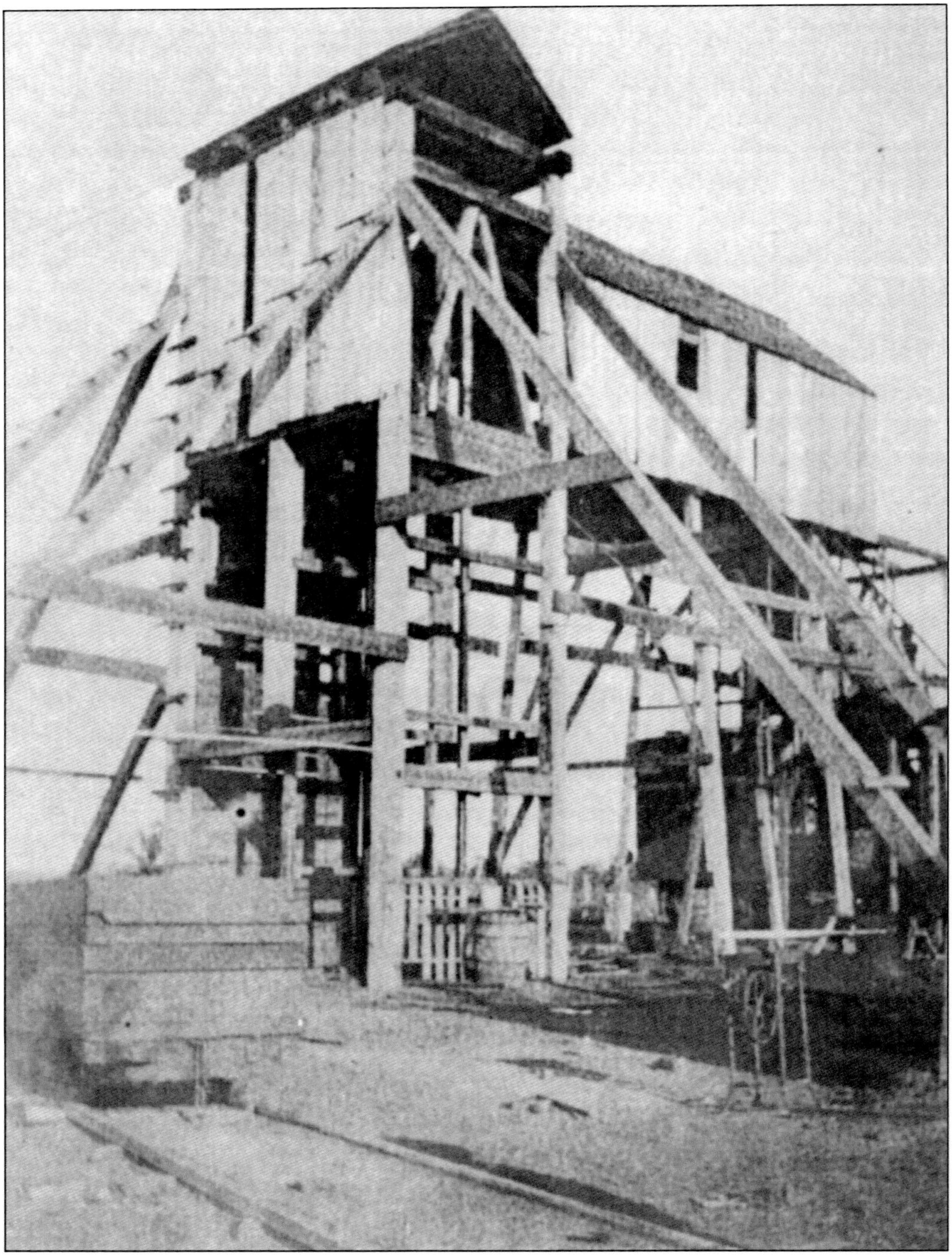

Workers operate in the tunnel mines near the site of the Vogel mines north of Rockdale, where Escuelita is now located. (Photograph courtesy of Alcoa Inc.)

Five

Rockdale Grows and Grows

The economic growth of Rockdale began with the establishment of Loewenstein's Store on Christmas Eve in 1873. Around the same time, E.M. Scarborough came to town. He represented H.P. Hale and Company of Hearne. Scarborough bought a building on Main Street and was a silent partner until Hale's death in 1882. At that time, R.H. Hicks became a partner, and the firm of Scarborough and Hicks was established. Theirs became a leading mercantile store in central Texas. Scarborough moved to Austin, where he established a branch house. The firm continued in Rockdale until 1935, when an early-morning fire destroyed the building, killing two firemen.

Cotton and corn also contributed to the economic growth of the thriving little city. In 1870, a total of 5,143 bales of cotton were produced, and by 1880, the number was 10,844 bales. By 1900, a total of 66,555 bales of cotton were produced in Rockdale, along with 201 bushels of corn.

By the mid-1890s, there were six mining operations in Rockdale, which brought a large number of Hispanics to the area. By 1914, a total of 20 railroad cars of coal were produced daily.

The first bank, the Rockdale Bank, was organized in 1874; but it failed after a year or two, and the structure became the Wolf Hotel. The early city was also filled with sundry stores: millinery shops, drugstores, and even a photographer, John Scott.

A significant change in the economy of Rockdale occurred in 1951 when construction began on the Alcoa plant. It continued to be a vital part of the Rockdale economy until 2008, when the plant ceased operation.

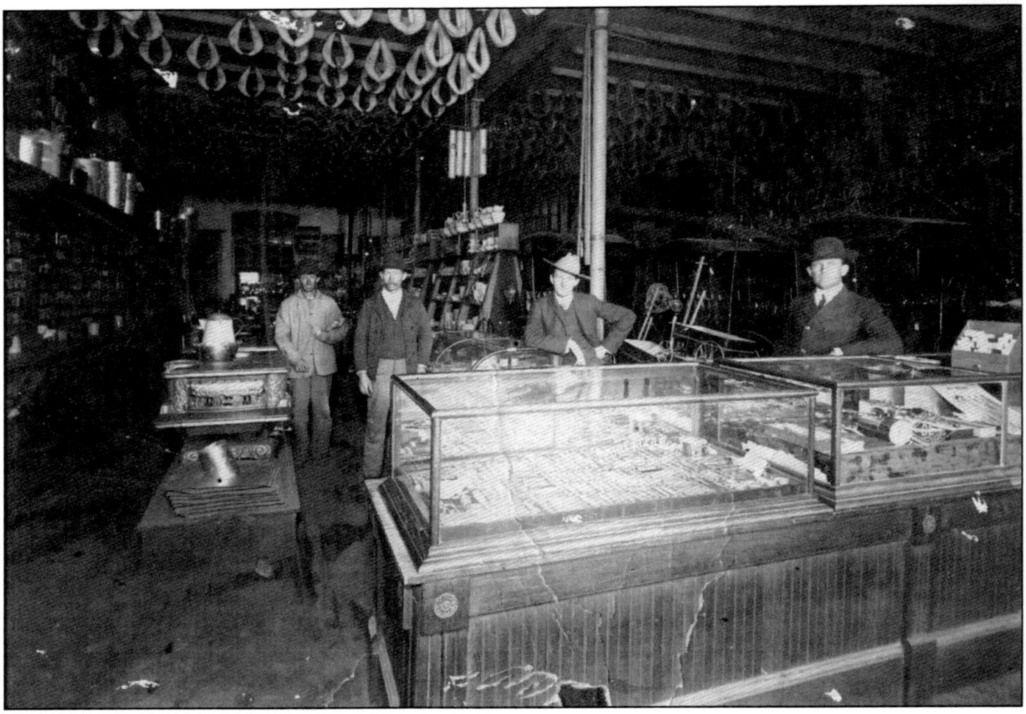

Coffield Hardware was run by Jules Coffield (second from right). On the far right is Preston Perry Sr. (Photograph courtesy of Tommy Coffield.)

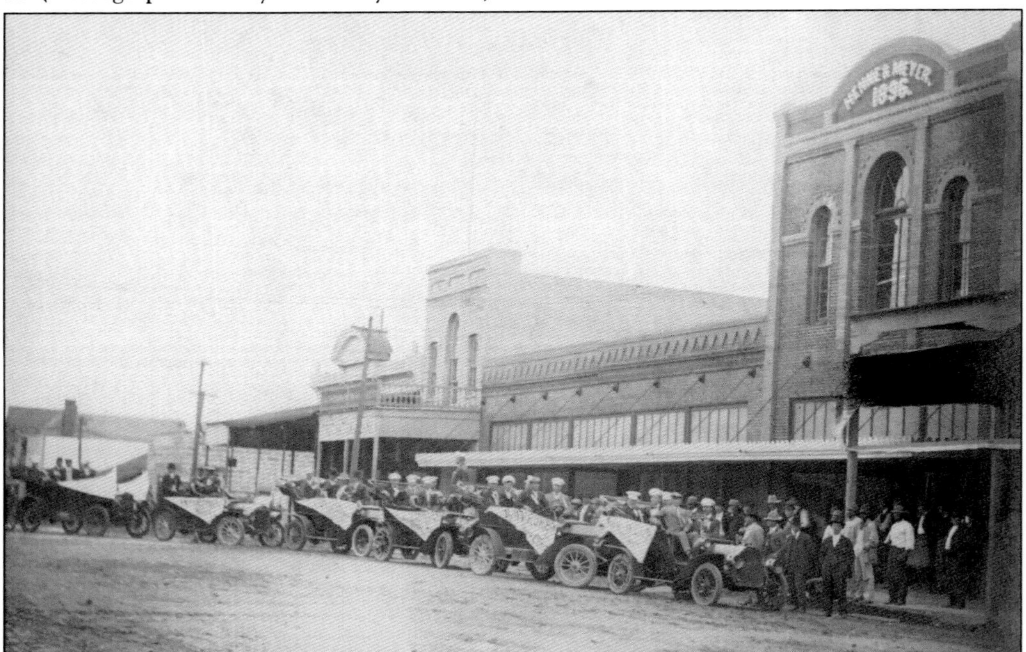

Cars line up in front of Henne and Meyers for the beginning of a parade. (Photograph courtesy of Tommy Coffield.)

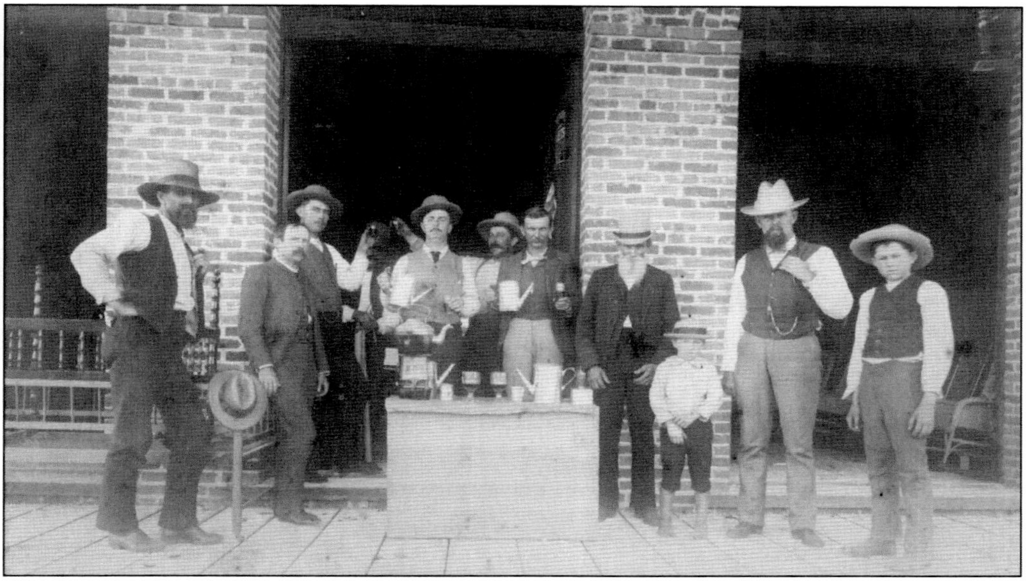

Jules Coffield (second from right) stands in front of Coffield Hardware with other townspeople. (Photograph courtesy of Tommy Coffield.)

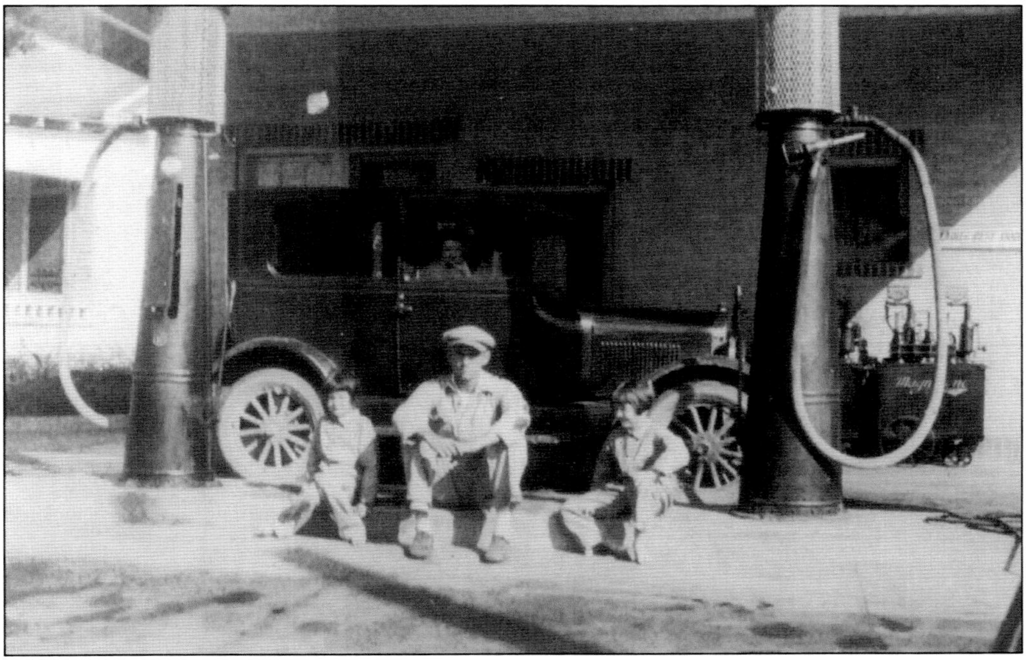

Eugenia Wolf (later Newton) (left) and Ella Frances Wolf (later Williams) sit beside an unidentified man in a service station at the corner of San Gabriel and Cameron Streets as their mother looks on from the car. (Photograph courtesy of Eugenia Wolf Newton.)

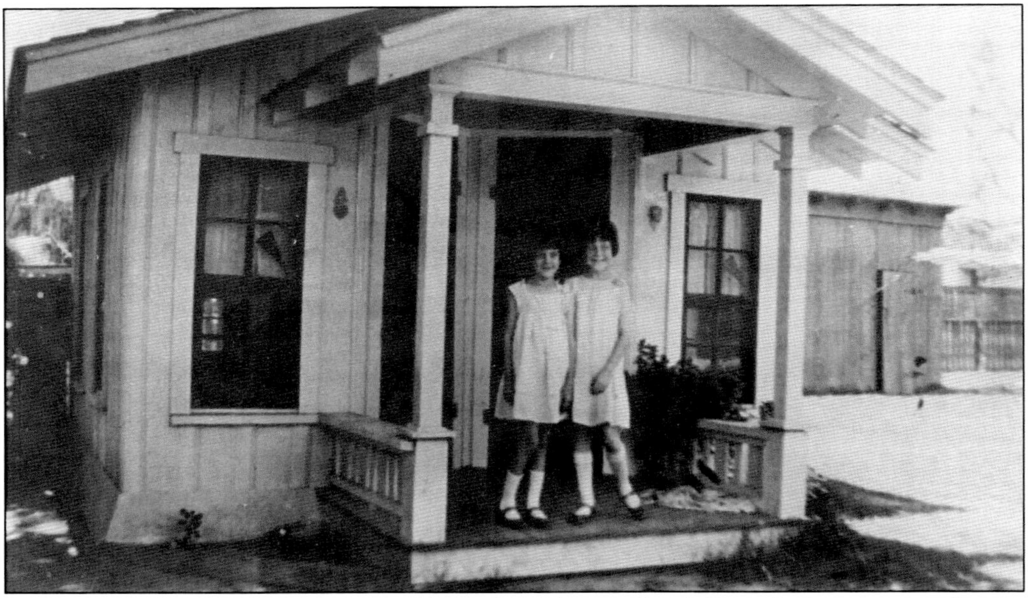

Sisters Eugenia and Ella Frances Wolf stand on the porch of their playhouse, one of many constructed by Tom Marrs, who built many of the homes in Rockdale—including the author's. (Photograph courtesy of Eugenia Wolf Newton.)

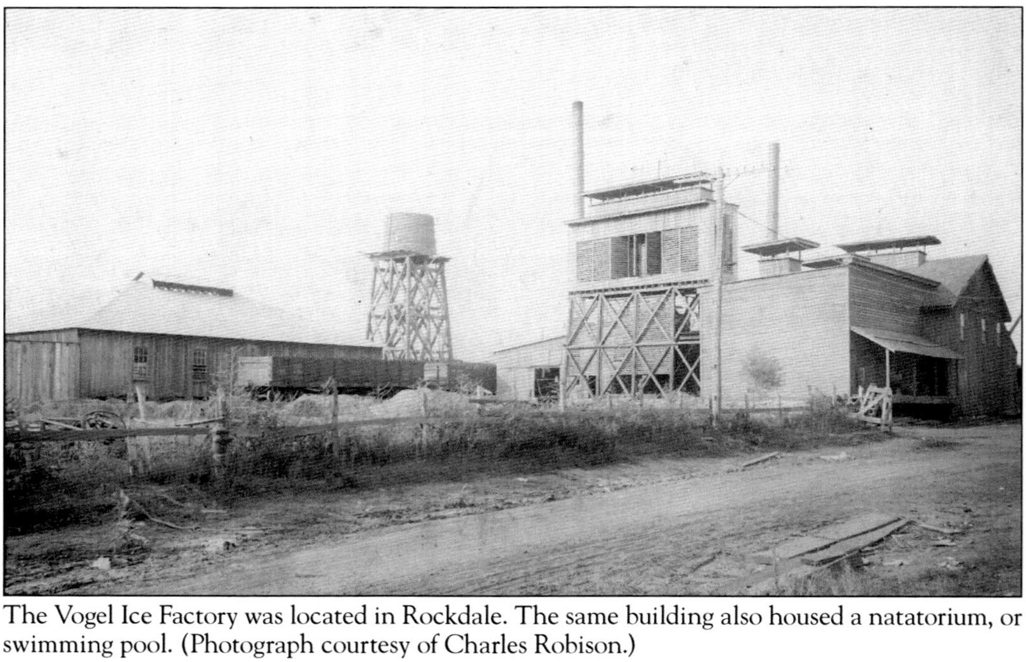

The Vogel Ice Factory was located in Rockdale. The same building also housed a natatorium, or swimming pool. (Photograph courtesy of Charles Robison.)

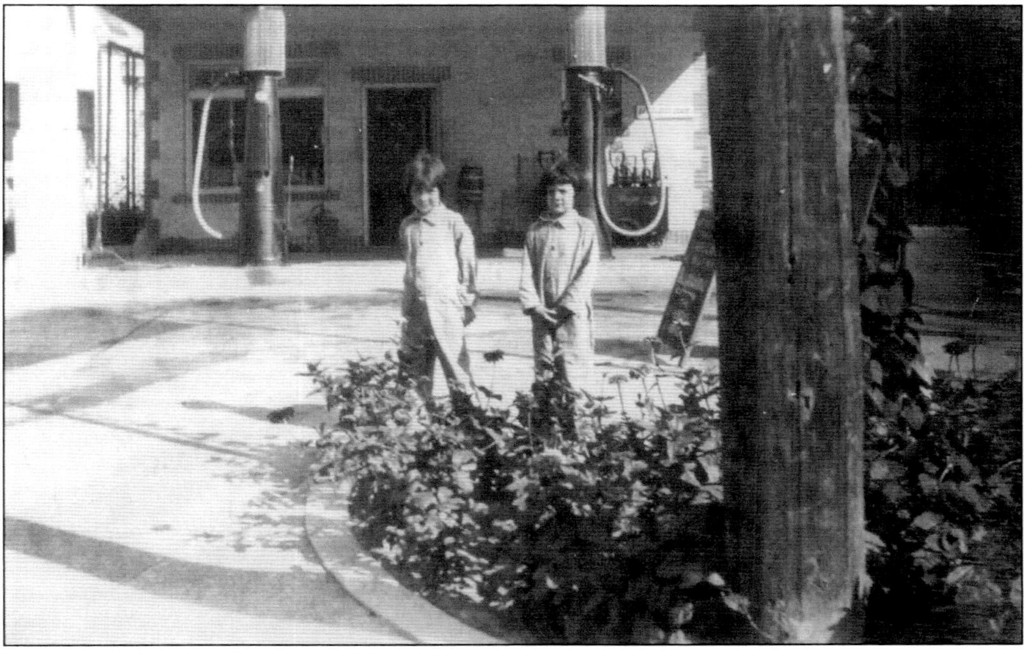

Eugenia and Ella Frances Wolf pose in the flowerbed located in front of the service station at the corner of San Gabriel and Cameron Streets. (Photograph courtesy of Eugenia Wolf Newton.)

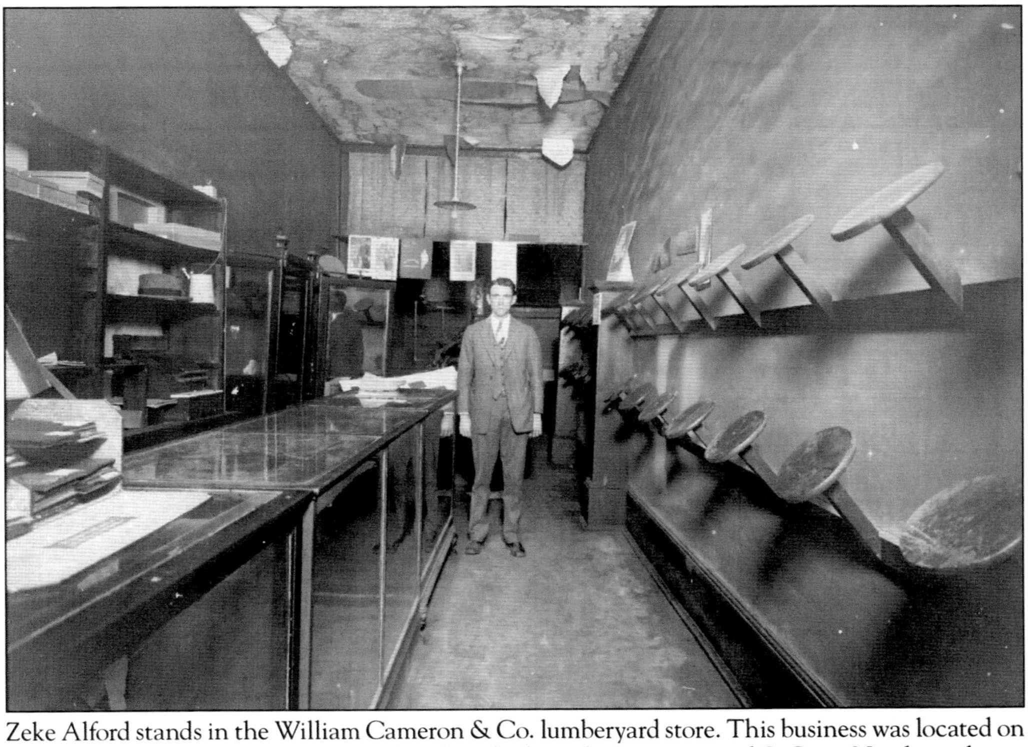

Zeke Alford stands in the William Cameron & Co. lumberyard store. This business was located on Route 908, immediately across the railroad tracks from the International & Great Northern depot. Brinkley Building Supply is now at this site. (Photograph courtesy of Eugenia Wolf Newton.)

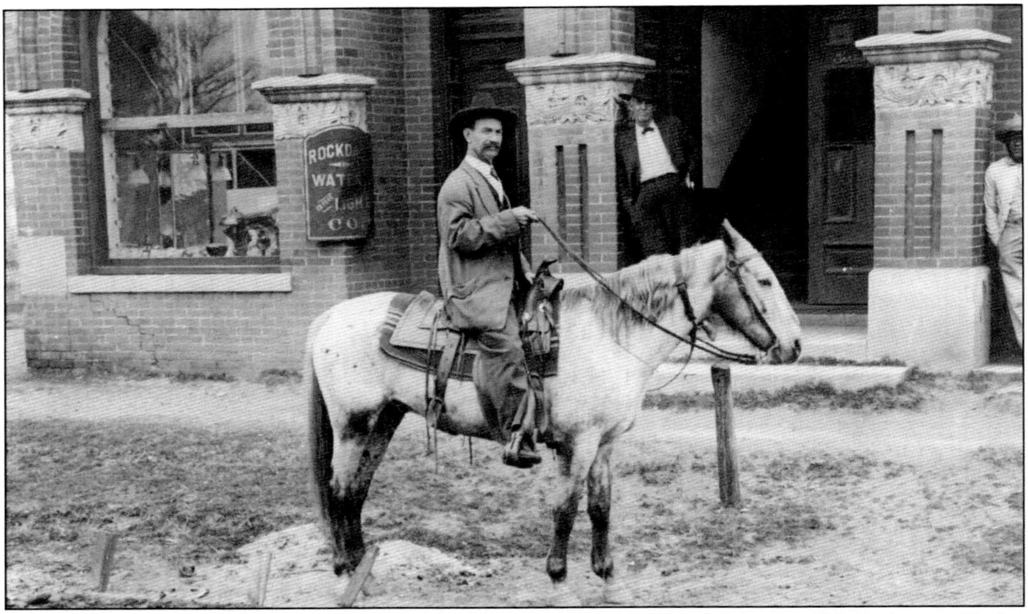

Constable Nathaniel Jefferson poses on his horse in front of Rockdale City Hall. At age 59, he was killed in a traffic accident near Cameron Street. Jefferson was the grandfather of Zeke Alford and Eugenia Wolf Newton. (Photograph courtesy of Eugenia Wolf Newton.)

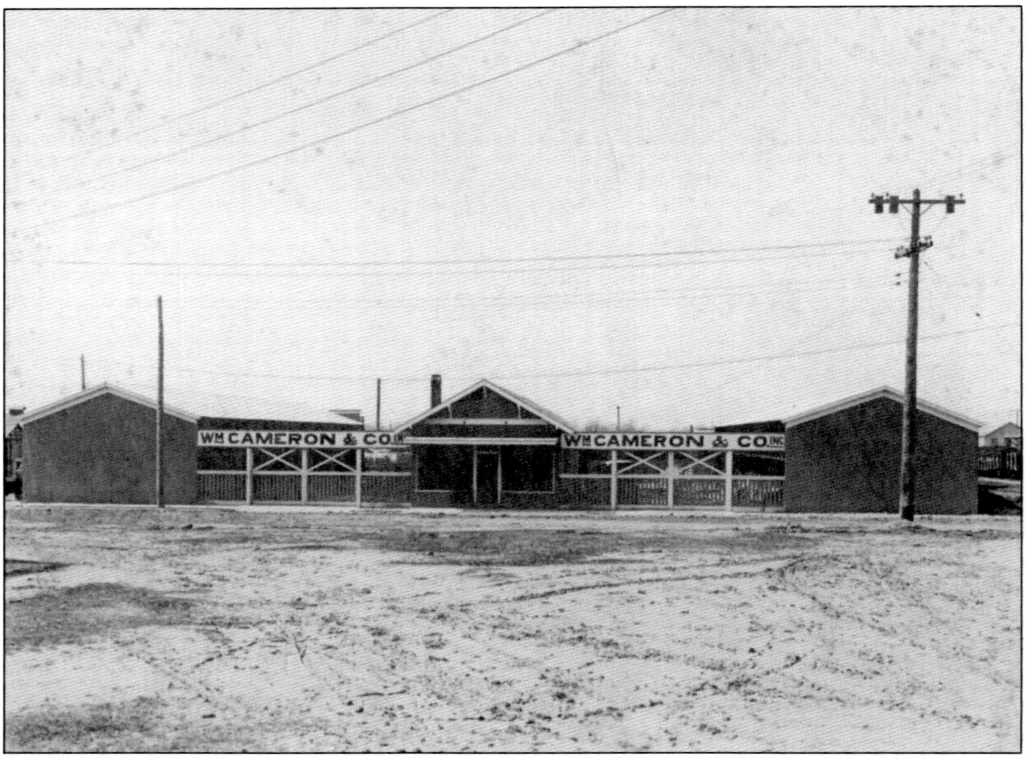

The William Cameron lumberyard was located at the current site of Brinkley Building Supply on Route 908. (Photograph courtesy of Eugenia Wolf Newton.)

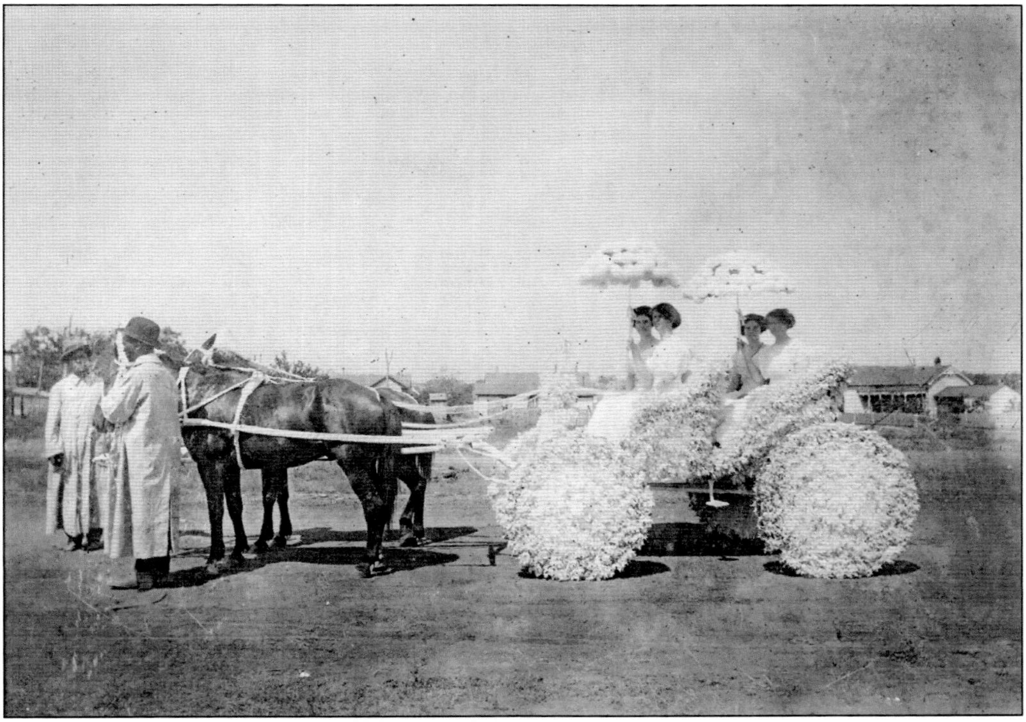

Eula Alford, ? Budman, Maude Alford, and Clara Fridge are out for a very festive carriage ride at the Old Schmidt Place. (Photograph courtesy of Eugenia Wolf Newton.)

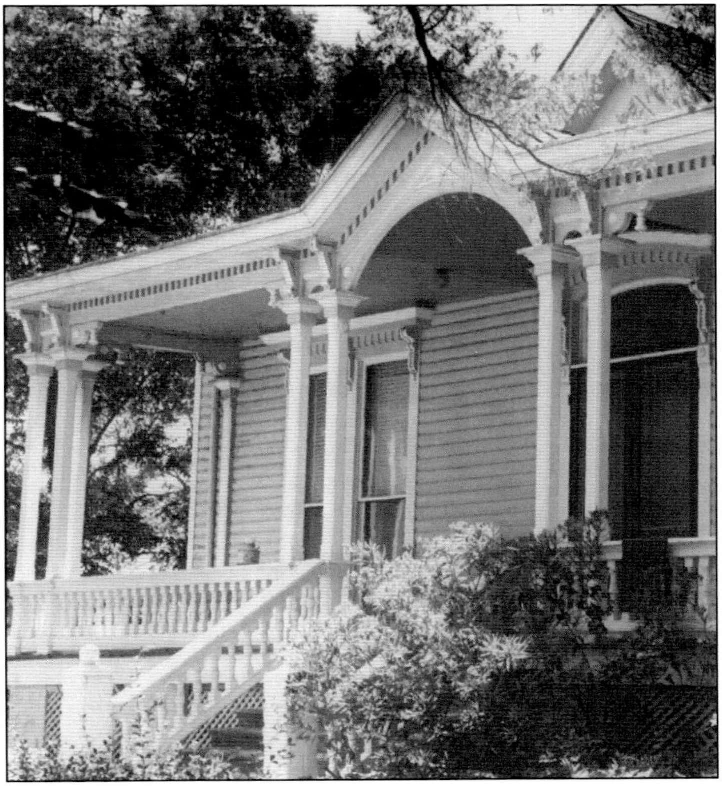

As the city grew and citizens prospered, beautiful homes sprang up all over town. Joseph Loewenstein built this home for his family in 1884. The house had a metal cistern, which was exposed to sunlight to provide hot water. (Photograph courtesy of Joseph Loewenstein, MD, Midland, Texas.)

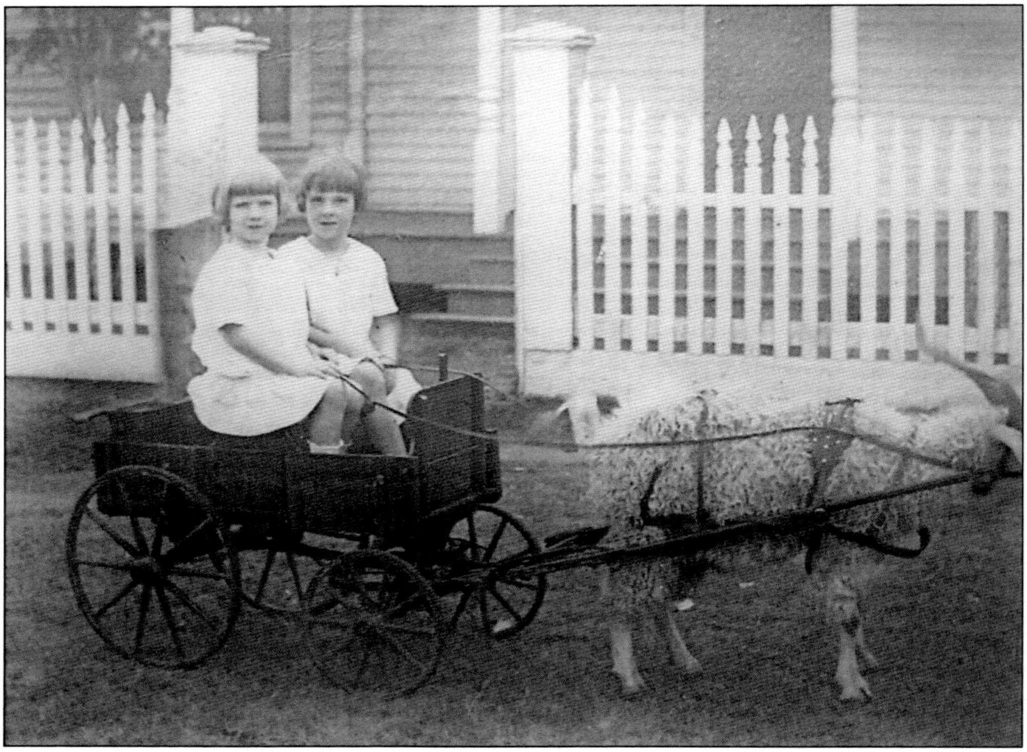

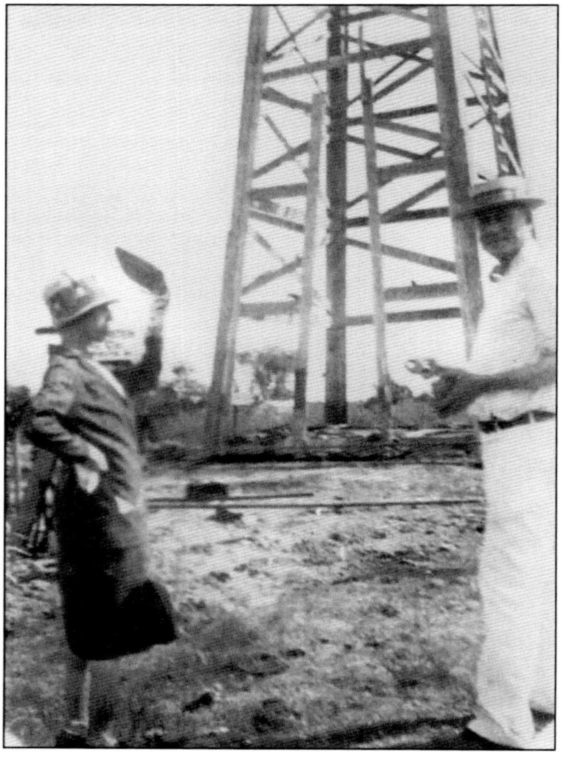

Carrie Loewenstein (left, born 1909) and her elder sister, Miriam (born 1908), were the daughters of Ben Loewenstein Jr. and his wife, Lena. Carrie was the last of the Rockdale Loewensteins, marrying Silas Tharp and living in Rockdale until her death in 1977. (Photograph courtesy of Joseph Loewenstein, MD, Midland, Texas.)

Oil was prominent in the Rockdale economy for a brief time. This photograph, taken in the early 1920s, shows Bertha Loewenstein Meyer, the daughter of Joe Loewenstein, and her cousin, Ben Loewenstein Jr., celebrating as a well came in on what is now Route 487. (Photograph courtesy of Joseph Loewenstein, MD, Midland, Texas.)

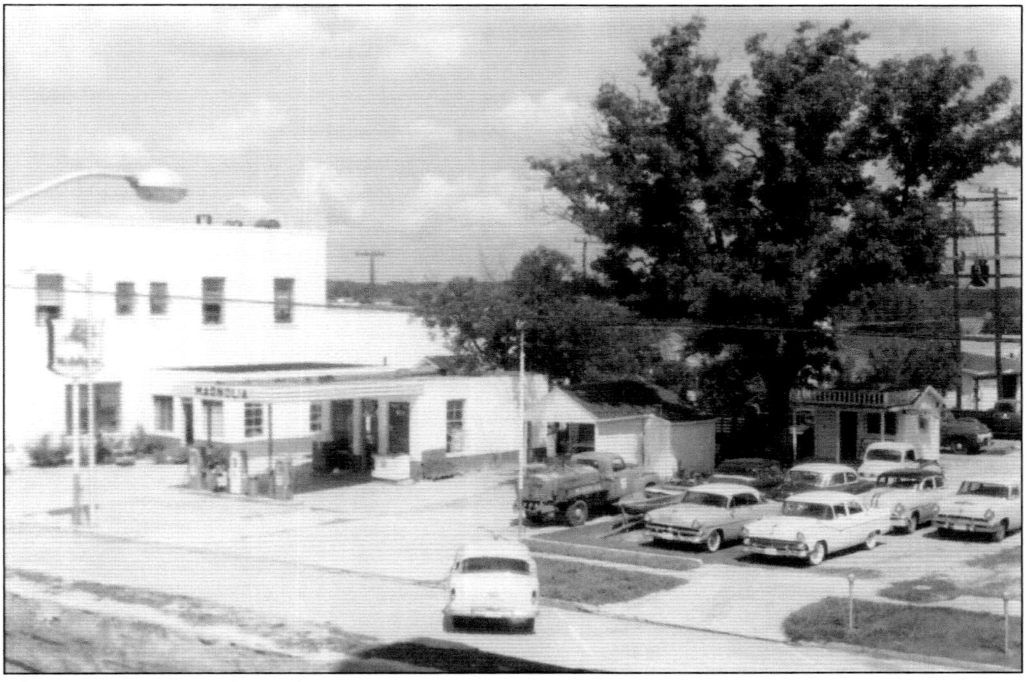

This service station, formerly George Lumpkin's Mobil dealership, is adjacent to Rockdale City Hall. It also used to be a Sinclair station. The site is now an auto detail shop, but the large tree is still there. (Photograph courtesy of Gary Jackson.)

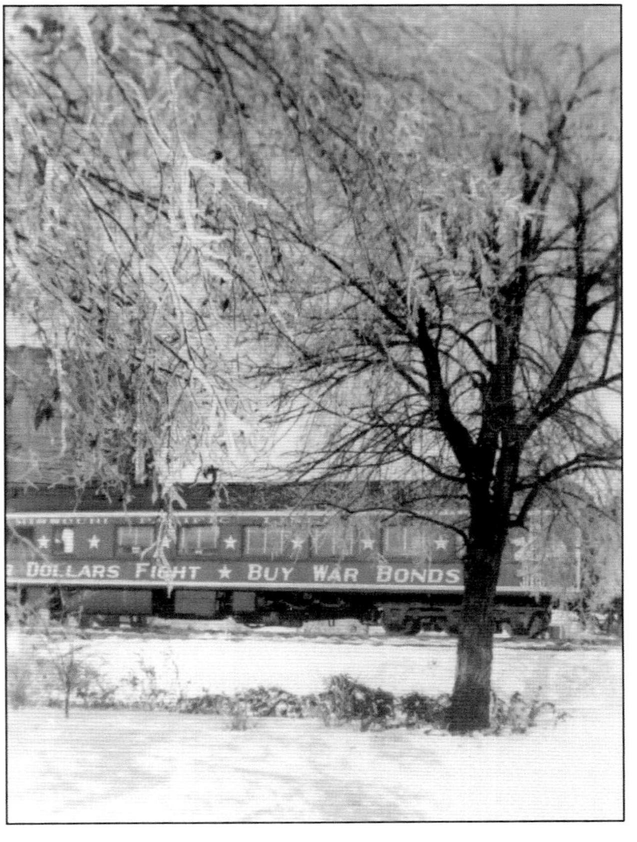

This train stopped in Rockdale to promote war bonds. This type of advertising was used frequently, both on passenger trains and troop trains. (Photograph courtesy of Gary Jackson.)

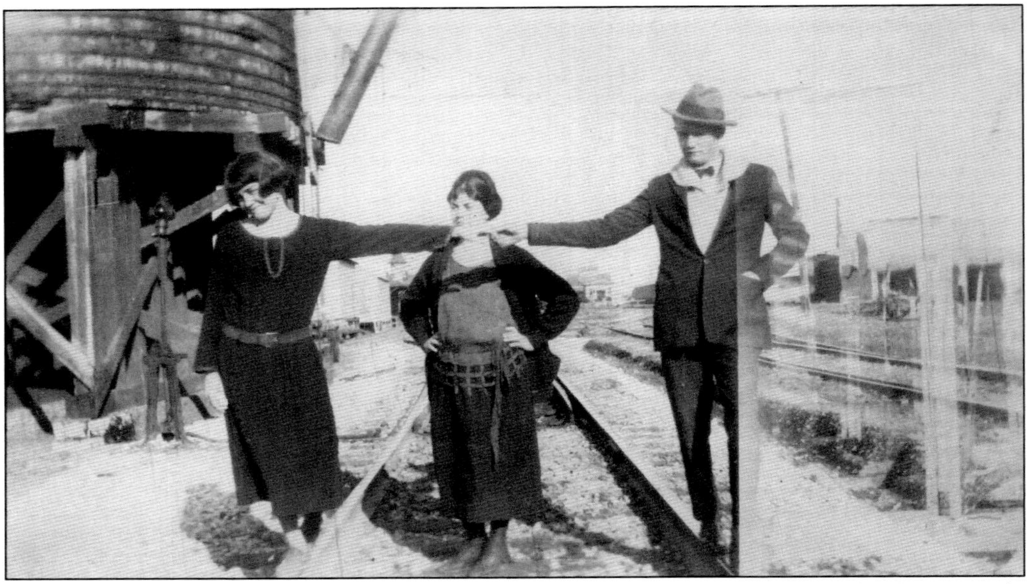

Lela Dean (left), Luine Dean, and Bill Allen have fun on the train tracks. Note the depot cupola in the background. (Photograph courtesy of Gary Jackson.)

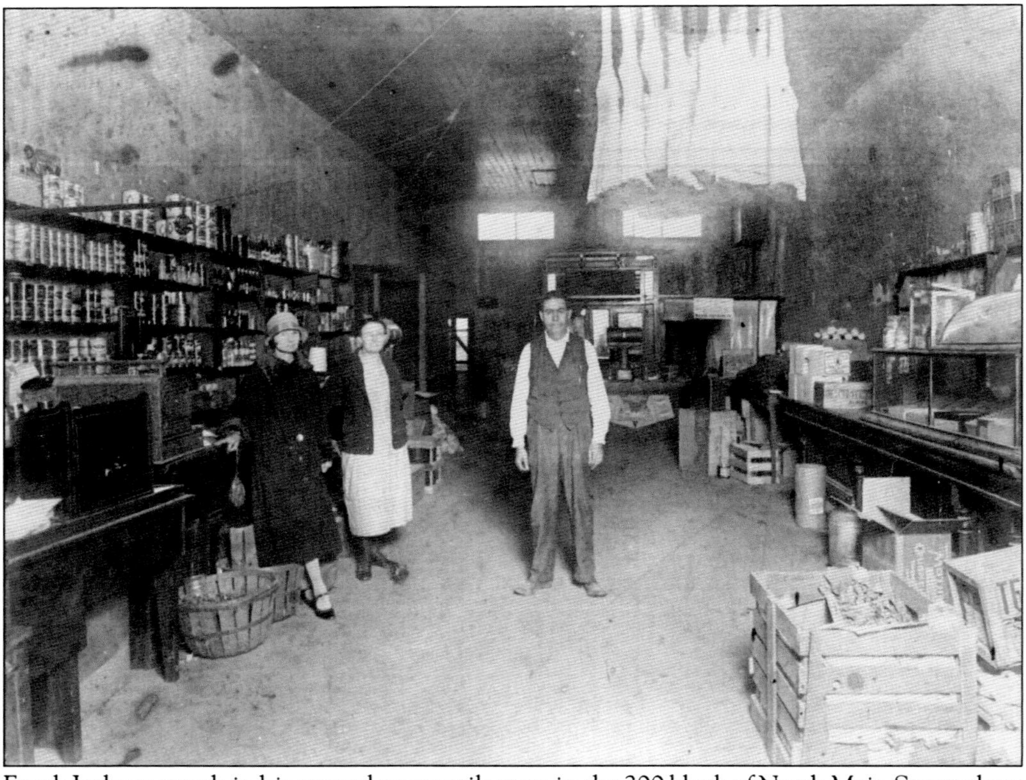

Frank Jackson stands in his general mercantile store in the 200 block of North Main Street along with Willie Mae Jackson (left) and an unidentified woman. The store operated in the 1920s. (Photograph courtesy of Gary Jackson).

Peggy Salisbury Nicholson, who grew up in Rockdale and graduated from Rockdale High School in 1951, was one of many students in the area with an interest in tennis. (Photograph courtesy of the author.)

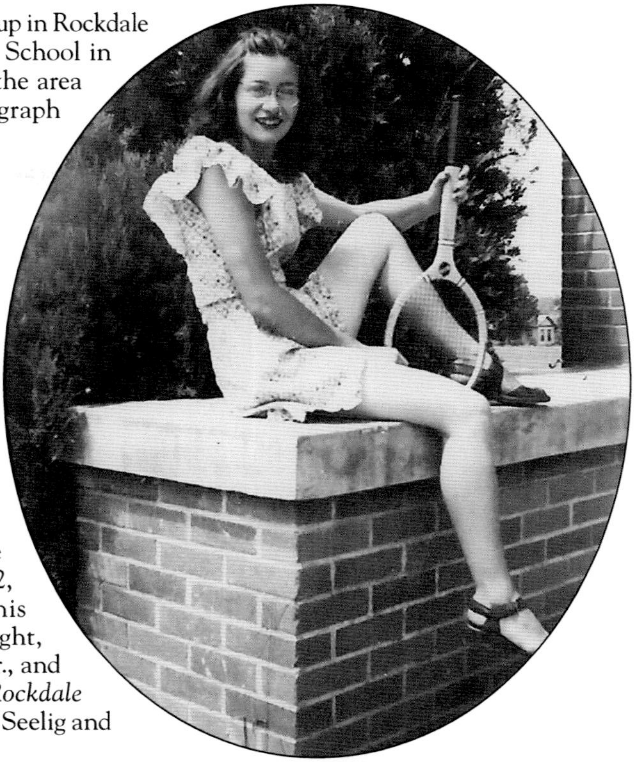

Backhaus Brothers Grocery opened in Rockdale in 1922 and operated until the store was sold in 1956. The business became an IGA store in 1932, an event pictured elsewhere in this book. Pictured here, from left to right, are John Backhaus, Gus Backhaus Jr., and Eddie Backhaus. (Photograph by *Rockdale Reporter*, courtesy of Doris Backhaus Seelig and Ruth Backhaus Storey.)

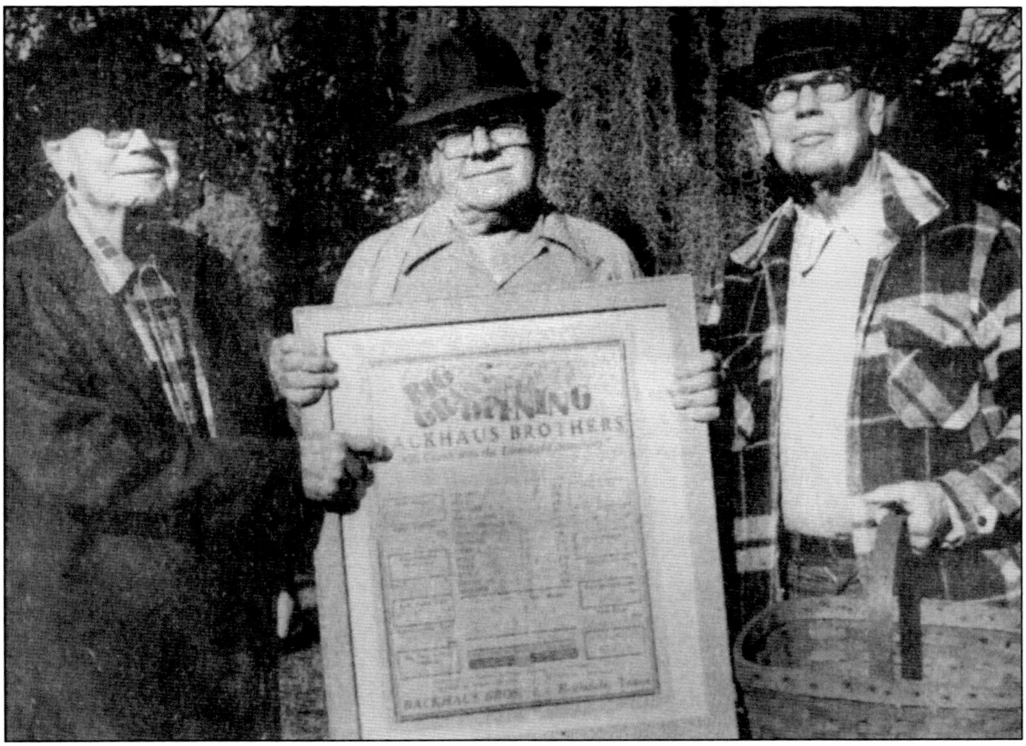

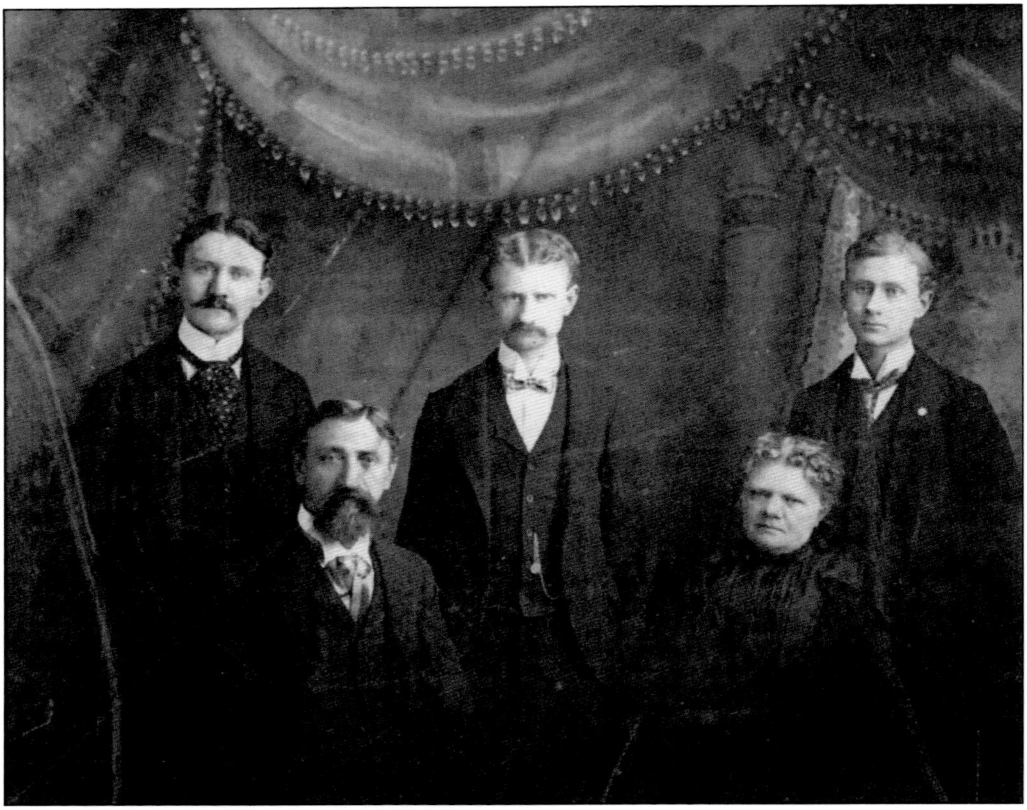

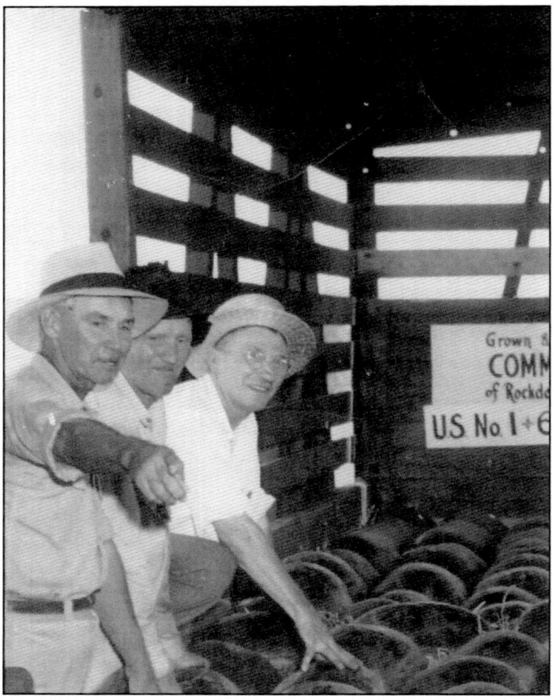

The Ben Loewenstein family poses for this family photograph around 1900. In front are Ben Loewenstein and his wife, Carrie. Behind them, from left to right, are Joe Loewenstein (born 1875), Robert (born 1874), and Ben Jr. (born 1880). (Photograph courtesy of Joseph Loewenstein, MD, Midland, Texas.)

Rockdale's agricultural background included watermelons, like these waiting to be shipped out around 1955. (Photograph courtesy of Gary Jackson.)

Six

George Sessions Perry

by Garna Christian, PhD,
University of Houston–Downtown

George Sessions Perry never really left Rockdale. The National Book Award winner and his beloved wife, Claire, spent their summers in a farmhouse in Guilford, Connecticut, for the last 15 years of his life before he died in 1956. Perry traveled widely on two European excursions: first in the 1930s as a World War II war correspondent, and later as a writer for the *Saturday Evening Post*. As gregarious as he was talented, Perry was welcomed at editorial offices in Philadelphia and New York City and hosted in the centers of power at Washington, DC. Nevertheless, Perry's heart and soul remained in the town of his birth.

Perry was Rockdale's ambassador to the world, a status he proudly flaunted. Rockdale, by its own name or fictionalized as Hackberry or Black Jack, formed the stage for most of his short stories as well as his major novels *Walls Rise Up*, *My Granny Van*, *Tale of a Foolish Farmer*, and the award-winning classic *Hold Autumn in Your Hand*. Perry never missed an opportunity to hail Rockdale as his favorite place in his interviews and writings.

Inevitably, chance and success pulled Perry away. Determined to serve his country despite a fall that left him physically unfit, he reported from the front lines of World War II. His *Saturday Evening Post* series on cities and families in the 1940s and 1950s required strenuous travel, which he endured despite the excruciating spinal arthritis that eventually immobilized him. After a nervous breakdown, Perry was unable to return to his Texas birthplace.

Ironically, his tragic drowning in an icy river near his Connecticut residence brought George Sessions Perry home, where he rests today, in the words of a reporter, "among magnolia and pine-clad hills."

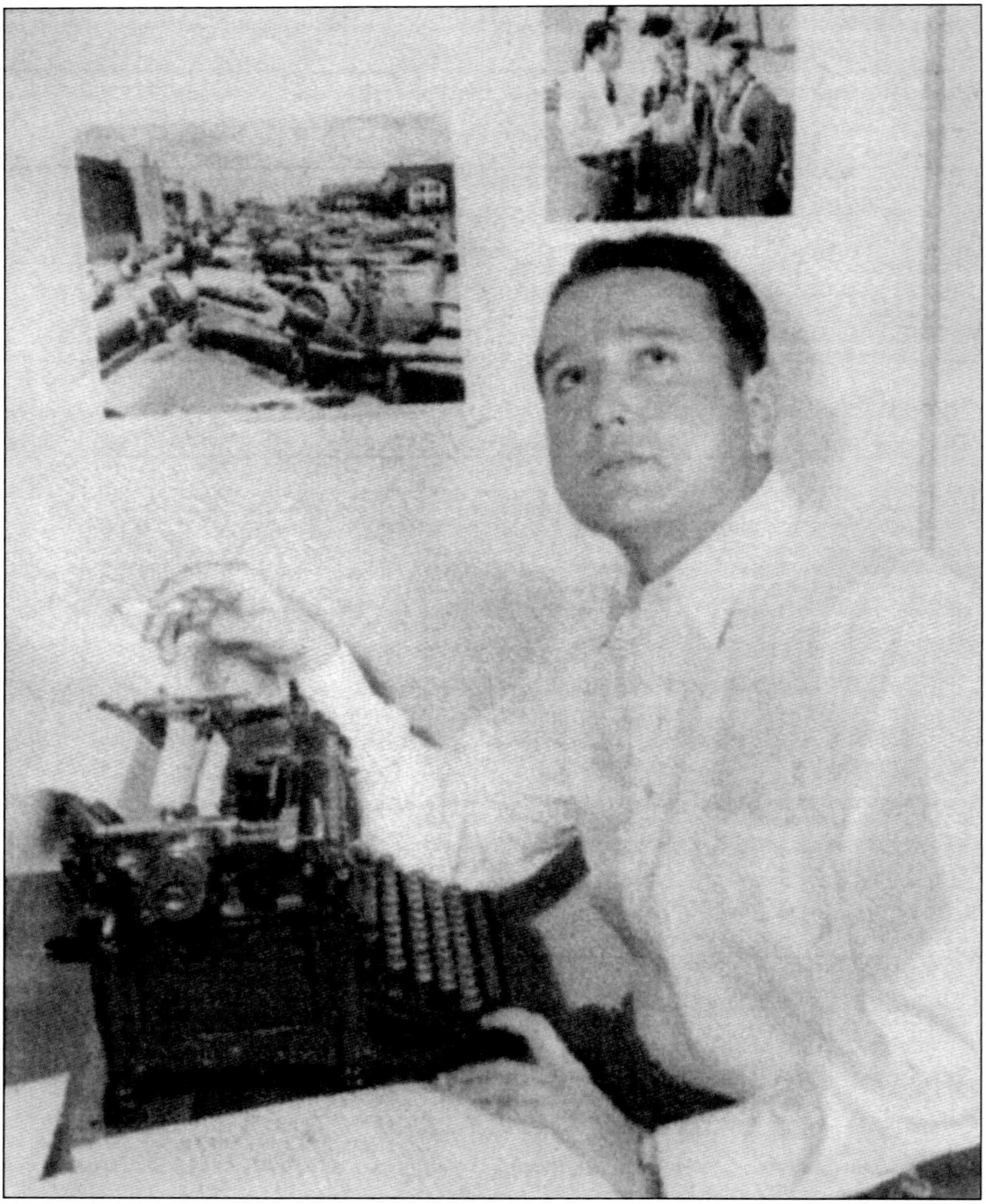

Declared ineligible for the military in World War II because of a recent fall from a horse that broke his left arm, Perry volunteered as an adjunct public relations officer at Randolph Field in Schertz, Texas. He wrote articles on air training and met novelist John Dos Passos and his wife. Discontented with his contribution, Perry applied for "a broader scope of action" with the Department of Air Force Public Relations. (Photograph courtesy of *Rockdale Reporter*.)

Four-year-old George Sessions Perry poses on the porch of his Rockdale home. Although his autobiographical novels depicted a troubled childhood, neighbors remembered a fun-loving boy who rode his pony through the streets shirtless and a charming schoolmate and athlete. A friend recalled Perry selling him a very expensive ring for only $4 for his graduation. (Photograph courtesy of *Rockdale Reporter.*)

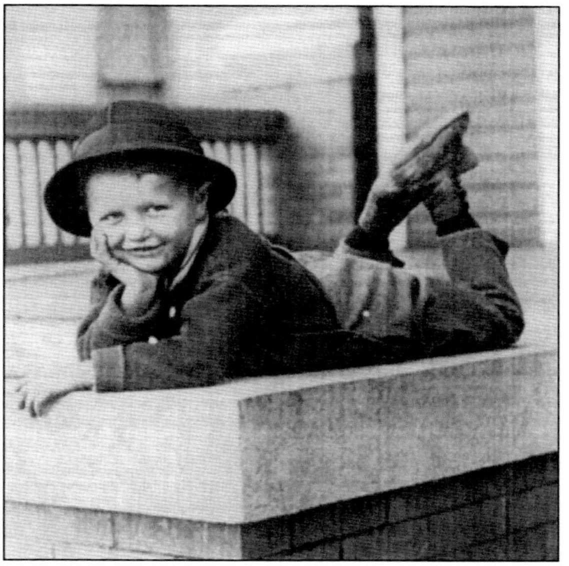

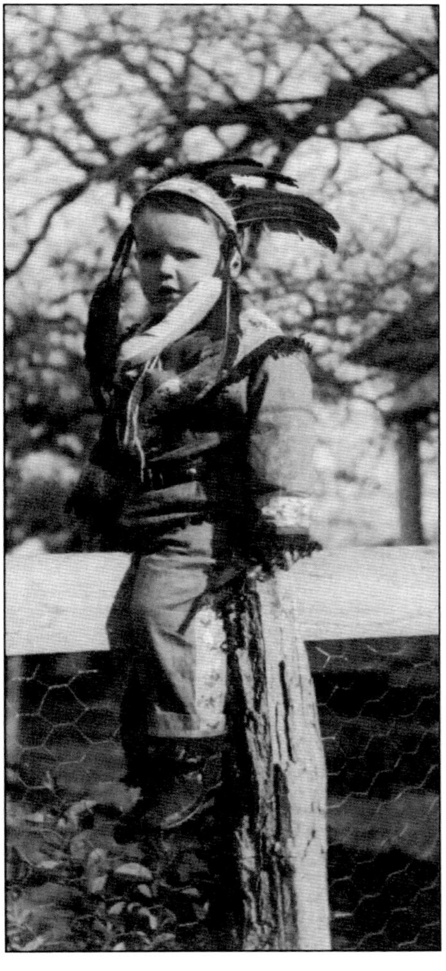

Young George sits on a fence post as "Chief Rain-in-the-Face," his first remembered character. As a child, he unwittingly started a fire that burned the fence and brought out the volunteer fire department, of which his father was a member. The incident embarrassed and humiliated the sensitive child, according to the adult Perry's fictionalized account. (Photograph courtesy of *Rockdale Reporter.*)

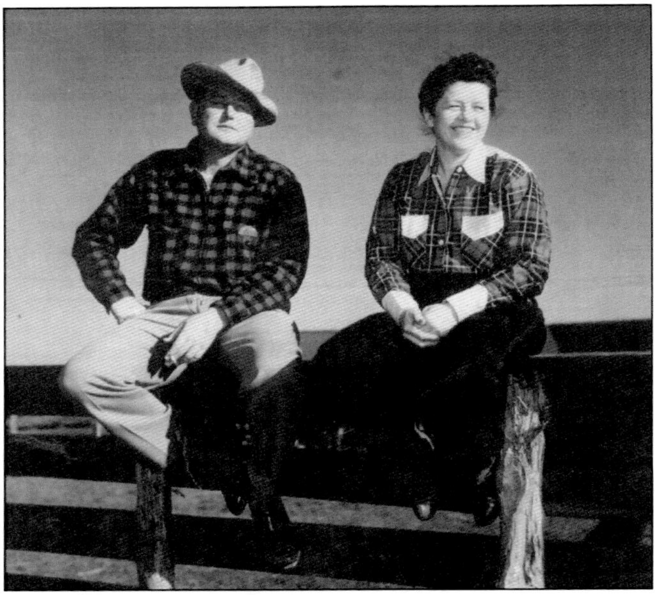

George and Claire Perry pose at their Hold Autumn in Your Hand Farm. The Perrys bought the property with proceeds from his National Book Award–winning novel of the same name. George recounts with humor the tribulations of running the farm in *Tale of a Foolish Farmer.* He confided that he named the farm animals after people they resembled. (Photograph courtesy of *Rockdale Reporter.*)

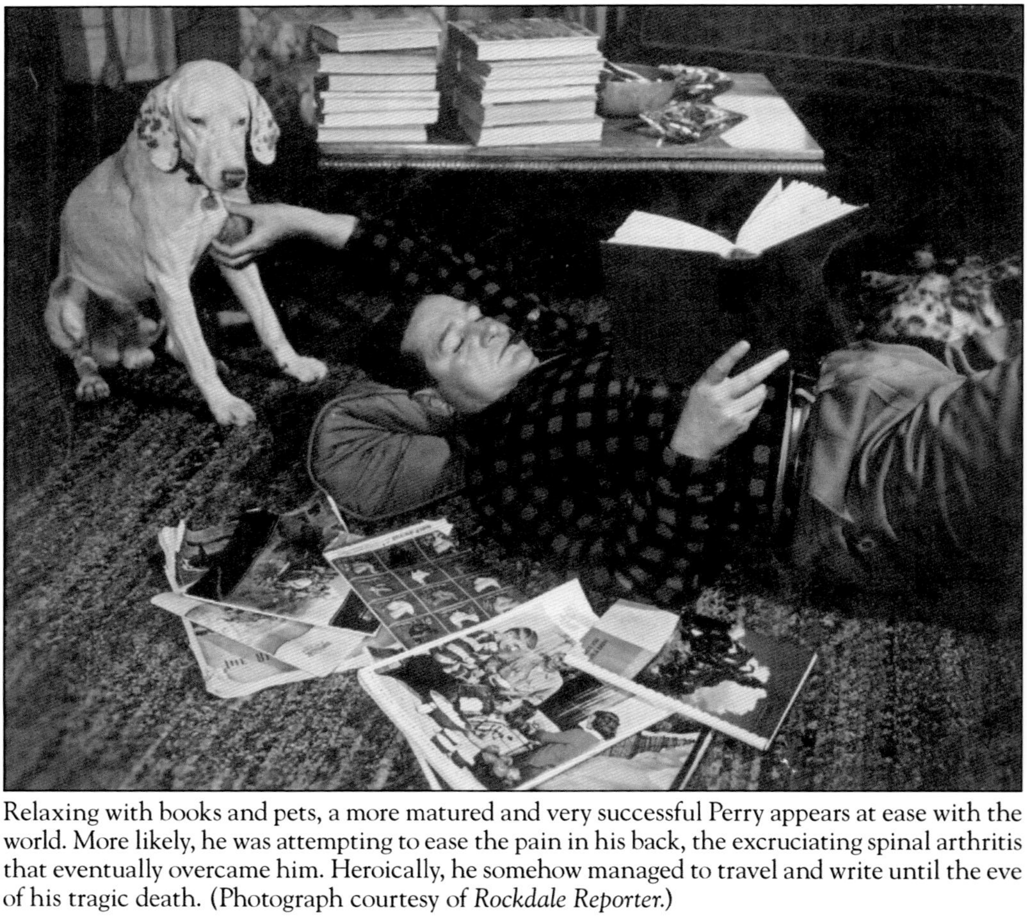

Relaxing with books and pets, a more matured and very successful Perry appears at ease with the world. More likely, he was attempting to ease the pain in his back, the excruciating spinal arthritis that eventually overcame him. Heroically, he somehow managed to travel and write until the eve of his tragic death. (Photograph courtesy of *Rockdale Reporter.*)

Perry is seen here in his study with an unidentified guest. The gregarious Rockdalean made friends and was befriended instantly, often creating lifelong relationships with interviewees and passersby. Although he met and corresponded with major literary figures, Perry remained outside their social circles—with the exception of Texas folklorist J. Frank Dobie, whom he and Claire always addressed respectfully as Mr. Dobie. (Photograph courtesy of *Rockdale Reporter.*)

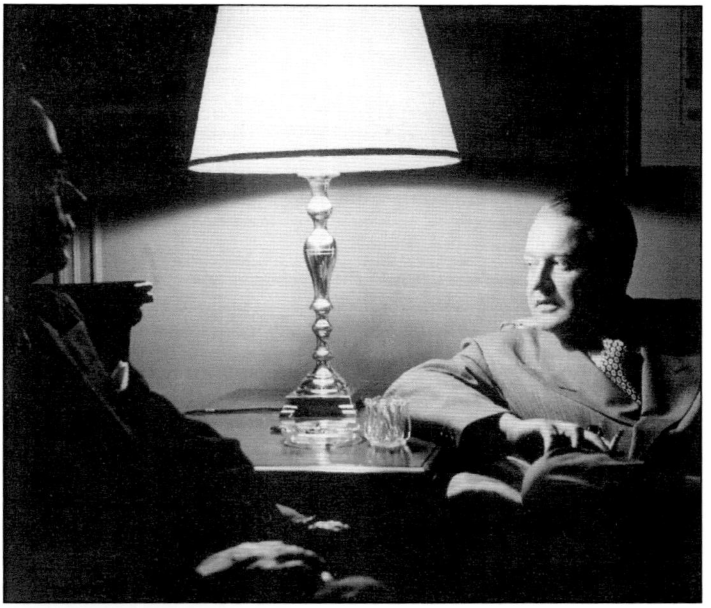

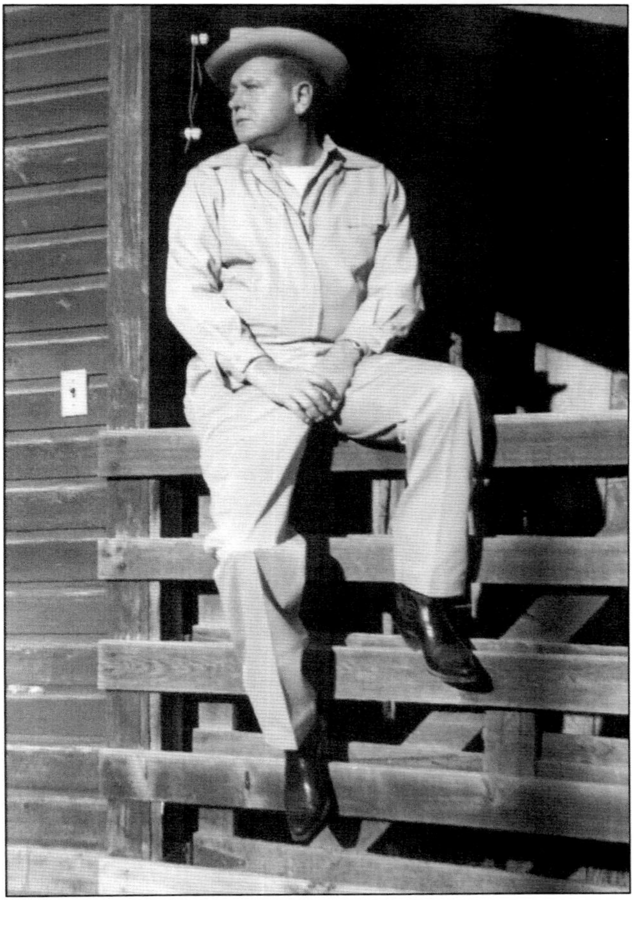

Perry relaxes in western gear at his Rockdale farm. As a welcome relief from the business suits and tuxedoes that he wore to big-city editorial meetings and social functions, Perry liked to kick back at his farm in more comfortable dress. He was famously assisted by Mary Arnwine and her family, who performed the daily chores and managed the property during his extensive absences. (Photograph courtesy of *Rockdale Reporter.*)

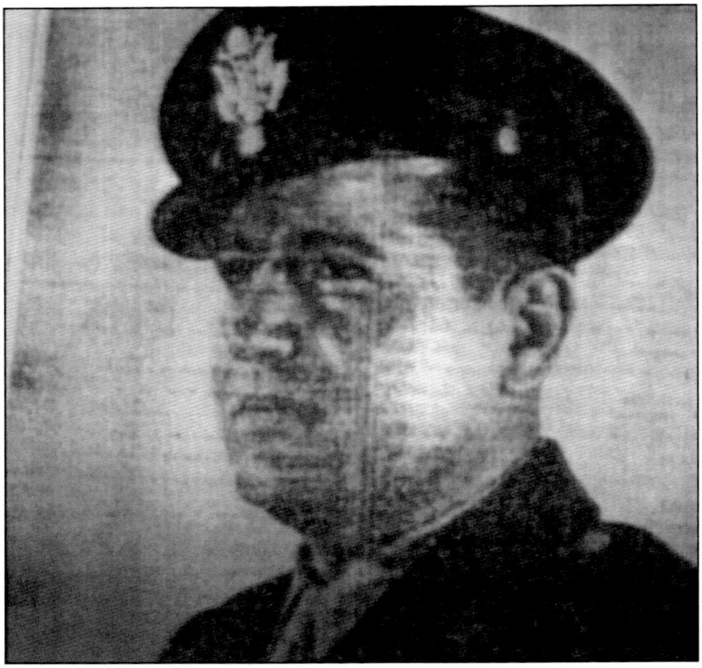

As a World War II correspondent, Perry was in the first wave of American troops in the Sicilian invasion and experienced bombing and submarine attacks. The Texan followed in the footsteps of Winston Churchill, Ernest Hemingway, Martha Gelhorn, Richard Harding Davis, and the inestimable Ernie Pyle, all war correspondents who risked their lives in the same manner as military personnel, but without weapons. Many, including Perry, suffered long-term post-traumatic stress. (Photograph courtesy of *Rockdale Reporter.*)

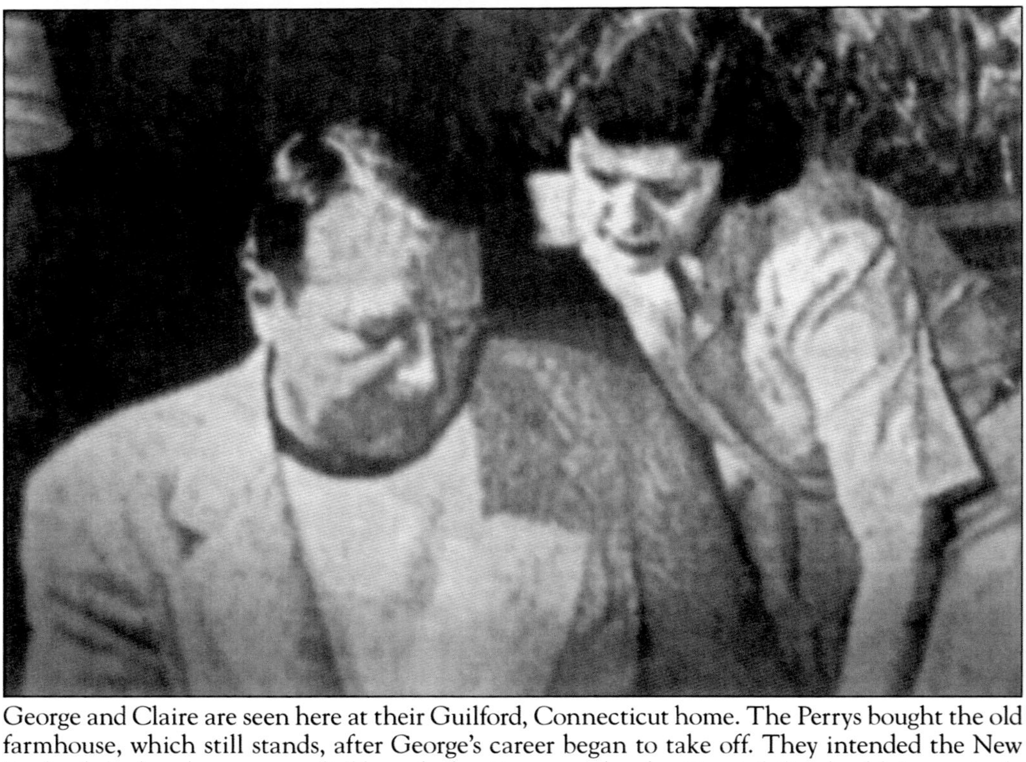

George and Claire are seen here at their Guilford, Connecticut home. The Perrys bought the old farmhouse, which still stands, after George's career began to take off. They intended the New England abode to be summer relief from the hot Texas weather, but Perry's failing health increasingly lengthened their visits. The colonial town's proximity to New York and Philadelphia placed him closer to his publishers' editorial offices. (Photograph courtesy of *Rockdale Reporter.*)

This is a map of Perry's pond, which he immortalized in one of his last articles for the *Saturday Evening Post*, "The Enchanted Pond." While reading Henry David Thoreau's *Walden Pond* at the edge of a swamp bordering his Connecticut property, George conceived the idea of damming a portion of the marshland, and he then created the pond. (Photograph courtesy of *Rockdale Reporter*.)

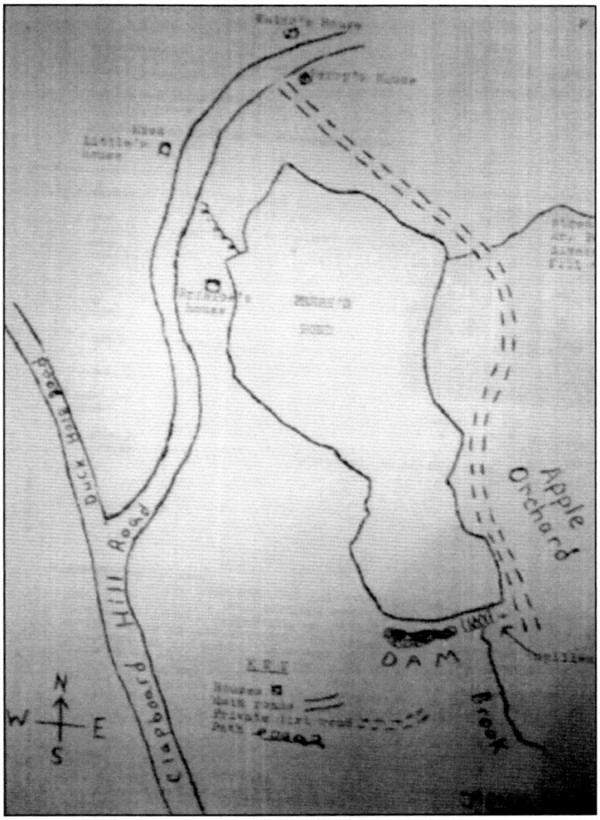

George and Claire lived in her parents' home in Beaumont, Texas, (seen here) in the 1930s when George was a struggling author. Like his houses in Rockdale and Guilford, it is a two-story structure and survives. Perhaps he associated hard times with the city, as Beaumont sometimes inspired George as a location for his fiction. (Photograph courtesy of *Rockdale Reporter*.)

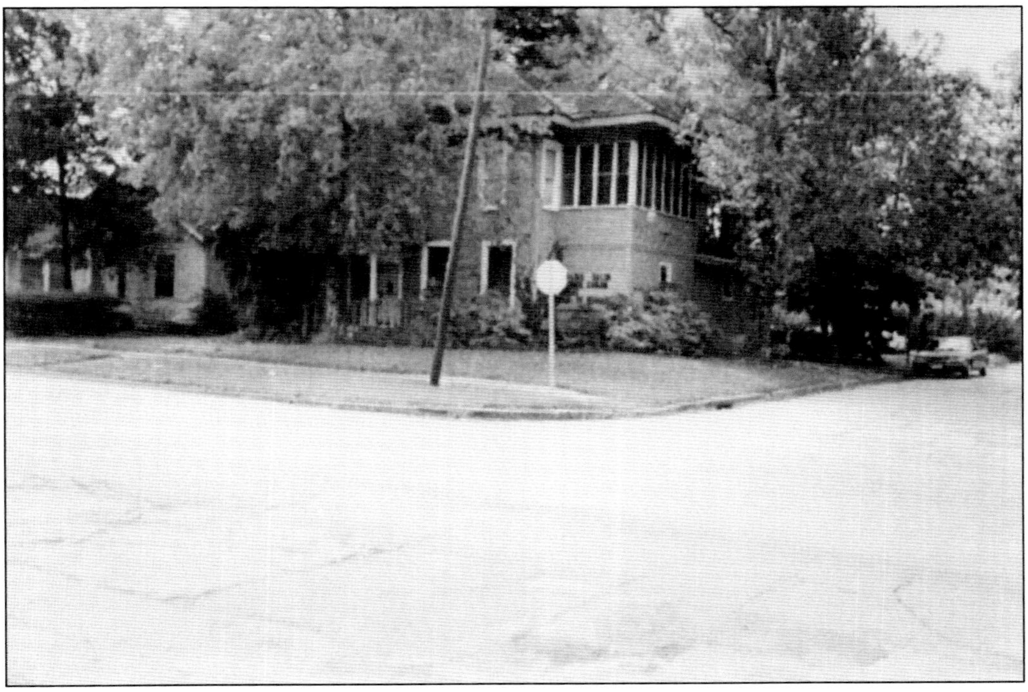

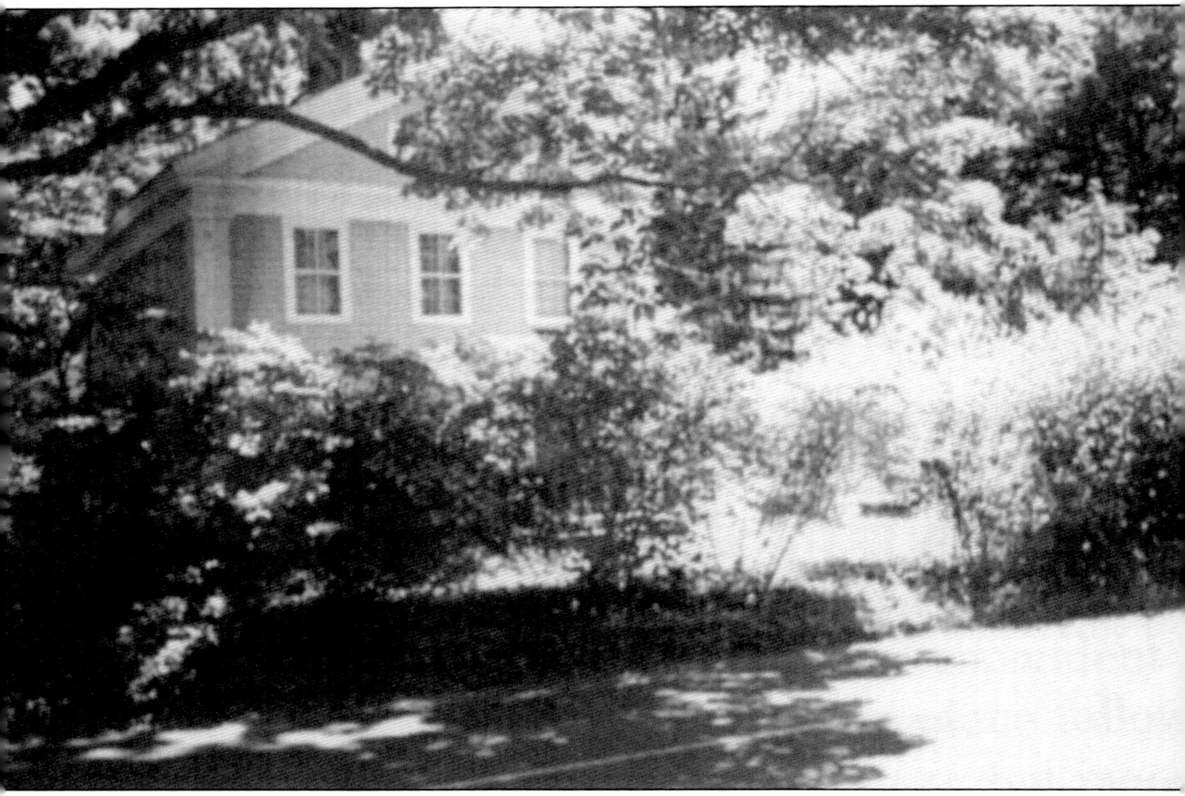

The Perry's Guilford farmhouse, where George spent his final months, is seen here. Immediately after publication of "The Enchanted Pond," the *Saturday Evening Post* printed his article, "There's Music in the Woods Again," which described a successful program by Perry and his neighbors to reintroduce songbirds into the adjacent woods. Incredibly, Perry continued to write into 1956, the last year of his life, even after suffering a mental breakdown and immobilizing physical pain. To the disappointment of many of his fans, Perry turned from fiction to journalism after his acclaimed novels *Walls Rise Up* and *Hold Autumn in Your Hand* and the highly popular "Hackberry Cavalier" series in the *Saturday Evening Post*. Nevertheless, his war reportage, which earned him a commendation from the US government, and the postwar series Cities of America and Families of America in the *Saturday Evening Post* made him one of the most widely read writers in the nation. (Photograph courtesy of *Rockdale Reporter*.)

Seven

School Bells Ring

Education was an integral part of life in Rockdale from the beginning. Soon after the town was founded in 1874, a school was organized by Milly Roby. She taught for six months, but the school had very few students and quickly closed. A private school was reopened in the fall of 1874 by Maggie Hall in a house on the corner of Davilla Avenue and Green Street. This school operated for one term, 1874–1875.

Soon after the town was incorporated, Texas governor O.M. Roberts strengthened the idea of public schools, and a board of trustees, chaired by E.M. Scarborough, was appointed. An old building located at the corner of Cameron and Green Streets was selected as the site for a school. It soon outgrew that site, moving next to the Brooks Hotel and, after the hotel sold, to the Methodist church.

On February 5, 1883, the first official board was elected. Bonds in the amount of $10,000 were voted on, and a school was constructed on what was to become known as College Hill. In 1922, another school was built at a cost of $75,000. The old school became the building for primary grades.

More construction occurred in 1958 and in 1962 and, finally, in 2008, when Rockdaleans opted for a new intermediate school and extensive renovations and additions to Rockdale High School and Rockdale Junior High School.

Prior to 1904, black students attended Rockdale Colored Public Schools. When the principal, S. Adams, resigned to accept another position, trustees selected B.Y. Aycock as principal. The last principal to serve was O.E. Wilhite. In 1965, Aycock School was closed, and black students began attending Rockdale High School.

La Escuelita was in the Mexican community near the mines. The community has been very active in preserving it as a historic site.

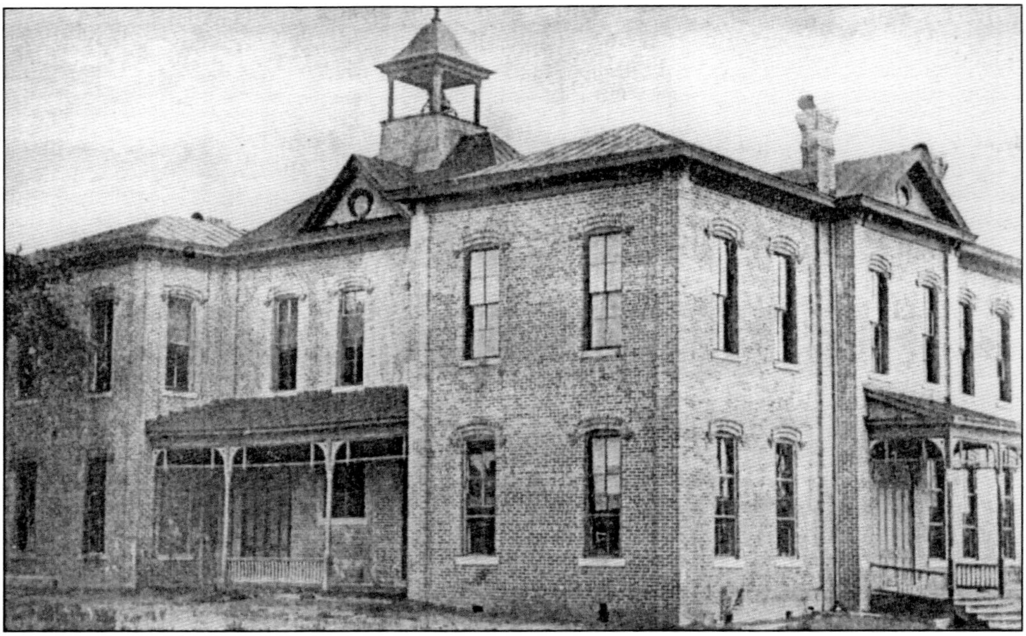

The first permanent school building in Rockdale, authorized in 1883, was built on College Hill. It was replaced by a newer high school building in 1922. (Photograph courtesy of *Rockdale Reporter.*)

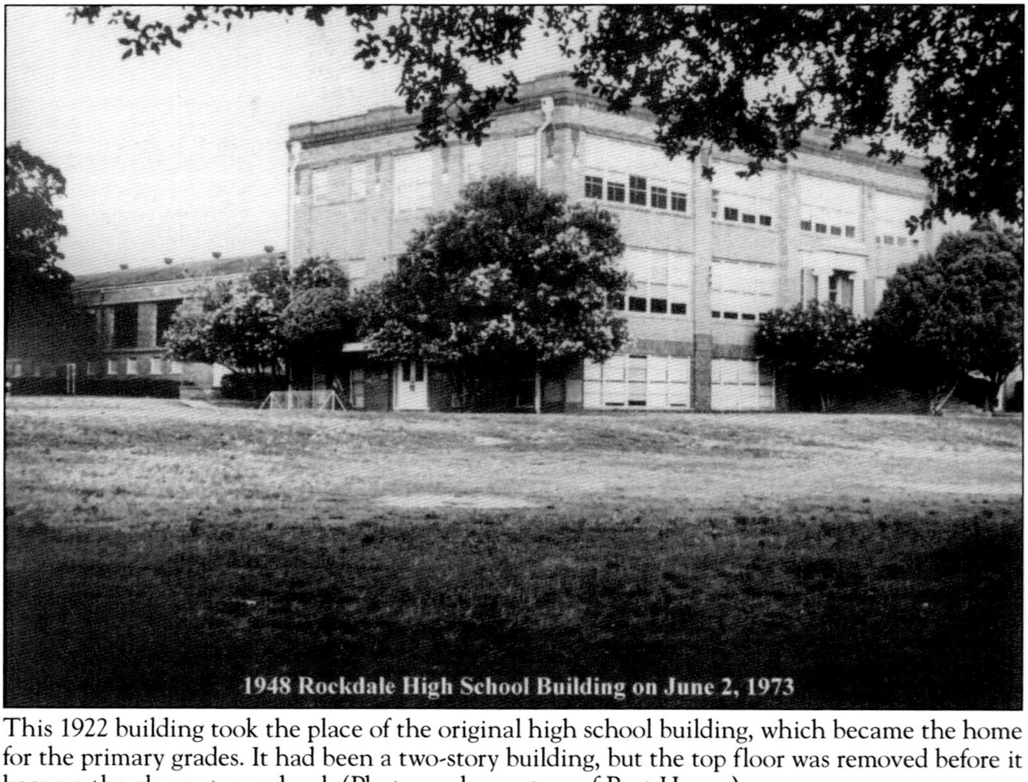

This 1922 building took the place of the original high school building, which became the home for the primary grades. It had been a two-story building, but the top floor was removed before it became the elementary school. (Photograph courtesy of Bert Henry.)

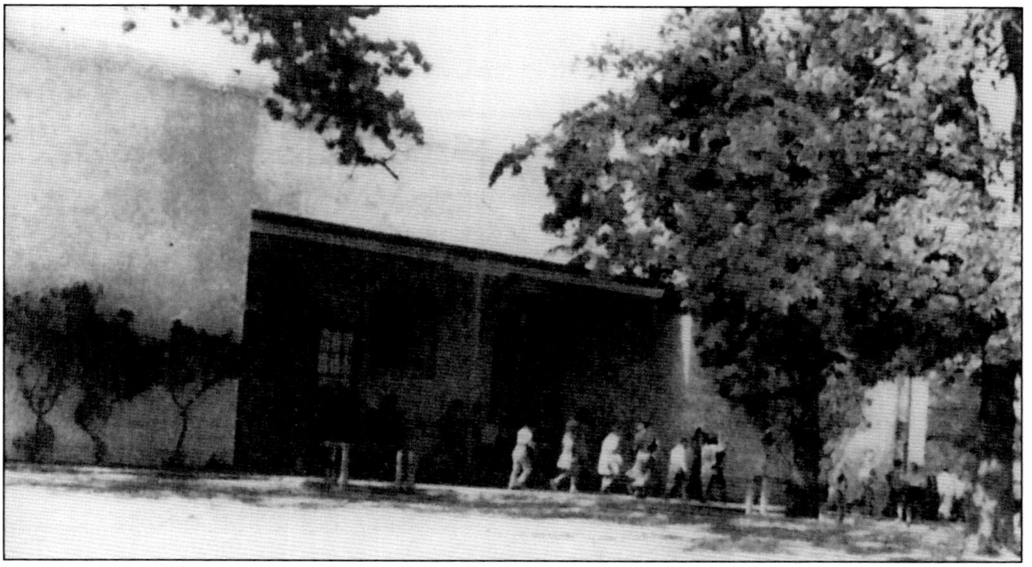

The Rockdale Elementary School, shown here about 1946, is still in use for prekindergarten through third grade. (Photograph courtesy of Bert Henry.)

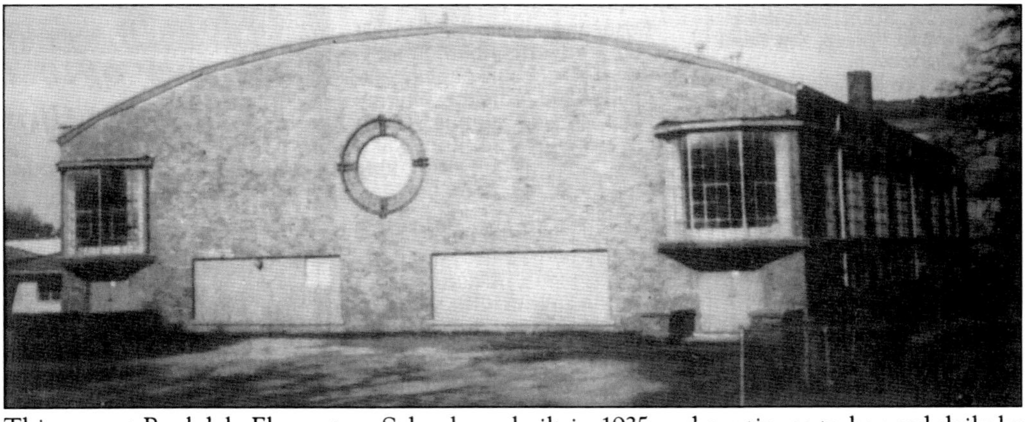

This gym at Rockdale Elementary School was built in 1935 and continues to be used daily by students at the school. (Photograph courtesy of Robert Edwards.)

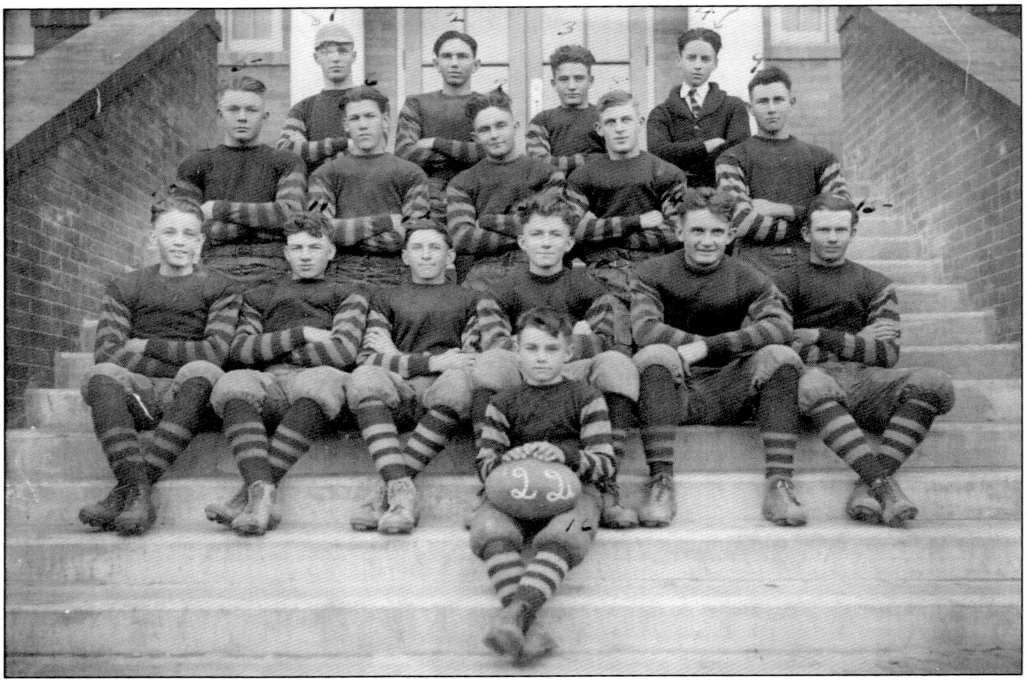

The 1922 Rockdale High School football team poses for a team photograph on the school steps. (Photograph courtesy of *Rockdale Reporter.*)

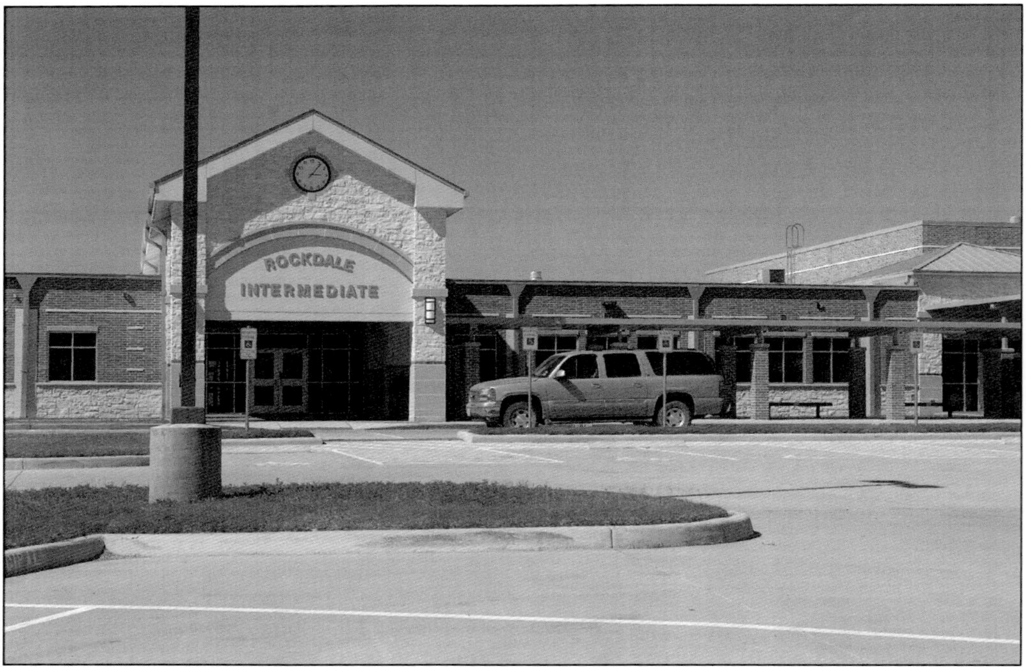

Rockdale Intermediate School was completed in 2010. It houses grades four through six. (Photograph courtesy of the author.)

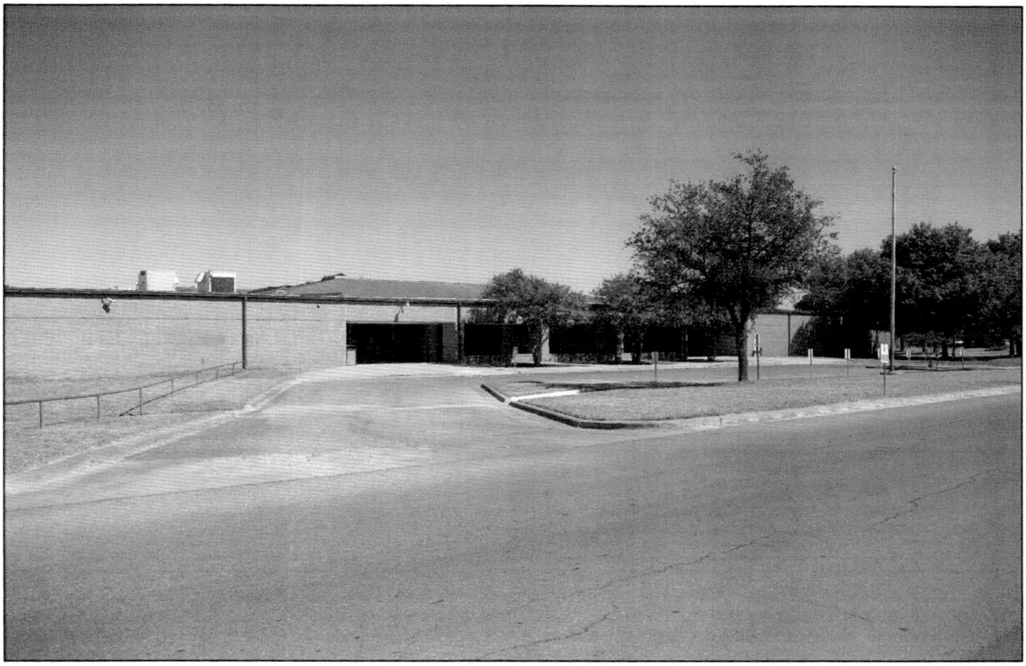

Rockdale Junior High School was completed in 1980 and is still in use. (Photograph courtesy of the author.)

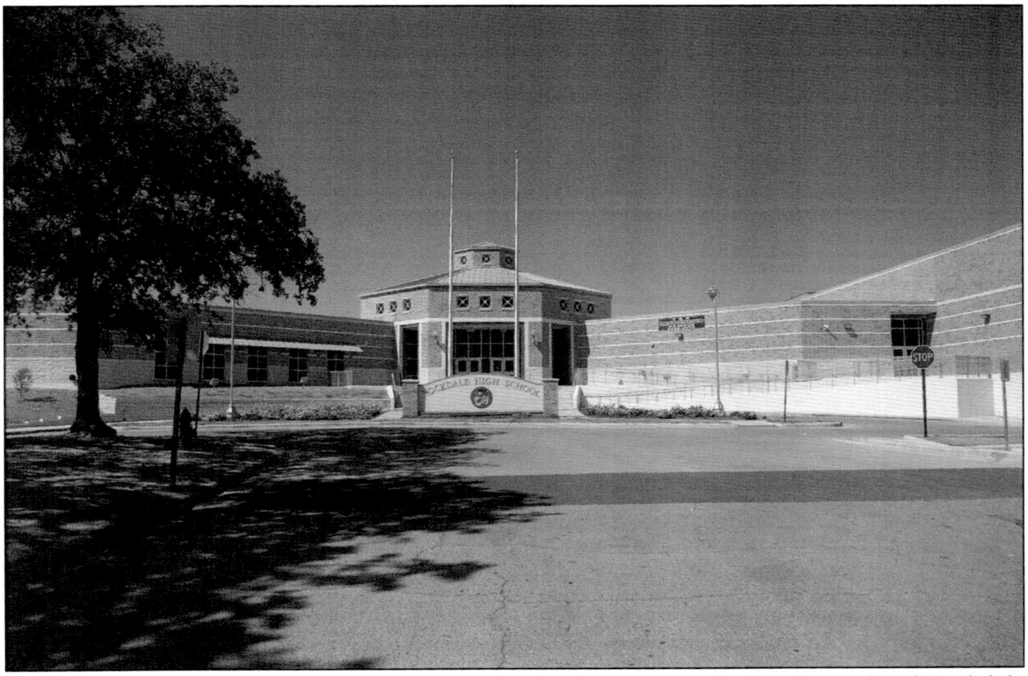

Extensive additions and renovations to the high school in 2010 resulted in this updated Rockdale High School. (Photograph courtesy of the author.)

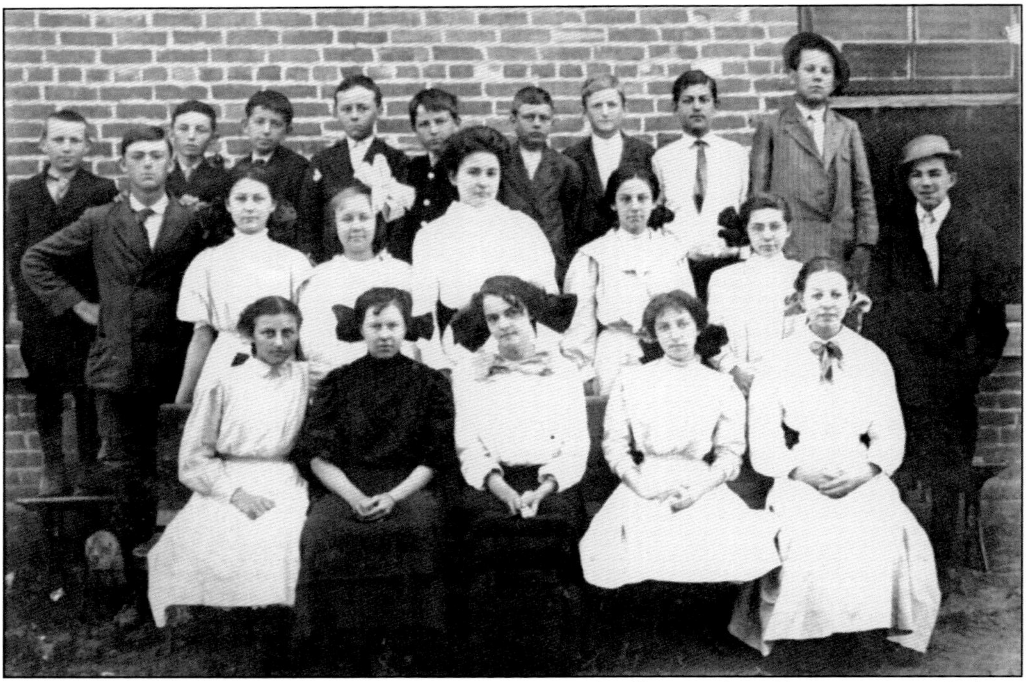

The seventh grade class of 1910 includes, from left to right, (first row) Molly Stein, Irma Shelton, I.G. Bonds, Annie Laurie Whitehurst, and Gussie McDaniel; (second row) Homer Turner, Mabel Harris, Lucile Poole, teacher Bertie Wooten, Naomi Williams, and Pearl Woody; (third row) Urguhart Wise, Charles Duffy, Will Norris Hale, Layfayette Joyner, Ed Prewitt, Ed Lengert, Otto Diehl, Holloway Smith, and Vilas Kennoe. (Photograph courtesy of the author.)

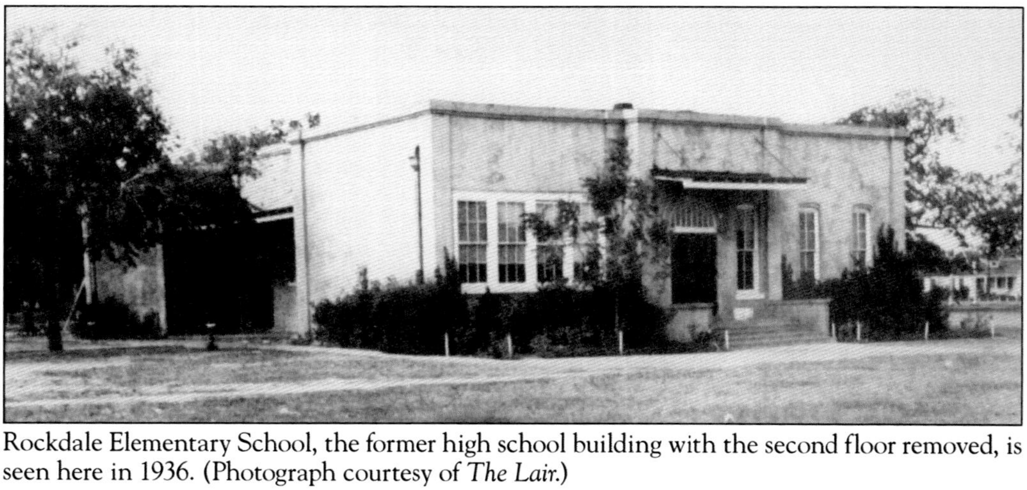

Rockdale Elementary School, the former high school building with the second floor removed, is seen here in 1936. (Photograph courtesy of *The Lair.*)

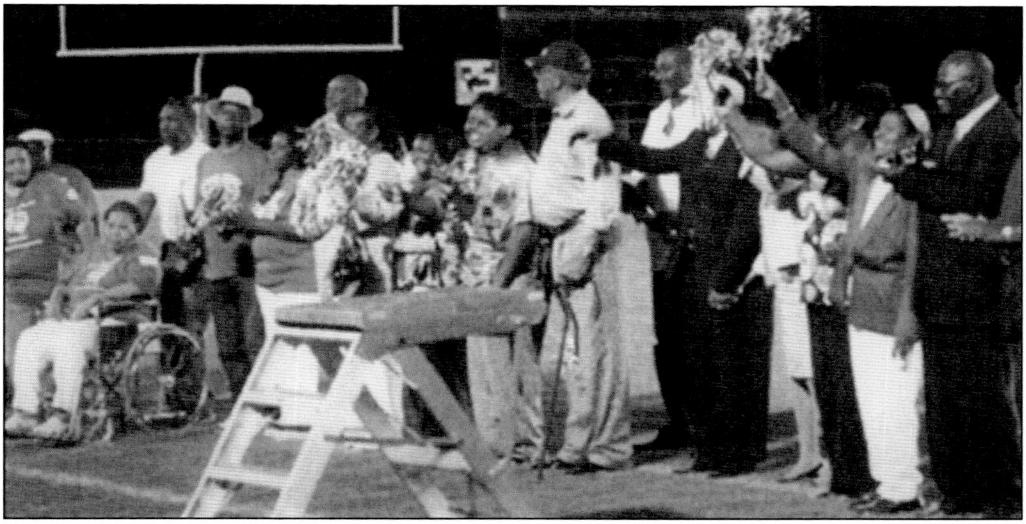

Members of the Aycock High School state champion football team and their families celebrate the 55th anniversary of their state championships in both football and basketball in the same year. (Photograph courtesy of *Rockdale Reporter.*)

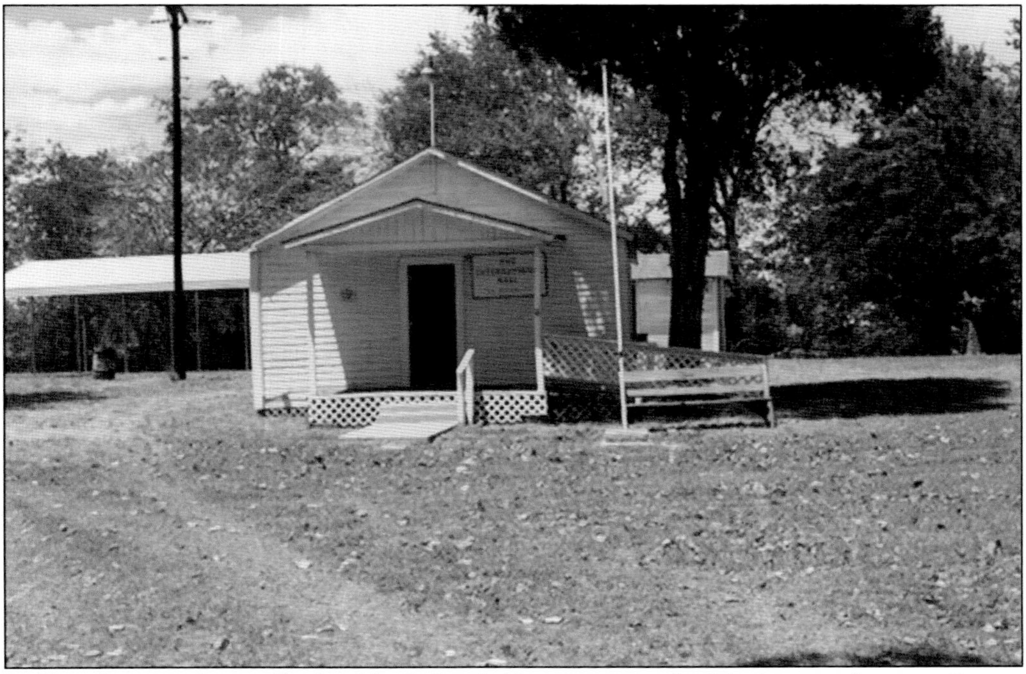

La Escuelita was the small school built for children living in the Mexican settlement adjacent to the Vogel Mines. As a part of the Talbott Ridge School District, they were transferred to the Rockdale schools in 1944. La Escuelita has been preserved and is recognized as a historic site by the Texas Historical Commission. (Photograph courtesy of the author.)

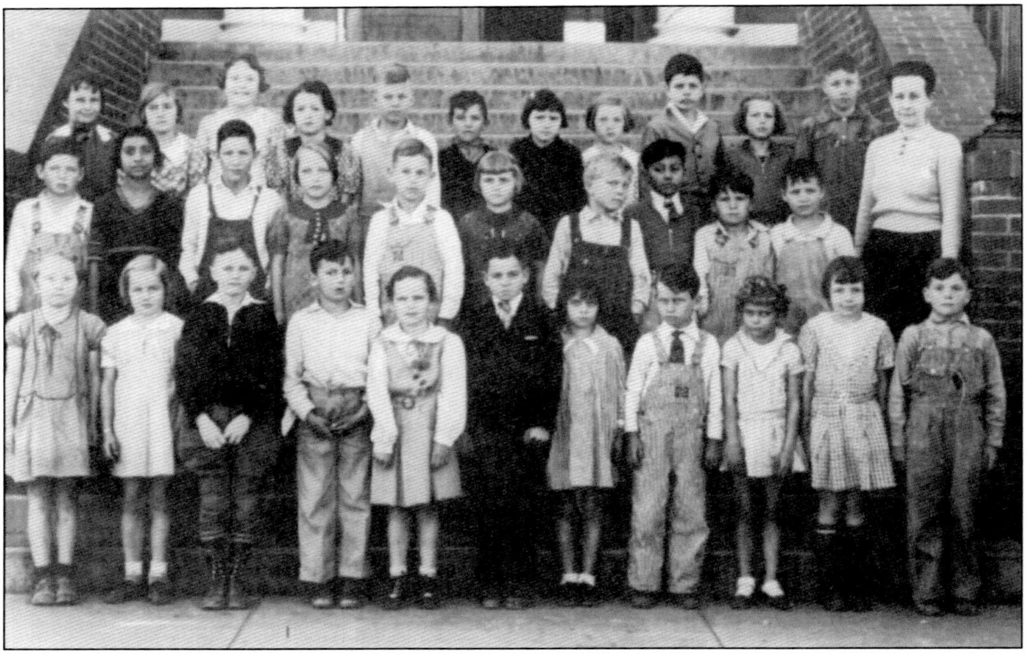

The second-grade class at Rockdale Elementary School has gathered for this class photograph in 1936. (Photograph courtesy of school annual for 1936, *The Lair.*)

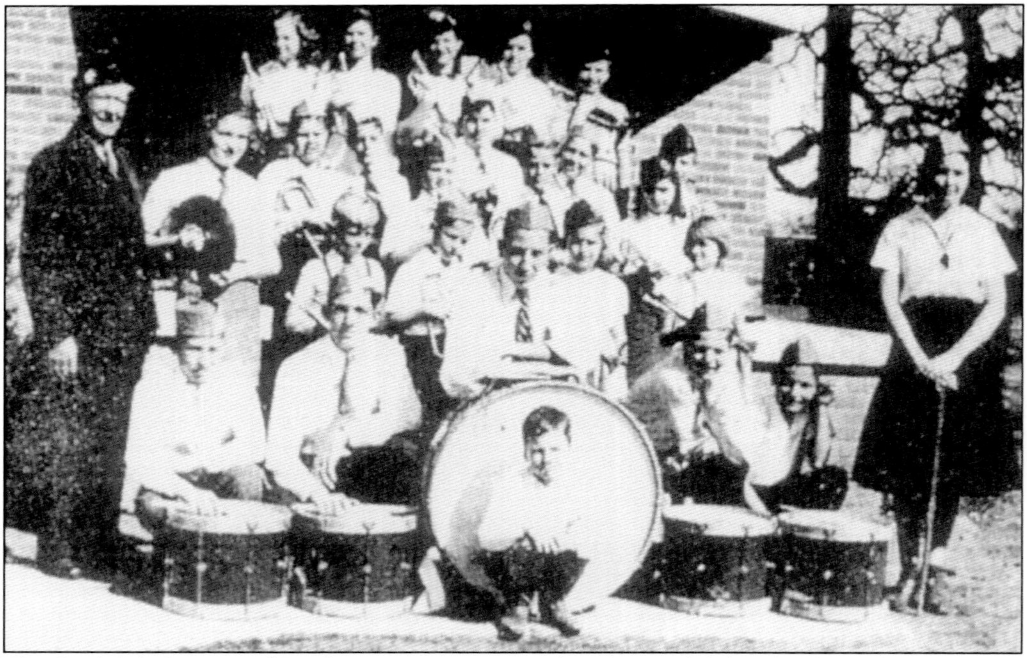

The Rockdale Drum and Bugle Corps was operated in the Rockdale schools by the American Legion from 1937 to 1939. This predated the school's band program. (Photograph courtesy of *Rockdale Reporter.*)

Eight

And the Church Bells Chime

Faith and trust in God was evident from the start in Rockdale. In the very beginning, church services were held on the second floor of Branch Brothers Furniture Store and conducted by a Baptist minister, a Mr. Vandivere. The singing was led by a Mr. Stewart.

Baptists, Methodists, Presbyterians, Episcopalians, and Christians formed a Union Church in 1876. The first church to leave this group and organize separately was St. Thomas Episcopal Church, the oldest remaining house of worship in Rockdale. The frame chapel of this first church was preserved and is still a part of the church today. The building has been modernized, but the original structure is still in place. In 1977, the Texas Historical Commission approved a historical marker for this site.

Soon after, other denominations began to build their own churches. The First Presbyterian Church was organized in 1874, and in 1876, the First Baptist Church of Rockdale was built. St. Joseph's Catholic Church was built around 1880 and eventually became a part of Rainbow Courts, now owned by Joan and Dan Ratliff. In 1883, St. John's Methodist Church built its first sanctuary, on Cameron Street.

As the population of Rockdale increased, so did the number of churches and the denominations represented. Today's telephone book lists more than 20 churches of many denominations. Peace Lutheran Church was organized in 1883, and in 1887, the First Christian Church (Disciples of Christ) was created. Hope Lutheran Church was organized in 1955.

Other churches and their dates of organization include Meadowbrook Baptist Church (1954), Church of the Nazarene (1955), Springfield Church (1873), Allen Chapel African Methodist Episcopal (AME) Church (1875), New Hope Baptist Church (1891), Rising Star Baptist Church (1907), Pecan Street Church of Christ (1948), and West Bell Church of Christ (1963). Not every church is pictured in this book, but all have played a valuable part in the history of Rockdale.

Many time-honored traditions emanated from the churches of Rockdale. For many years, when a death occurred on the east side of town, church bells would toll in announcement of the event. Church bells also rang in the new year and tolled in honor of other important events.

The churches of Rockdale unite each year to celebrate the week before Easter as Holy Week.

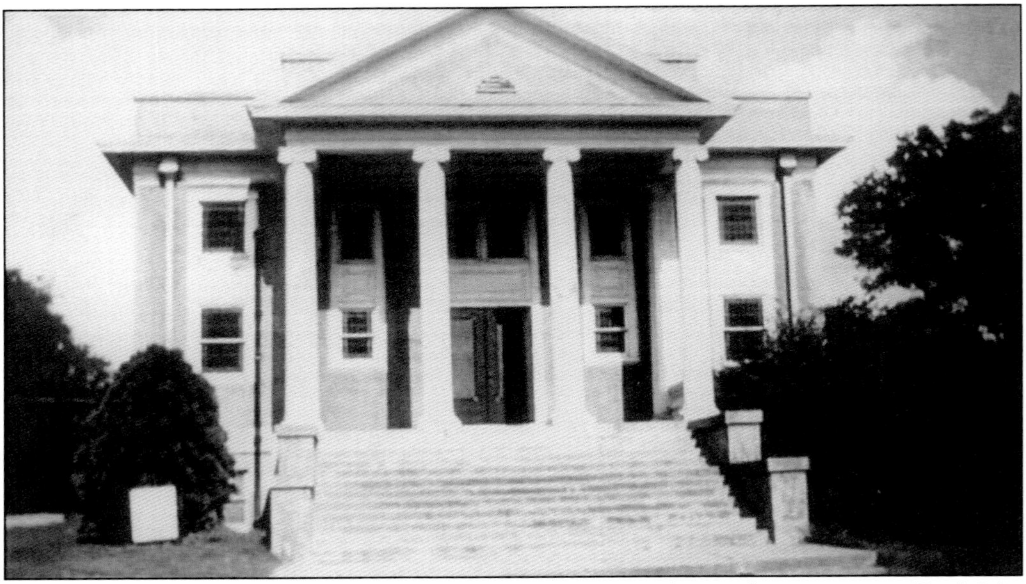

Peace Lutheran Church was organized in Rockdale in 1883 in the small community of Bushdale. A Rockdale chapel was built and later enlarged to accommodate a growing congregation. In 1966, a new building was constructed on Meadow Drive. (Photograph courtesy of Bert Henry.)

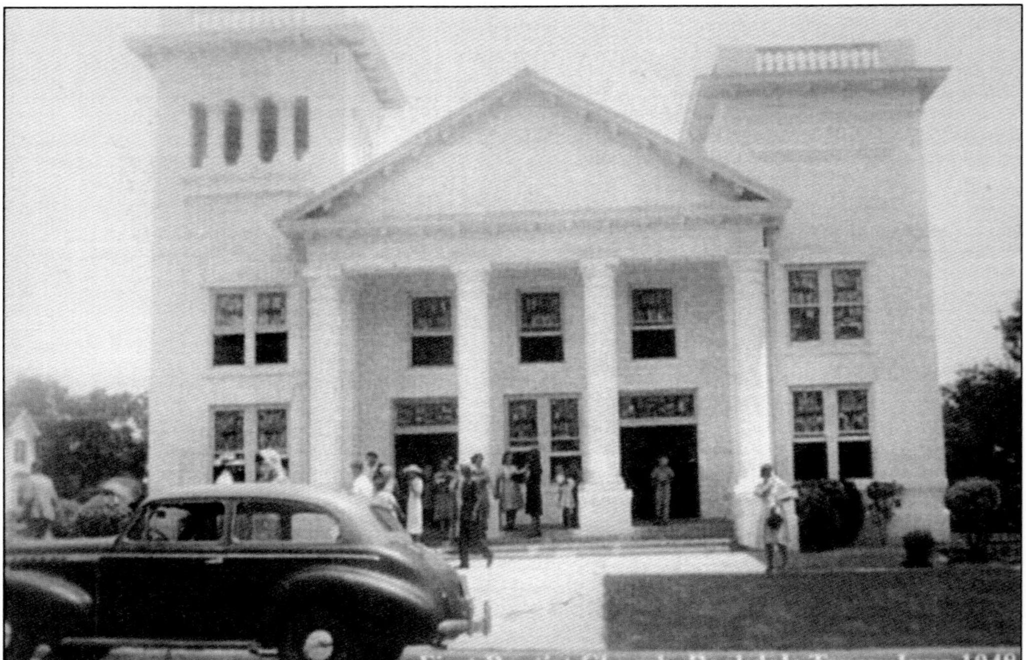

The First Baptist Church in Rockdale was organized in 1876. This building has been replaced by a more modern structure on the same site. One of the most famous pastors of this church was the father of the well-known film actor Dana Andrews. (Photograph courtesy of Bert Henry.)

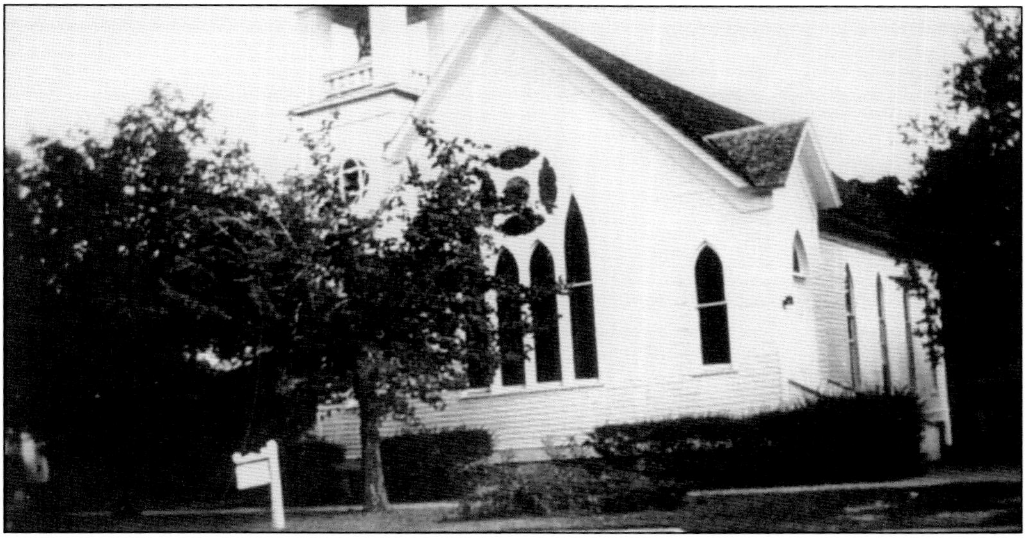

St. John's United Methodist Church was first located on Cameron Street. A new structure on Calhoun Street is the present home of the congregation. (Photograph courtesy of Bert Henry.)

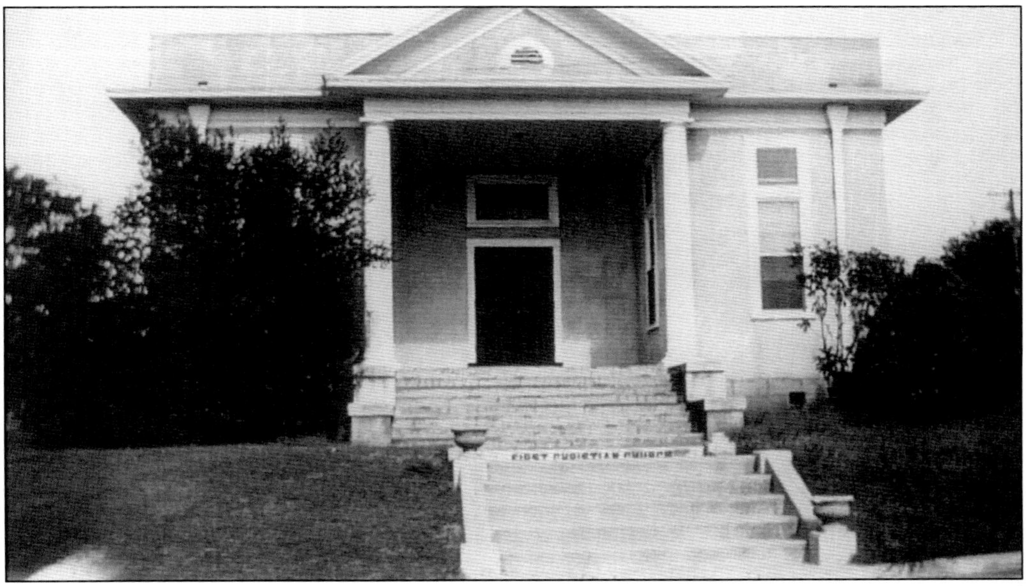

The First Christian Church of Rockdale was organized in 1887. It moved to the corner of Bell Avenue and Scarborough Street in 1891 and still operates from that site today. (Photograph Courtesy of Bert Henry.)

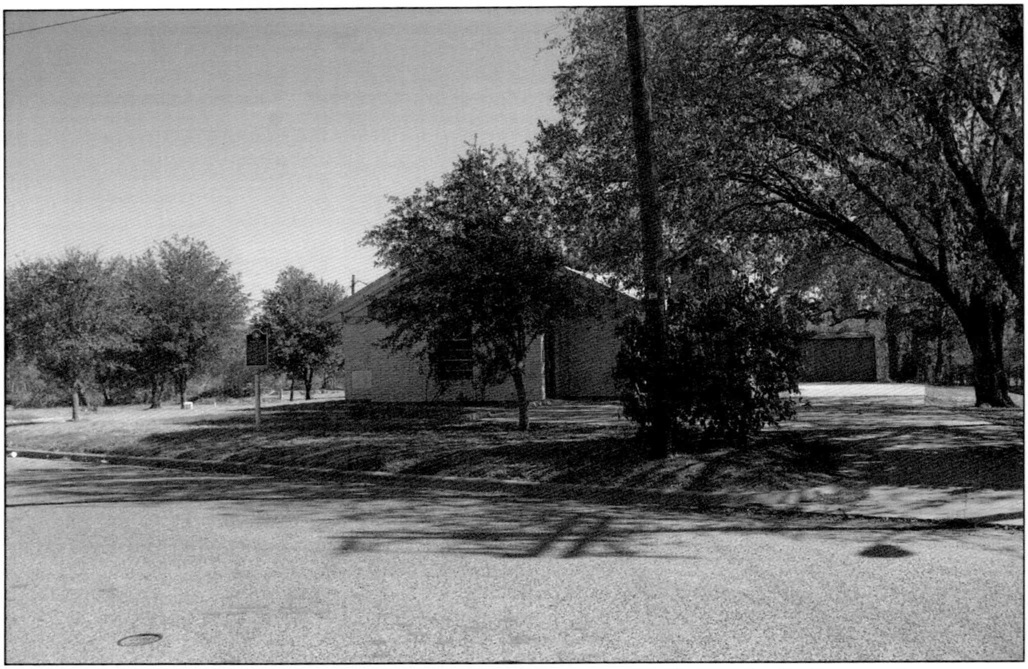

Springfield Baptist Church was organized in 1872. It was a member of the LaGrange Association. (Photograph courtesy of the author.)

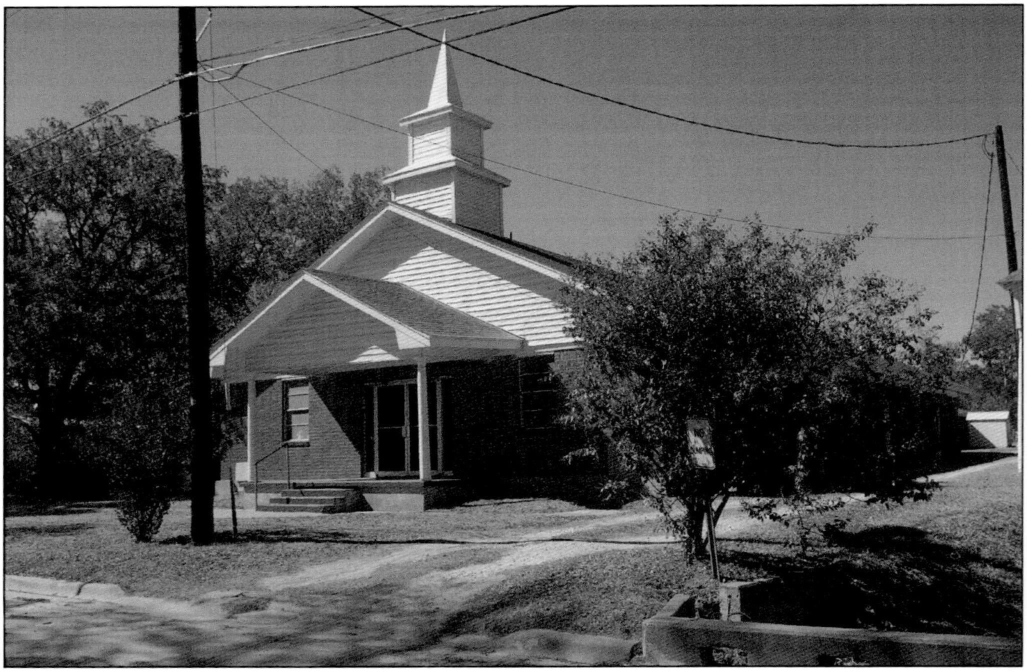

New Hope Baptist Church first met in a tent on Rice Street, later moving to the Henry Smith properties before arriving at its present location on East Third Street. (Photograph courtesy of the author.)

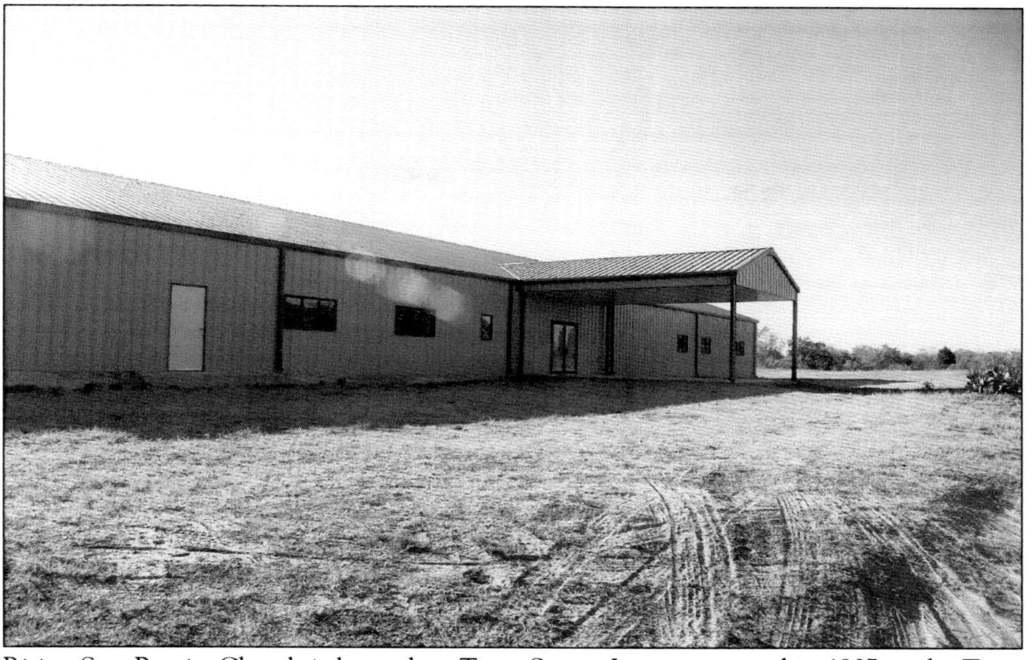

Rising Star Baptist Church is located on Texas Street. It was organized in 1907 in the Tracy Community and moved to its present location in 1960. This church is known for its outstanding choir. (Photograph courtesy of the author.)

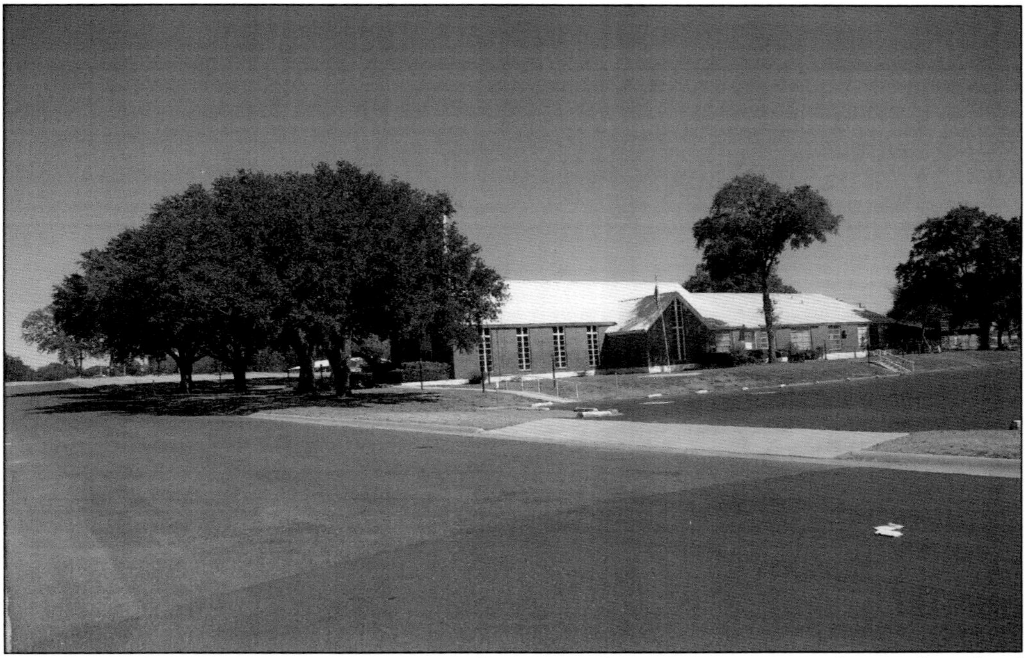

Meadowbrook Baptist Church was organized in 1954. The congregation met first in the school cafeteria and in other school locations. The present building was completed on Colorado Street in 1955. (Photograph courtesy of the author.)

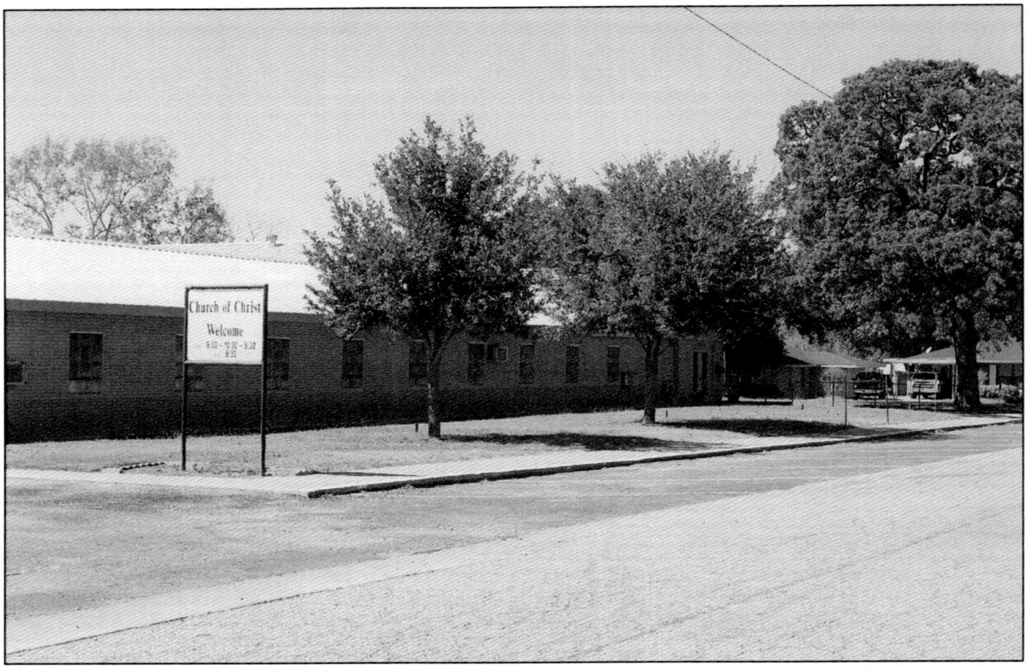

The Church of Christ was organized in 1922. In 1954, it moved into a new building on Murray Street, where the congregation still meet today. (Photograph courtesy of the author.)

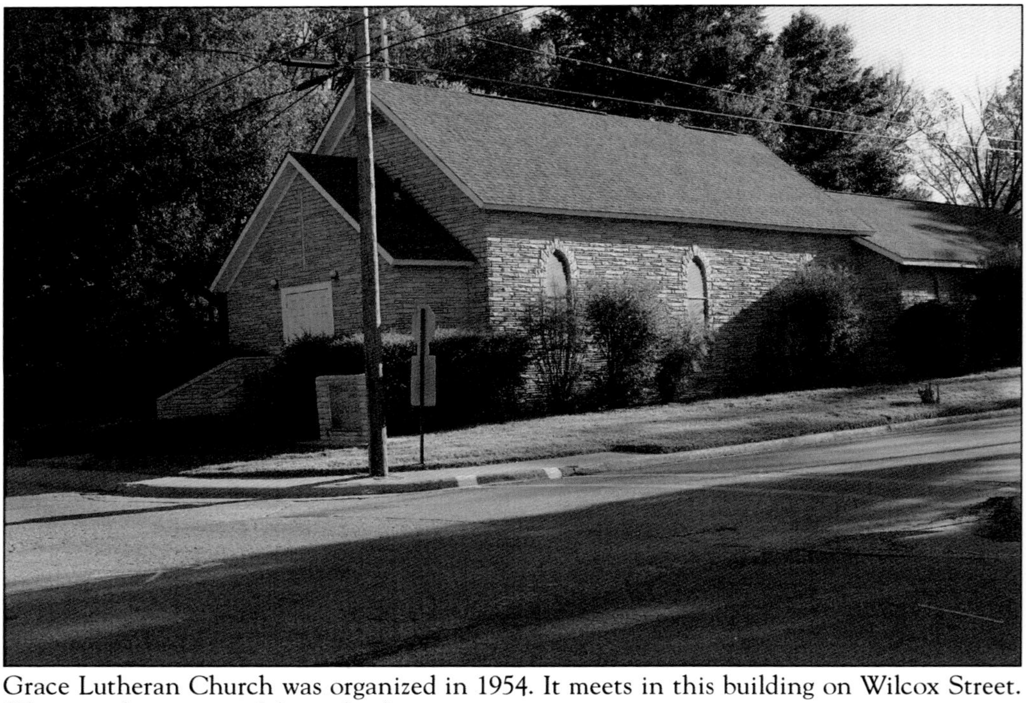

Grace Lutheran Church was organized in 1954. It meets in this building on Wilcox Street. (Photograph courtesy of the author.)

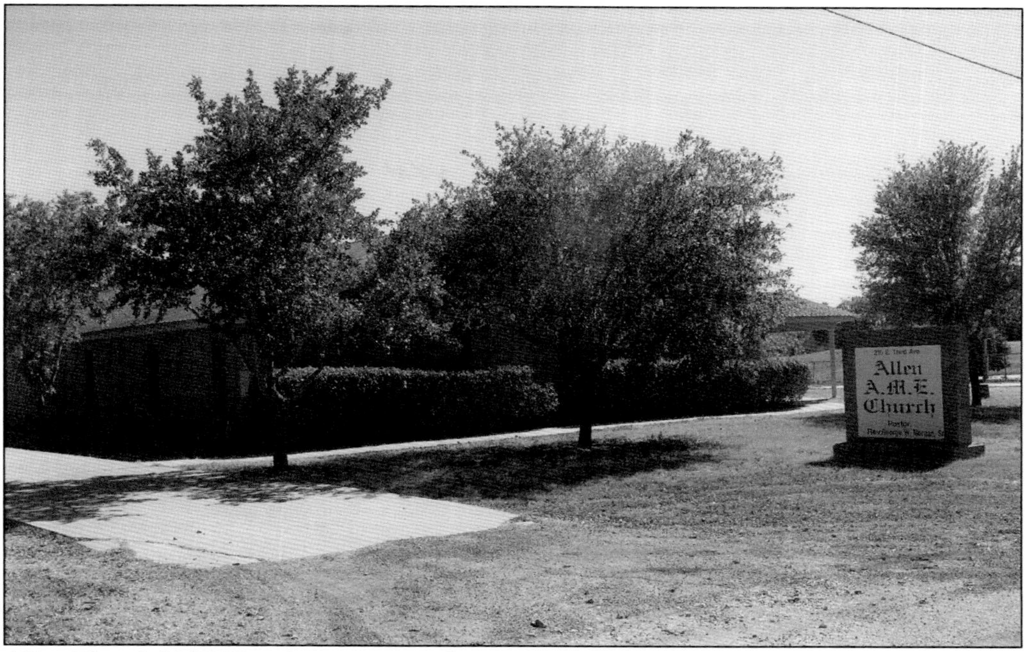

Allen Chapel AME Church was organized in 1875, moving to its present location 100 years later, in 1975. (Photograph courtesy of the author.)

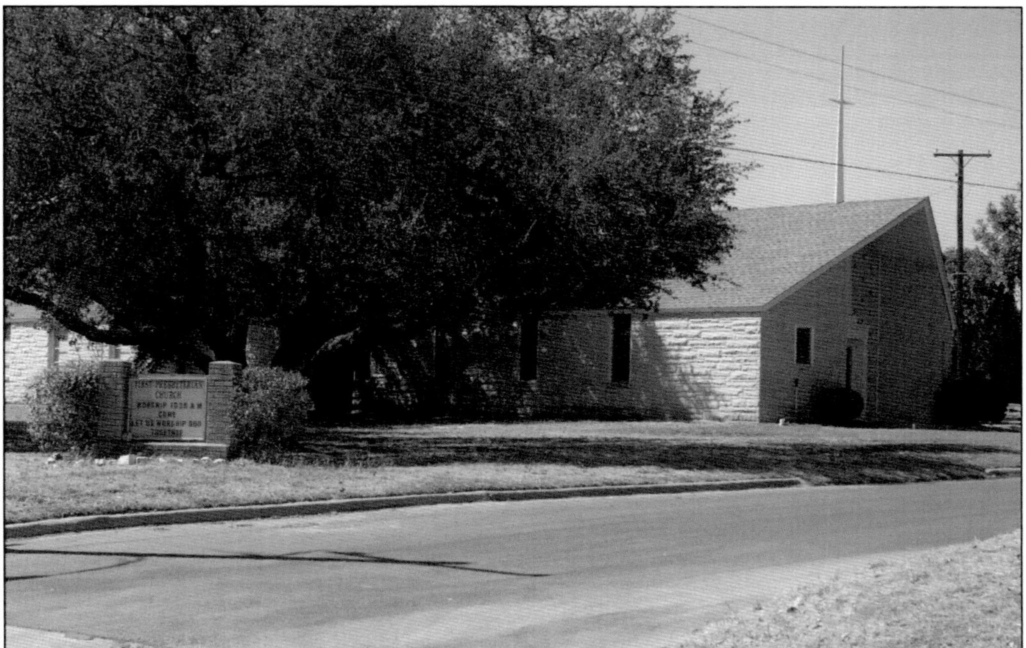

The First Presbyterian Church was organized in 1874. It met in various locations before moving to its present location in 1954. (Photograph courtesy of the author.)

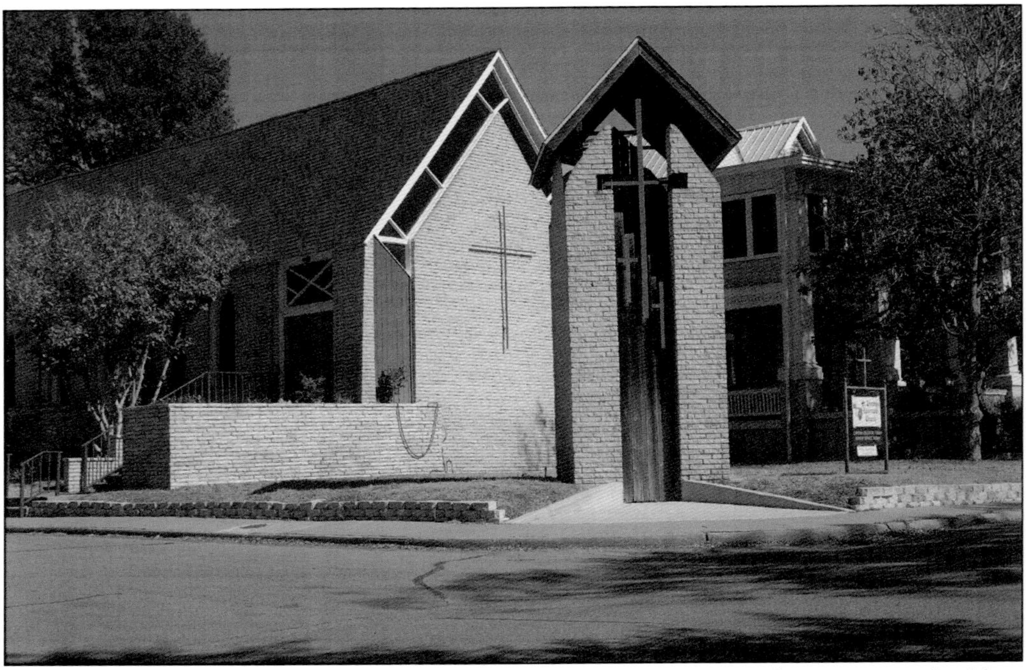

St. Thomas Episcopal Church was organized in 1873. For a time, it met downtown in a building called McCawley's Corner, but in 1952, the church moved into its current building. (Photograph courtesy of the author.)

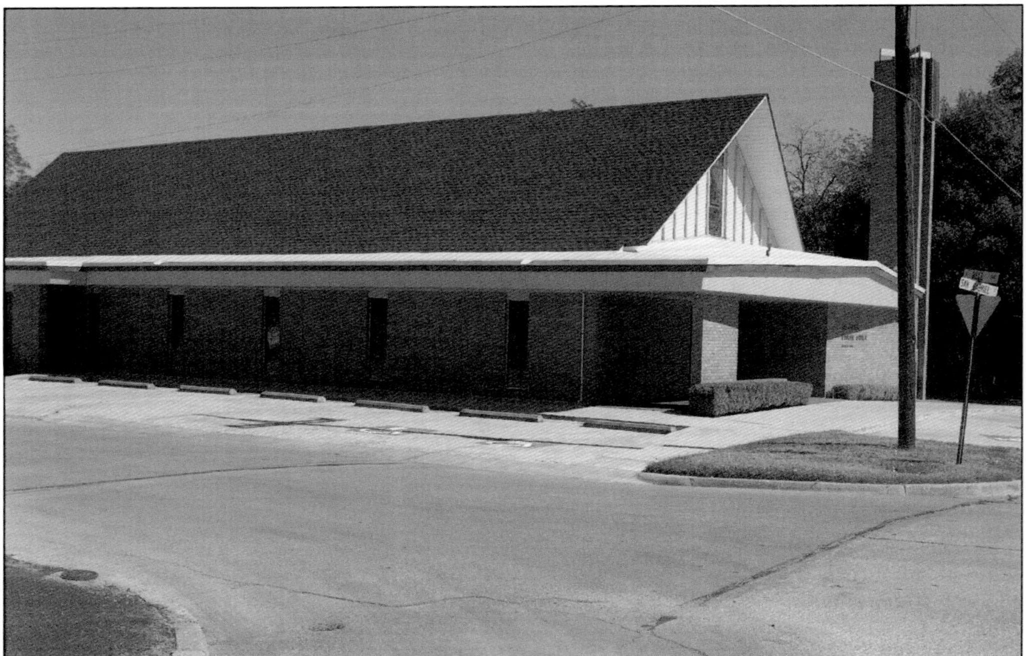

St. Joseph's Catholic Church was organized in 1880. The present structure was completed on San Gabriel Street in 1967. (Photograph courtesy of the author.)

Nine

Ramblin' 'Round Rockdale

No stronger influence can be found on Rockdale than the *Rockdale Reporter.* This family-owned newspaper has exerted a positive influence in Rockdale for a century. One popular column in the *Reporter* was the Ramblin' Round Rockdale column by W.H. Cooke, the editor and publisher. A favorite was his Thanksgiving column in 1989, which reads: "We give thanks for our blessings, for important things like love and life and family and friends and peace."

Three major ethnic groups comprise the population of Rockdale. Whites followed the railroads to town in large numbers. Rockdale's dependency on agriculture, especially cotton, attracted many blacks, both former slaves and freemen. A strong force in the black community today is the organization known as the Original Twelve. It provide scholarships and other academic assistance to encourage young people to pursue education. The mines also attracted large numbers of Mexicans. Each group today maintains a distinct identity, but the spirit is generally one of cooperation and respect. La Escuelita is a historic site, focusing on the history and achievements of the Hispanic community. Rockdale enters its 36th year of sponsoring an annual old-time fair at the Rockdale Fairgrounds. In 2004, Pres. George W. Bush signed legislation creating the El Camino Real de los Tejas National Historic Trail, which will have an impact on Rockdale's future.

Rockdale's history was simmering on the back burner for many years, but now it is promoted with vim and vigor by Dr. Kathleen Kirk Gilmore. With Alcoa gone, locals will not be making aluminum any more, but they will be making memories and helping the young people understand one small slice of American heritage. Readers are invited to come and ramble 'round Rockdale.

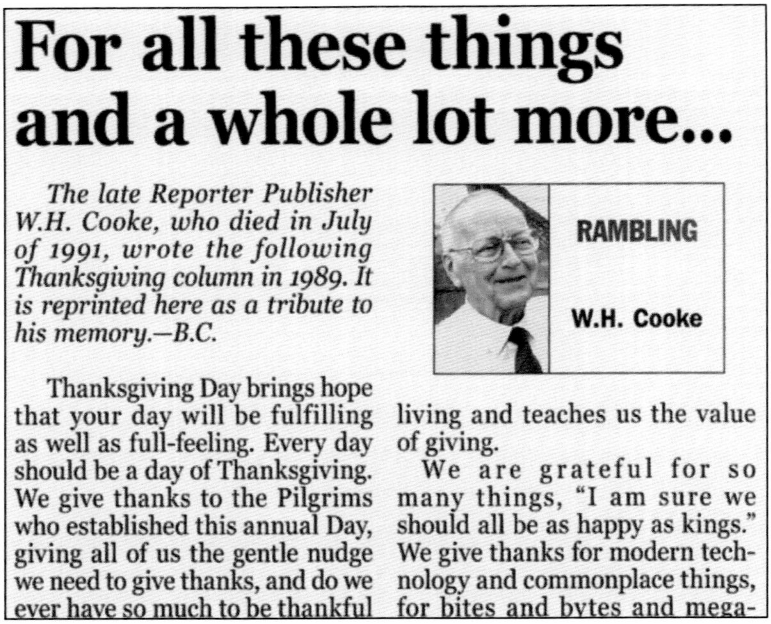

For all these things and a whole lot more...

The late Reporter Publisher W.H. Cooke, who died in July of 1991, wrote the following Thanksgiving column in 1989. It is reprinted here as a tribute to his memory.—B.C.

RAMBLING

W.H. Cooke

Thanksgiving Day brings hope that your day will be fulfilling as well as full-feeling. Every day should be a day of Thanksgiving. We give thanks to the Pilgrims who established this annual Day, giving all of us the gentle nudge we need to give thanks, and do we ever have so much to be thankful living and teaches us the value of giving.

We are grateful for so many things, "I am sure we should all be as happy as kings." We give thanks for modern technology and commonplace things, for bites and bytes and mega-

Ramblin' Round Rockdale, written by editor and publisher W.H. Cooke for so long, is still a favorite in the *Rockdale Reporter*. (Courtesy of *Rockdale Reporter*.)

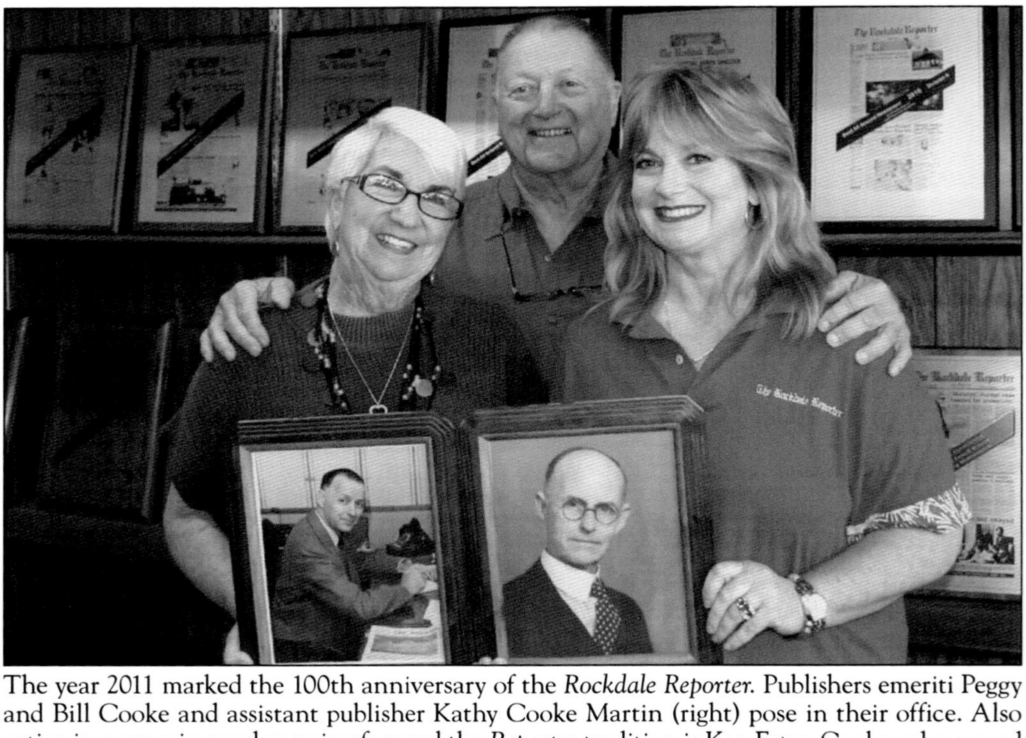

The year 2011 marked the 100th anniversary of the *Rockdale Reporter*. Publishers emeriti Peggy and Bill Cooke and assistant publisher Kathy Cooke Martin (right) pose in their office. Also active in preserving and carrying forward the *Reporter* tradition is Ken Esten Cooke, who served as editor and publisher of the *Reporter* for several years before moving to Victoria. He is now the editor and publisher of the *Fredericksburg Standard*. (Courtesy of *Rockdale Reporter*.)

El Paso girl

Granados' book shows gritty but humorous look at life in 'Chuco'

The mountains, the heat, the fights, the 1970s cars, the offbeat family members, the characters.

Christine Granados tucked away memories and retained a connection to all of these things and many more while growing up in El Paso.

Reflections on her decidedly non-Ozzie-and-Harriet upbringing influenced her decision to write.

Now, at 37, the El Paso native and Rockdale resident has published her first book of literary fiction, "Brides and Sinners in El Chuco" (Arizona University Press, $14.95).

Granados' stories are not "happily ever after" tales though plenty of humor is laced throughout. They show a sometimes disturbing side of life with "underbelly" characters in that border town.

"Some of it is loosely based on characters and relatives I knew growing up, but it's all fiction," Granados said. "

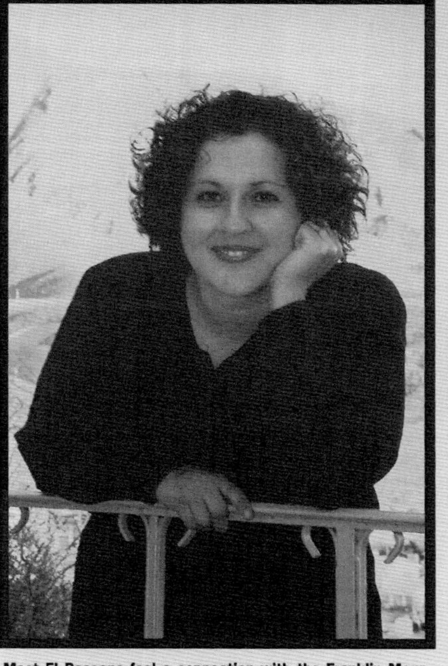

Most El Pasoans feel a connection with the Franklin Mountains and author Christine Granados is no different. She writes of the steamy border city in her new book "Brides and Sinners in El Chuco."

As Dagoberto Gilb, a PEN Hemingway Award winner and a 2003 finalist for the Book Critics Circle Award, wrote: "...Granados is helping to re-orient Latino literature away from poignant, romanticized goody-goodyism, toward stark, complex storytelling that will remind the many of us who have grown up imperfectly what it is to be living on the embattled *fronteras* of Mexican and American."

Book critic Rigoberto González wrote, "Brides and Sinners in El Chuco celebrates a community's prejudices, flaws, and shortcomings as lovingly as it critiques them."

Growing up in 'Chuco'

"El Chuco," the nickname given to the town by men there in the 1930s, was a colorful place to grow up, Granados recalls.

"We were raised in South El Paso and I didn't speak English until I was five years old. That's when my father worked for Coca Cola and moved us out to the suburbs," she said of the fast-growing east-side of town.

"But my transition into school life was easier than my brothers and sisters. I picked up English quickly since I was so young and they all struggled with it more," she said.

While her family was better off than many in that town, poverty is another thing that is rooted in her stories.

"It really affects your sensibilities—when you see people without electricity, running water or food to eat. It makes you appreciate everything so much more," she said of seeing the poorest neighborhoods and those across the border in Ciudad Juarez.

"Even here in Rockdale, the poor are a lot better off than in Juarez," she said. "It's just like growing up in Rockdale, the small town atmosphere and knowing all your neighbors affects who you are as an adult.

"Being raised on the border of a third world country affects who you are and the way you view life," Granados said. "It's made me more cautious, skeptical, resilient and not prone to take what I have for granted."

Learning her craft

Granados spent much of the past five years earning her master's degree in Creative Writing from Texas State University, which is becoming one of the top programs in the country. She wanted to begin exploring fiction after having written for many daily newspapers and editing a now-defunct Latina fashion magazine called *Moderna*.

"The second semester in the program, I got pregnant with my first child, which meant I had to slow down," she said. "And in this age of the 'Hurried Woman Syndrome', it was no easy task. I dropped out a semester, then took only one class per semester."

When child number two showed up, her time became more constrained.

"Every time I sit and type, I have blinders on to the chaos in my house," she laughed. "It's a constant battle I wage and it's something I think everyone, Latina or otherwise, will be able to relate to."

Under the tutelage and encouragement of Gilb, Granados managed to get her first book together and University of Arizona Press took an interest. Gilb invited her to share one of her stories with the audience at the Texas Book Festival and the response was encouraging.

"He's from El Paso and has a working-class background and has had articles in *The New Yorker*, *Harper's*, and he's been on National Public Radio's 'Fresh Air.' What *vato* from El Paso can claim that?" she said. "Having a similar background, he's been a real inspiration to me."

'Off-kilter'

Even the cover art reflects the quirky, funny-but-kind-of-pathetic characters. Photographer Joel Salcido, who worked with Granados at *The El Paso Times*, is now a photographer for *Texas Monthly* and other publications. He photographed mannequins in a Korean-owned wedding store near the downtown El Paso-Juarez International Bridge. The mannequins wigs and even a hand from a male dummy are off-kilter.

"I thought it was the perfect image," Granados said. "It's not at all about the stereotype of the Mexican mother making tortillas."

The book is not Granados' first publication—she penned five biographical books of celebrities for young readers for Mitchell Lane publishers in the late 1990s. But she counts this as her first "real" offering.

Between juggling duties with her husband, two young sons and some civic activities, Granados is working on her second book, which will be a novel. She plans to travel extensively throughout the Southwestern U.S. to promote "Brides and Sinners."

Christine Granados published her book *Brides and Sinners in El Chuco* while living in Rockdale with her husband, Ken Esten Cooke, and their two sons. She maintains strong ties with her El Paso heritage, a fact that is illustrated by her book. In it, she writes of her experiences growing up in the imaginary border town of El Chuco. Christine and her family now live in Fredericksburg, Texas, where Ken is editor and publisher of the *Fredericksburg Standard*.

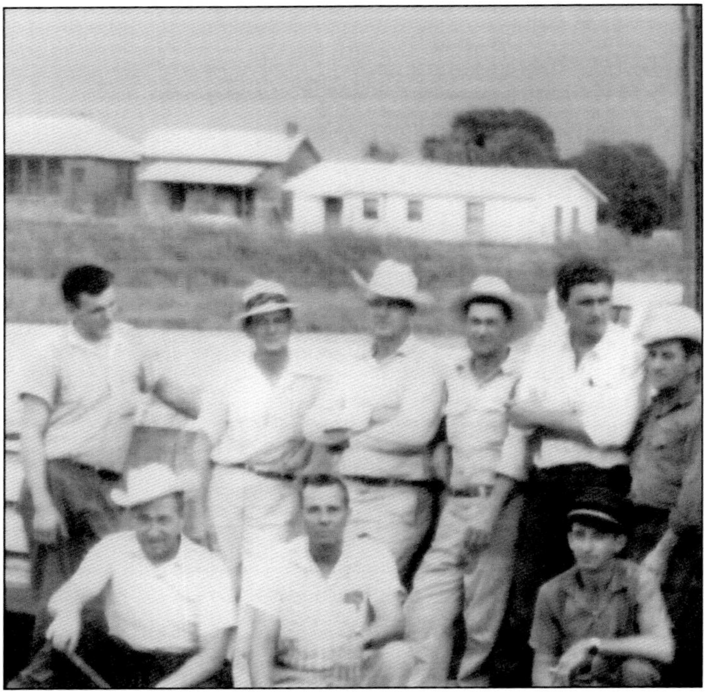

These growers, including Gary Jackson (second row, far left) wait for watermelons to be loaded and shipped in about 1955. (Photograph courtesy of Gary Jackson.)

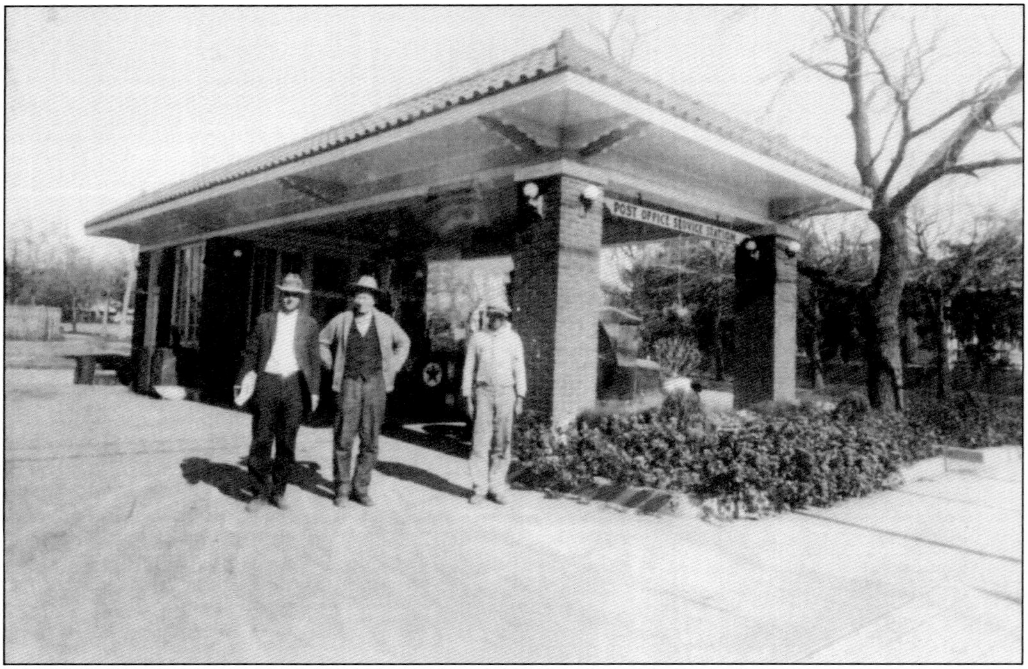

This service station, one of many located in Rockdale, was adjacent to city hall, which is now the present police department. For many years, the station was a Magnolia and later a Mobil dealership owned by George Lumpkins. Lumpkins sold it to Don Roddam, who moved the business to Cameron Street, where it was eventually replaced by the Sinclair dealership owned by Ernest Rinn. (Photograph courtesy of Gary Jackson.)

With no shoes and his lunch in his hand, Albert Gest from Gay Hill stands on the steps of Bushdale School, ready for school. Gest later worked as a carpenter in Gay Hill, and his son is a pediatrician and teaches at Ohio State University. (Photograph courtesy of Robert Edwards.)

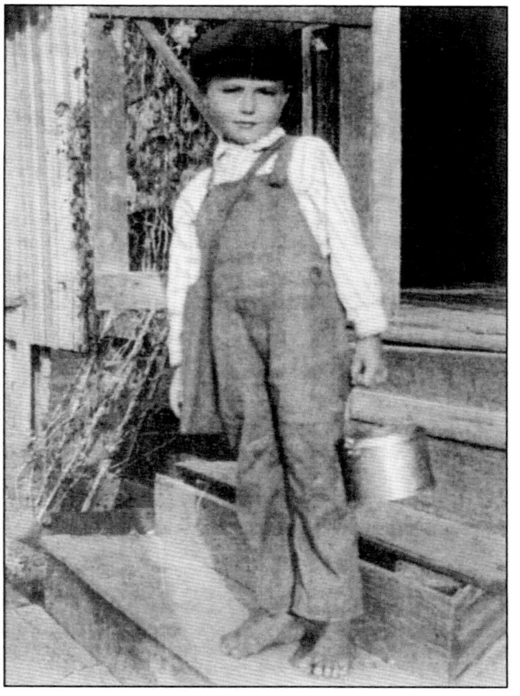

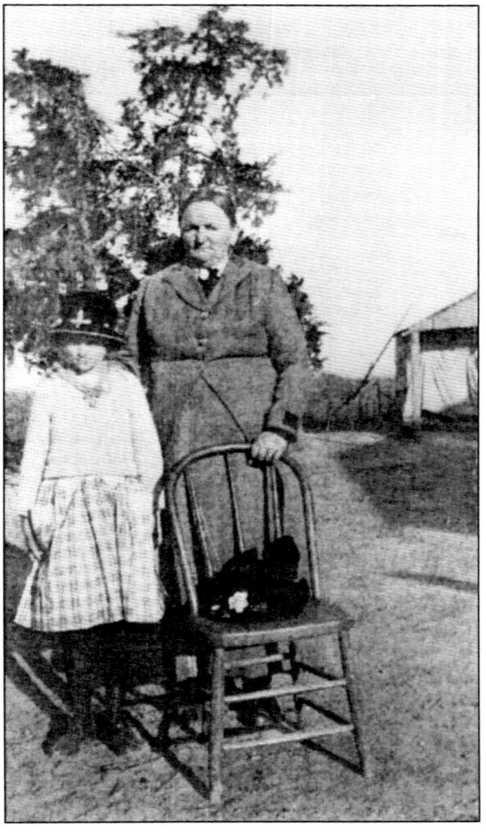

Emma Drescher, with her hat resting on the chair in front her, and little Ida Drescher appear to be ready for church. (Photograph courtesy of Robert Edwards.)

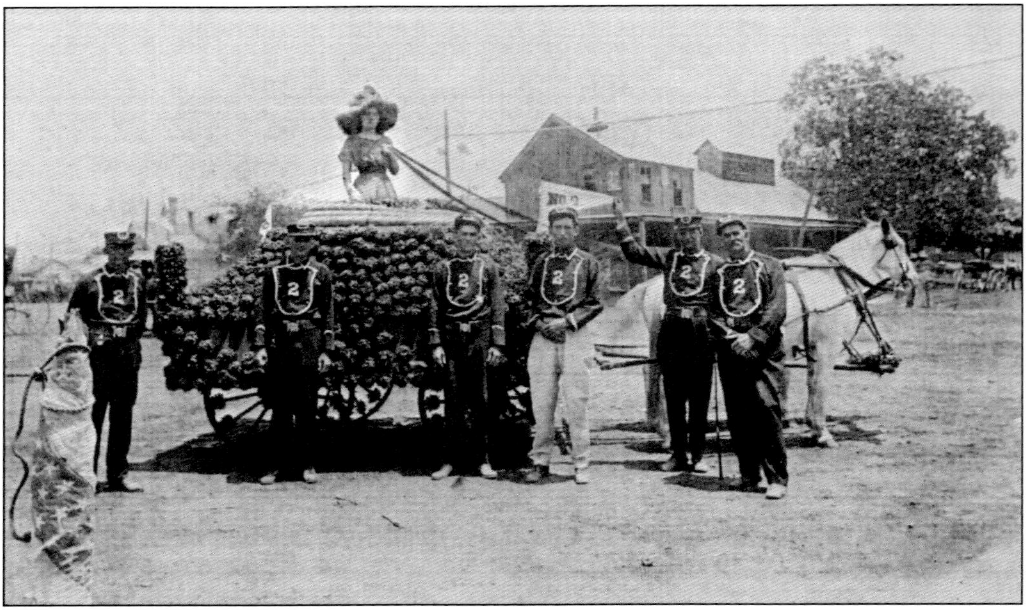

Parades have always been popular in Rockdale, and ornate decorations like those on this carriage were not uncommon. (Photograph courtesy of *Rockdale Reporter.*)

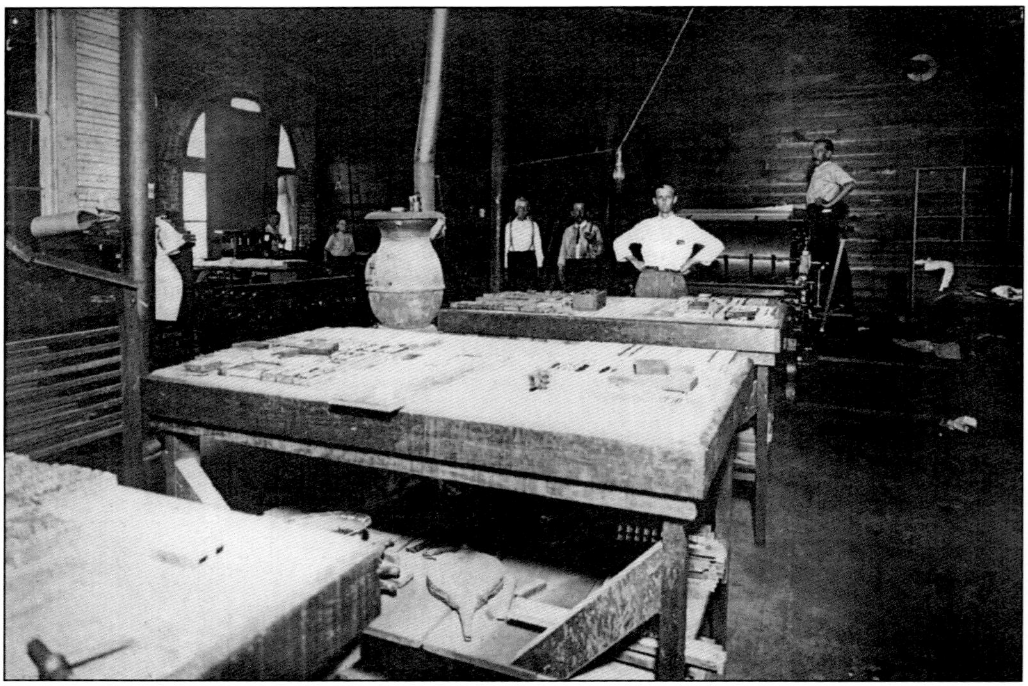

The *Rockdale Reporter* was purchased by John Esten Cooke, seen here in his printing department with his hands on his hips in May 1911. The makeup stone and the old press can be seen in the foreground. Note the potbellied stove. (Photograph courtesy of *Rockdale Reporter.*)

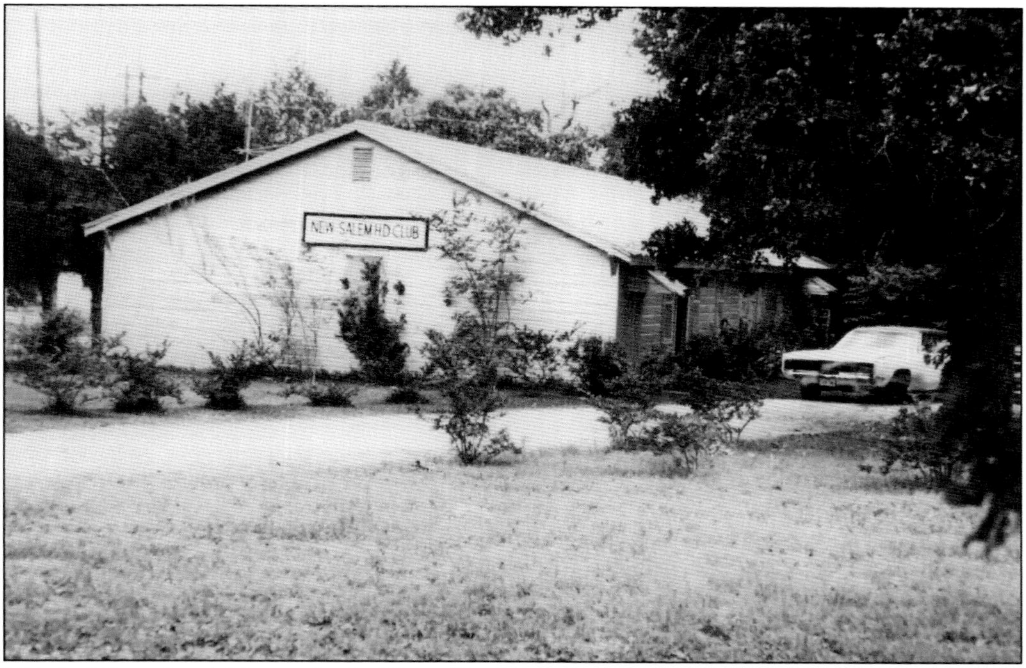

This building, the clubhouse for the Home Demonstration Club, is still used for many community events. (Photograph courtesy of Gary Jackson.)

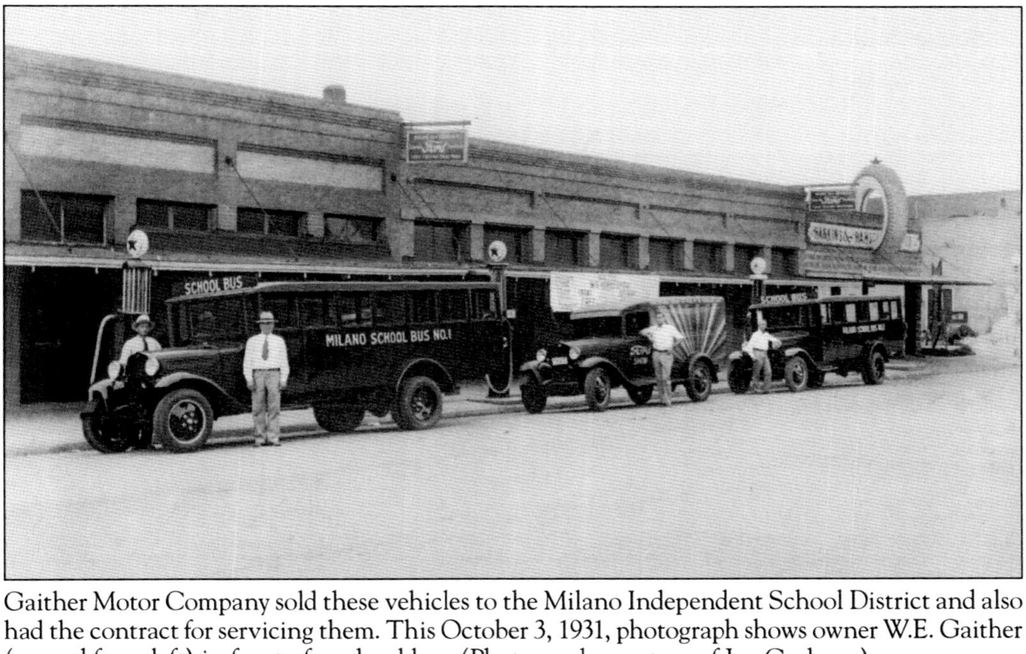

Gaither Motor Company sold these vehicles to the Milano Independent School District and also had the contract for servicing them. This October 3, 1931, photograph shows owner W.E. Gaither (second from left) in front of a school bus. (Photograph courtesy of Joy Graham.)

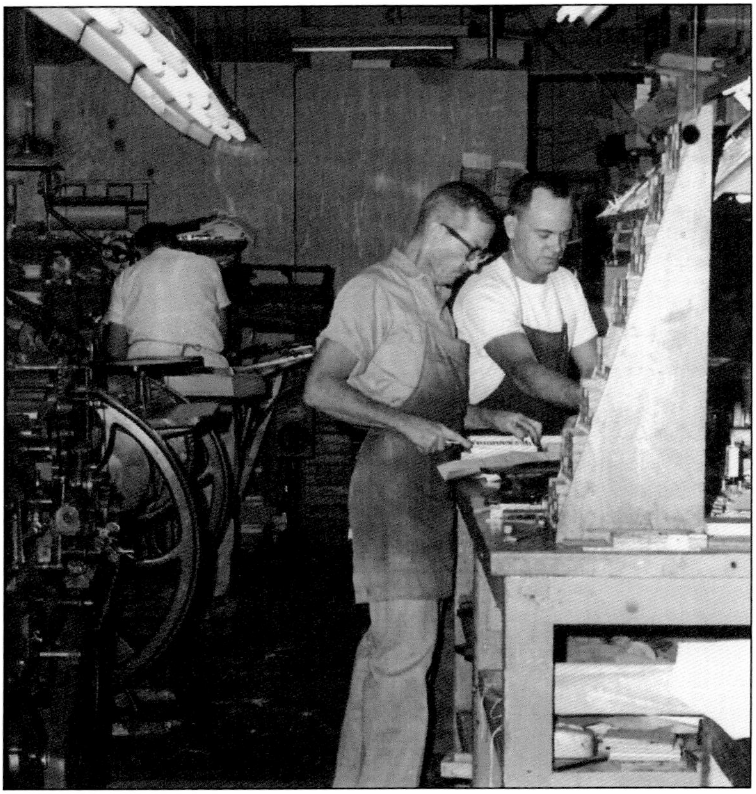

Wendell Dyer (left) and Roland Lawson work on the linotype machine in the office of the *Rockdale Reporter.* (Photograph courtesy of Wenda Dyer, Sharon Dyer Shoemake, and Judy Dyer Sivadon.)

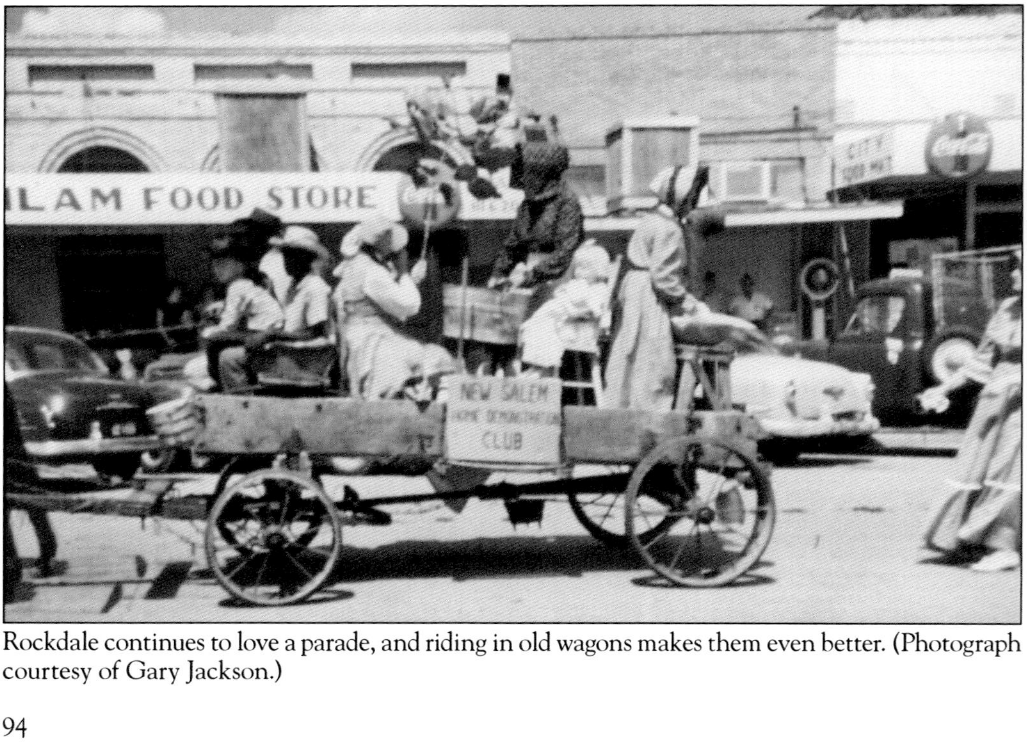

Rockdale continues to love a parade, and riding in old wagons makes them even better. (Photograph courtesy of Gary Jackson.)

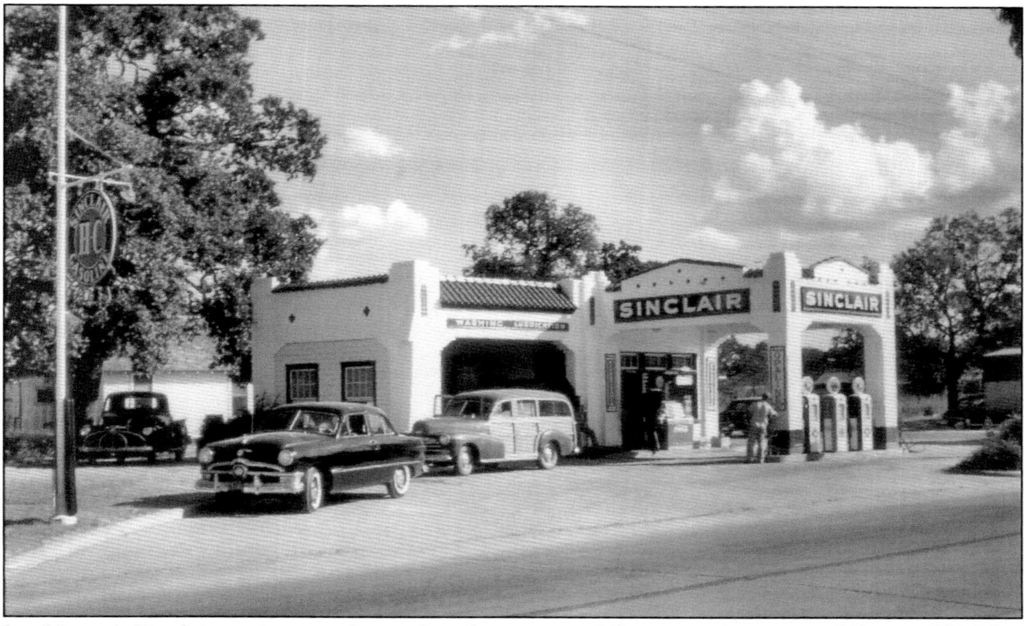

Joe Henry's Sinclair station was located at the corner of Cameron Avenue and Route 487. This was directly across from the current location of Rockdale City Hall. (Photograph courtesy of Bert Henry.)

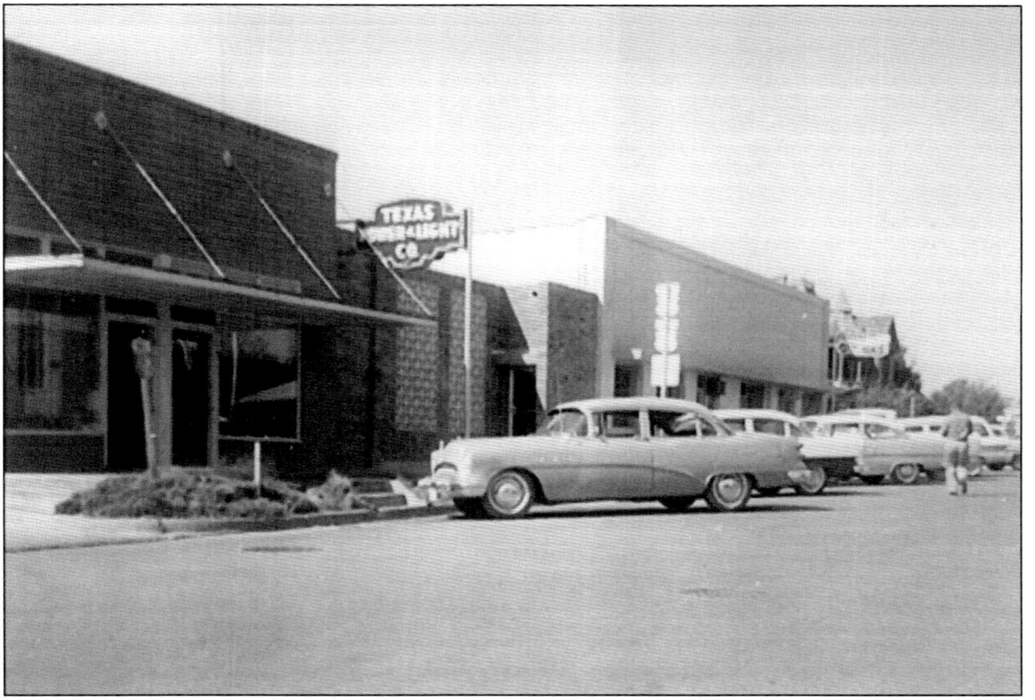

The Texas Power and Light Company on Ackerman Street is directly across from the post office. Note the Lockett home still visible in the background. (Photograph courtesy of Bert Henry.)

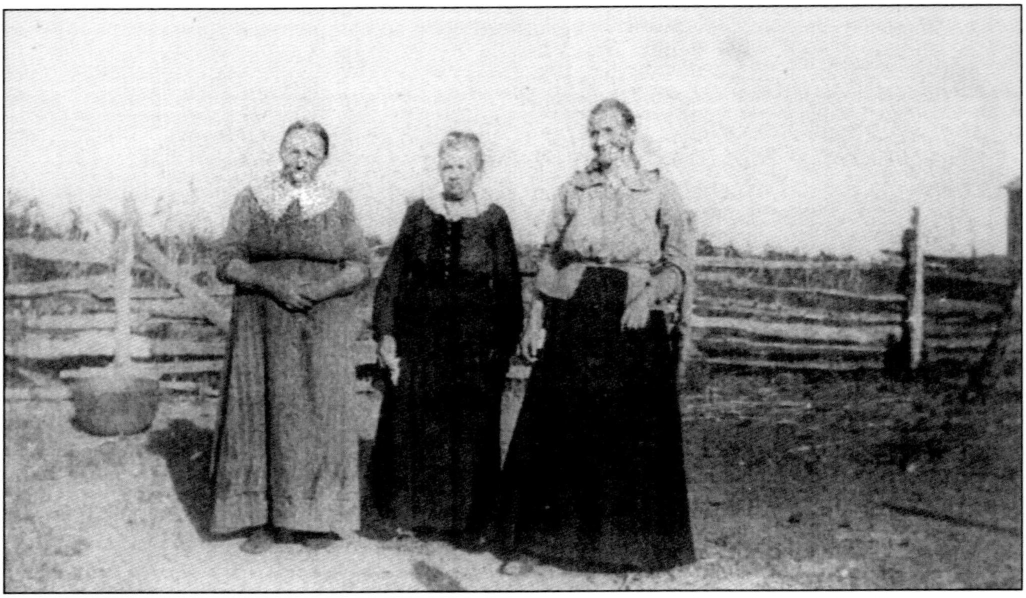

These three ladies from Bushdale pose for a photograph around 1922. They are, from left to right, Emma Drescher, a Ms. Helmeeke, and a Mrs. Palmer. (Photograph courtesy of Robert Edwards.)

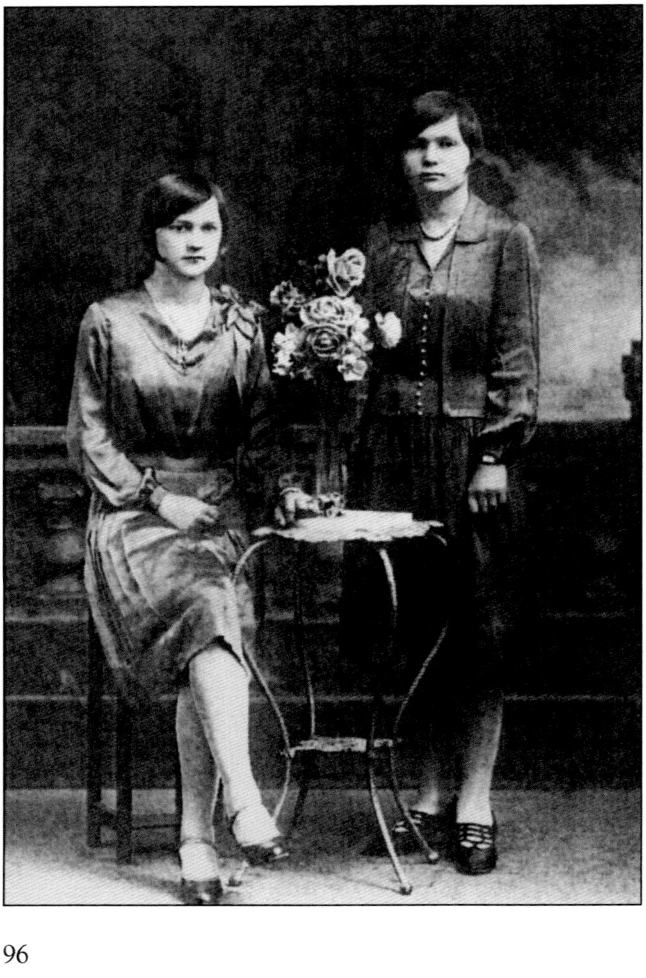

Ida (left) and Bertha Drescher pose in their finest fashions. (Courtesy of Robert Edwards.)

Lena Howse married Ben Loewenstein in 1905. They remained in Rockdale and were perhaps the best-known Loewensteins in the area. Ben died as the result of a pedestrian/car accident in 1934, and his wife continued to run the store, finally selling it in the 1940s or 1950s. She died in 1972. (Photograph courtesy of Joseph Loewenstein, MD, Midland, Texas.)

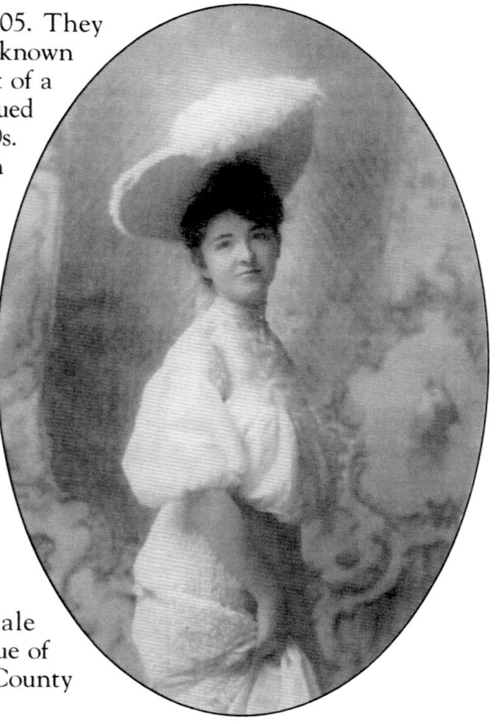

This aerial photograph showing the Rockdale Fairgrounds and Racetrack appears in a 1942 issue of *Life* magazine. (Photograph courtesy of Milam County Historical Commission.)

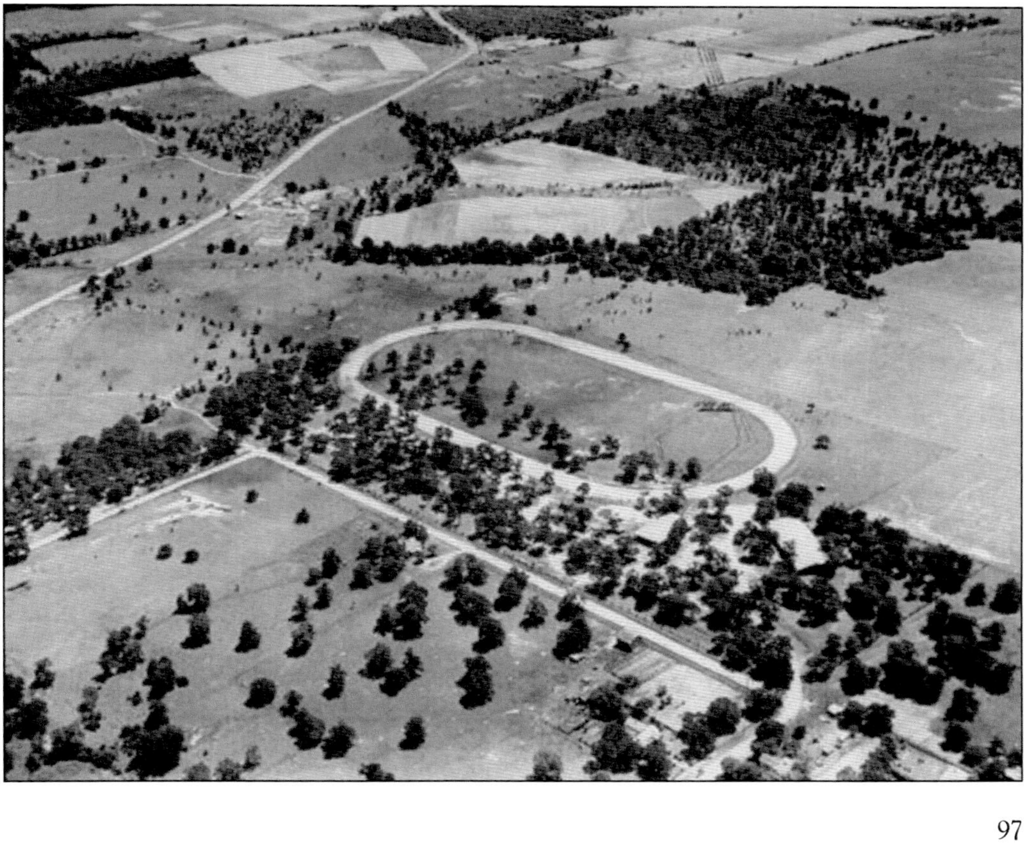

March 31, 1996. Actual Birthday, April 3

Mildred's Musings

On the Occassion of her 80th Birthday Party

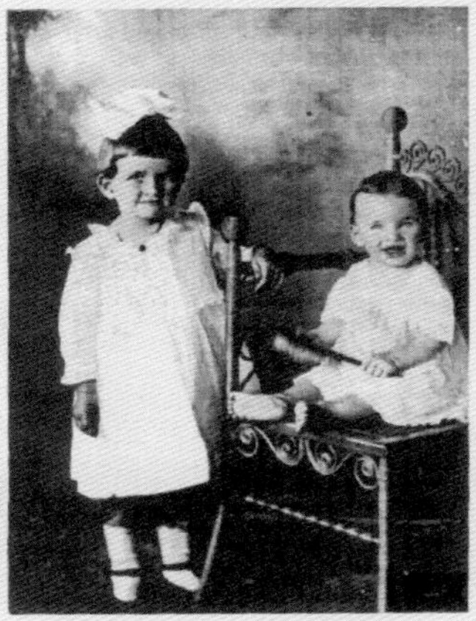

My Life at Pleasant Hill

To be asked to discuss the past, my past, is very flattering. At age 71 there is a lot of "past" My life, and that of my peers, has been spent in the greatest time in history. We've seen the advancement in travel from Model T to Space, in communications from U.S. Mail to more than I can describe. But we also have learned that the human race never changes. We all need love and attention. We need care. And when we get scratched we all bleed the same way, no matter the social level on which we live or the color of our skins.

of large post oak trees. The community of Pleasant Hill, established in 1874.

Houses in those days, in our part of the world didn't have living rooms, or dens. Our house had 3 bedrooms, dining room, and kitchen. The larger of the 3, where our parents slept, had a wood heater and some comfortable chairs. There was no heat, other than that, except from the wood cook stove in the kitchen. In the summers most of the sitting took place on the porches, front or back, and one "fanned" oneself a lot with one's straw hat!

I like old people,
young people,
fat people,
skinny people,
black people,
white people,
rich people,
poor people.
And all other kinds of people. Wouldn't it be dreadful, dull, and tiresome to be restricted to, or restrict one's self to only one kind.
MLHB

I guess a pencil and paper is about my favorite thing in the whole wide world
MLHB

The heart of Rockdale is its people, and there is no one soul who better typifies Rockdale and the heart of her generation than Mildred Harris Baker. In *Mildred's Musings*, written on the occasion of her 80th birthday, she provides a vivid insight into life and love in Rockdale. (Photograph courtesy of Leanna Harris Applegate.)

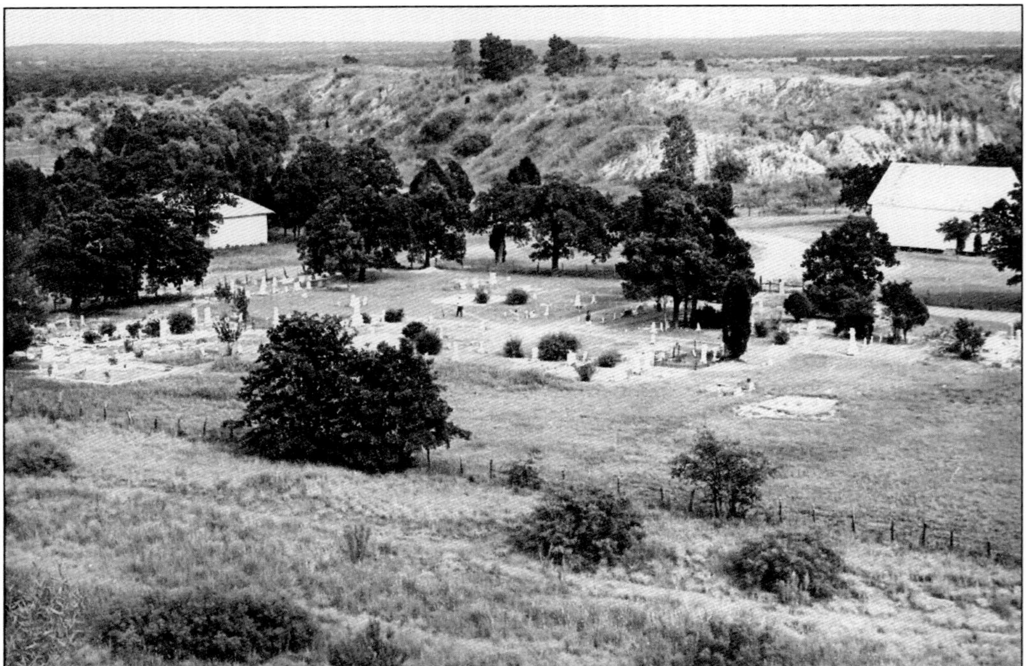

Mildred Baker chronicled the story of Pleasant Hill, a small community near Rockdale that was swallowed up by Alcoa as it moved into the area. This photograph shows the Pleasant Hill Methodist Church cemetery. The church was established in 1881. (Photograph courtesy of Leanna Harris Applegate.)

Pictured here, from left to right, are Katie Lee McNeil Luckey, Mildred Luckey (Harris Baker), Winifred Luckey (who would die at age 8), and Homer Luckey. (Photograph courtesy of Leanna Harris Applegate.)

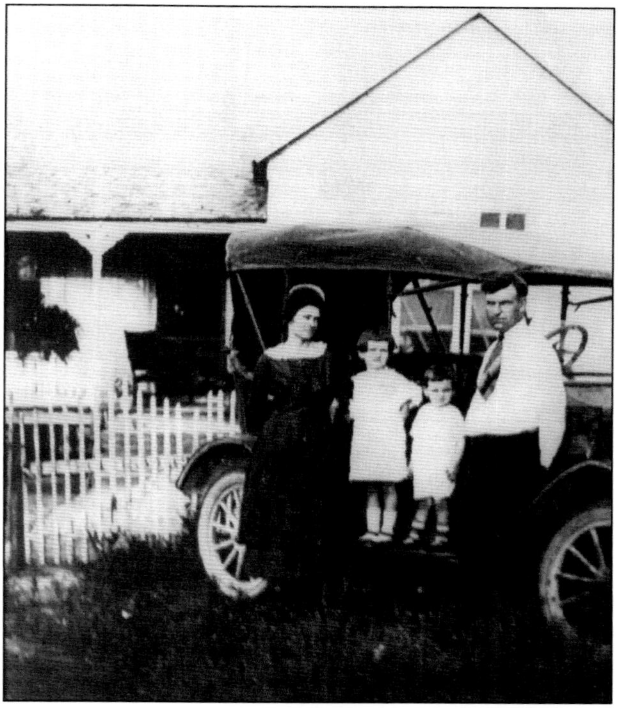

Vera Avrett drew this map of the layout of Pleasant Hill. (Drawing courtesy of Leanna Harris Applegate.)

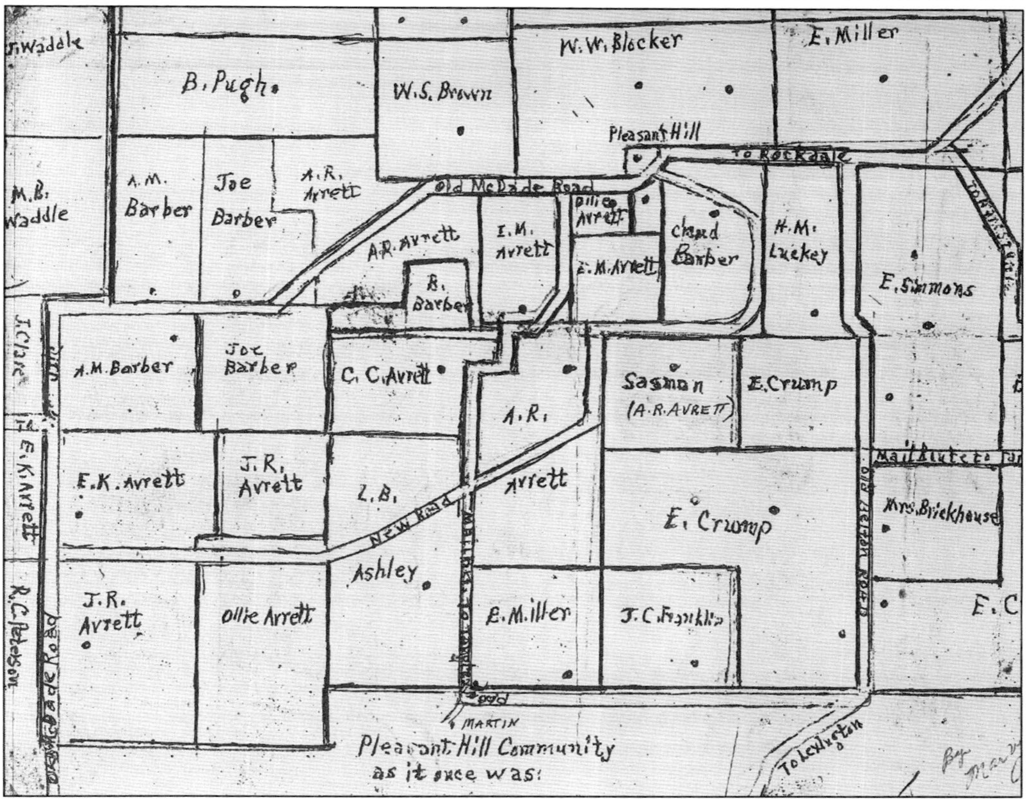

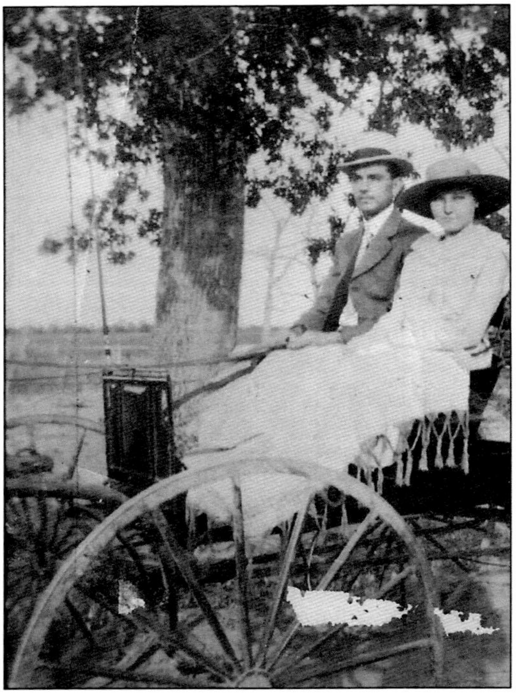

Bernard and Ethel (Peterson) Barber ride to church in style in Pleasant Hill. (Photograph courtesy of Leanna Harris Applegate.)

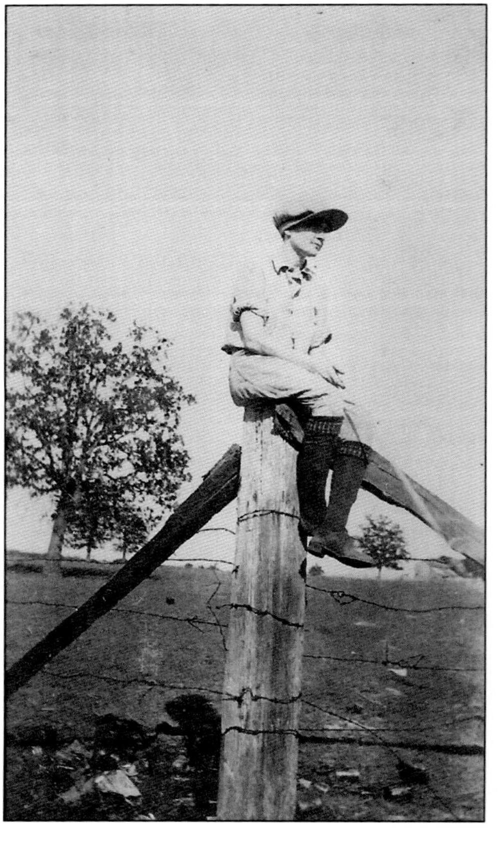

Hallie Mundine sits on the fence adjacent to the dog pen in Pleasant Hill. (Photograph courtesy of Leanna Harris Applegate.)

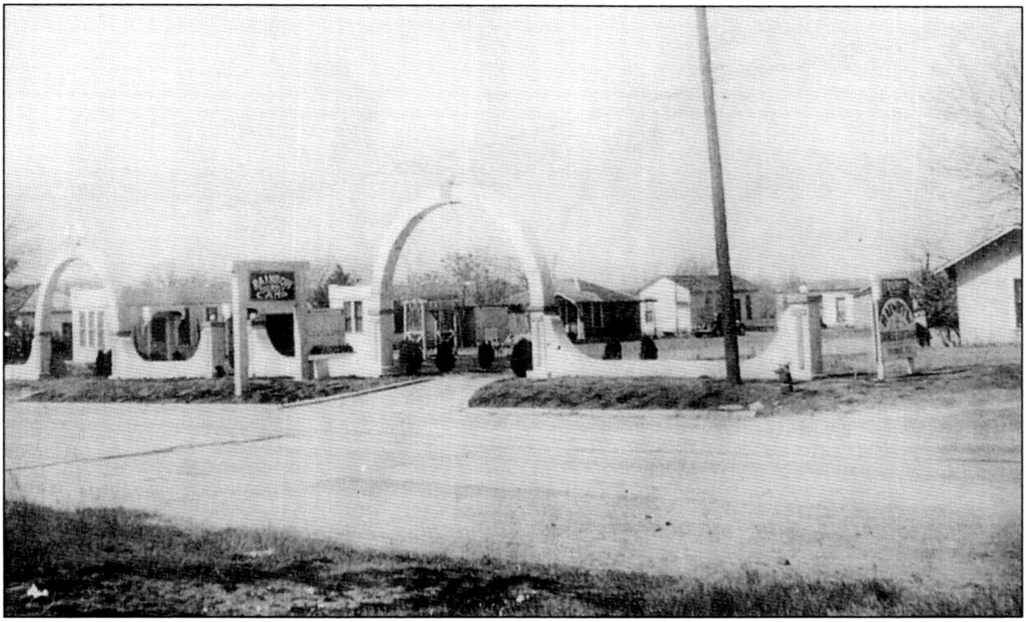

The land on which Rainbow Courts stands was purchased by Nathan Bullock and his wife, Johnnie, in 1918, for the purpose of establishing a tourist camp. In the 1930s, he sold it to his brother, Ira Benjamin Bullock, and Ira's wife, Algae, who moved to Rockdale to manage the courts. This is the oldest known photograph of Rainbow Courts. (Photograph courtesy of Joan and Dan Ratliff.)

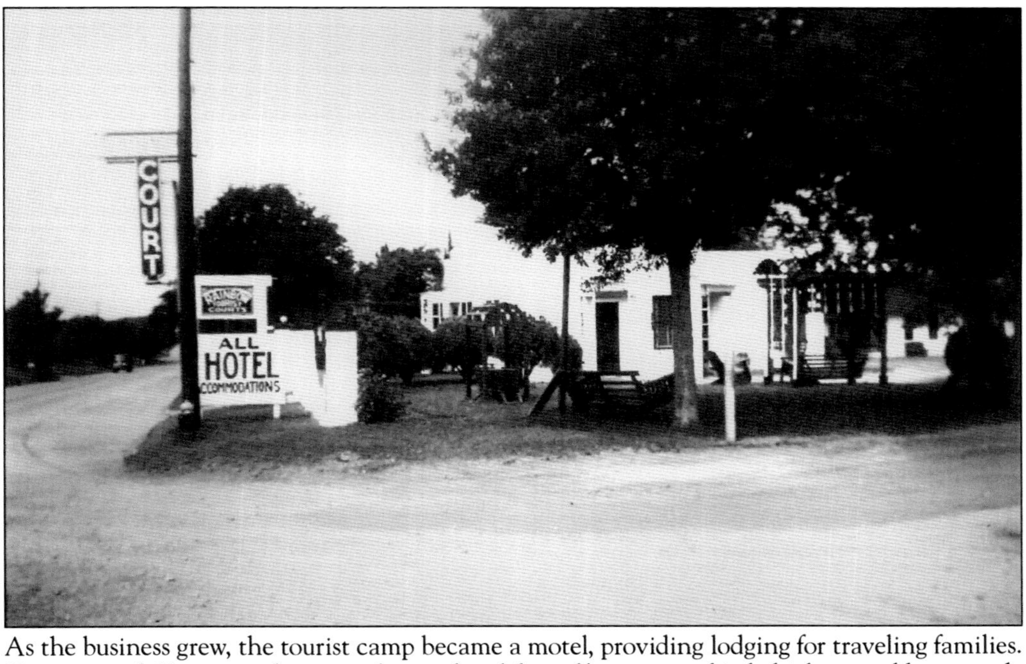

As the business grew, the tourist camp became a motel, providing lodging for traveling families. If guests paid 10¢ more, they got a hearty breakfast of ham, eggs, fried chicken, and homemade biscuit, which Algae Bullock rose at 3:30 each morning to cook. (Photograph courtesy of Joan and Dan Ratliff.)

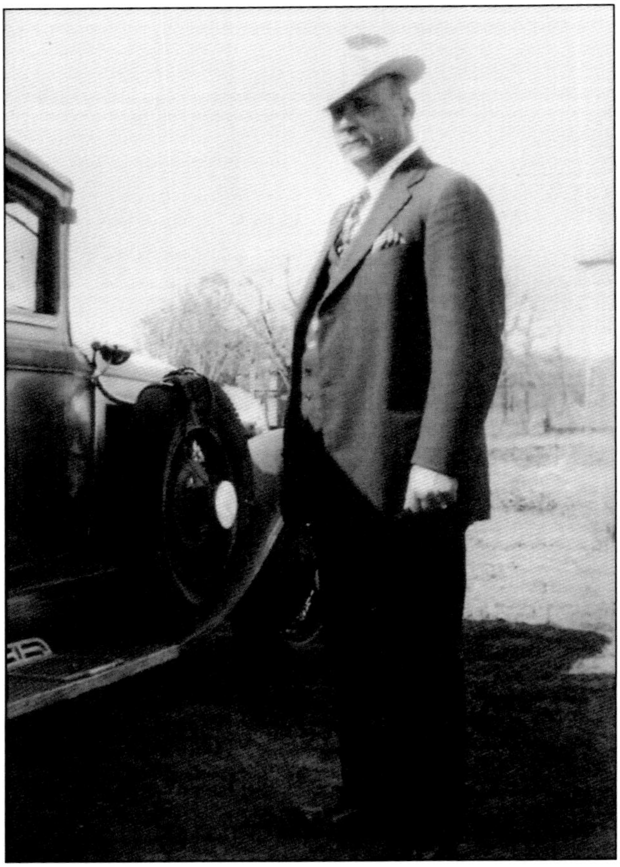

Nathan Bullock, seen here, purchased the land for Rainbow Courts in 1918 before selling it to his brother Ira. It was not uncommon for musicians to pay for their stay with a recording of their music, as Bob Wills did when he stayed here. The Bullocks did not have a record player, but they prized the album. (Photograph courtesy of Joan and Dan Ratliff.)

Ira and Algae's daughter, Marjorie, and her husband, Speedy Crockett, eventually took over the Rainbow Courts operation. (Photograph courtesy of Joan and Dan Ratliff.)

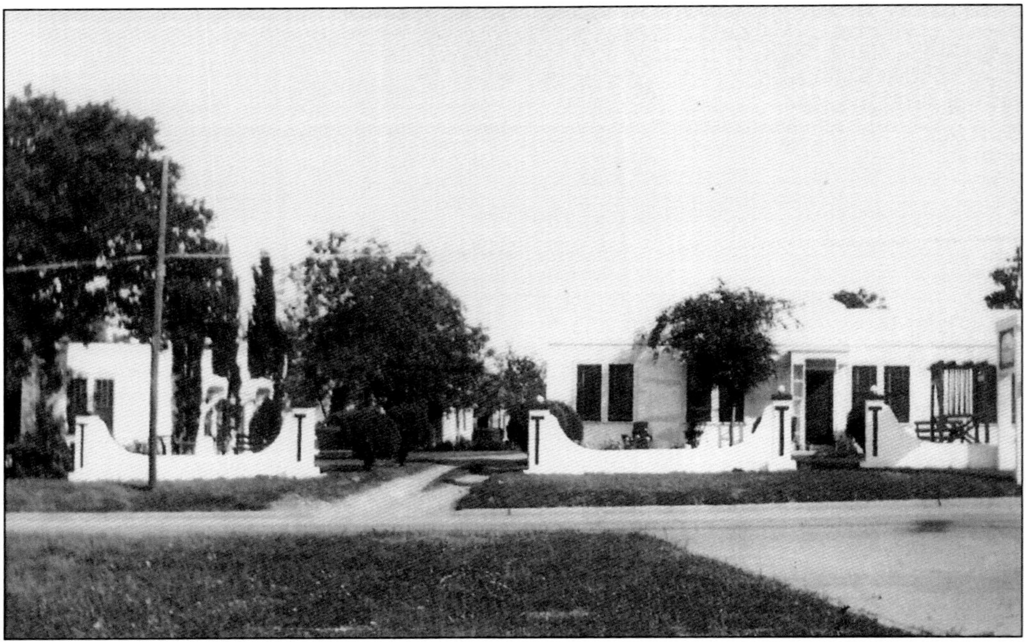

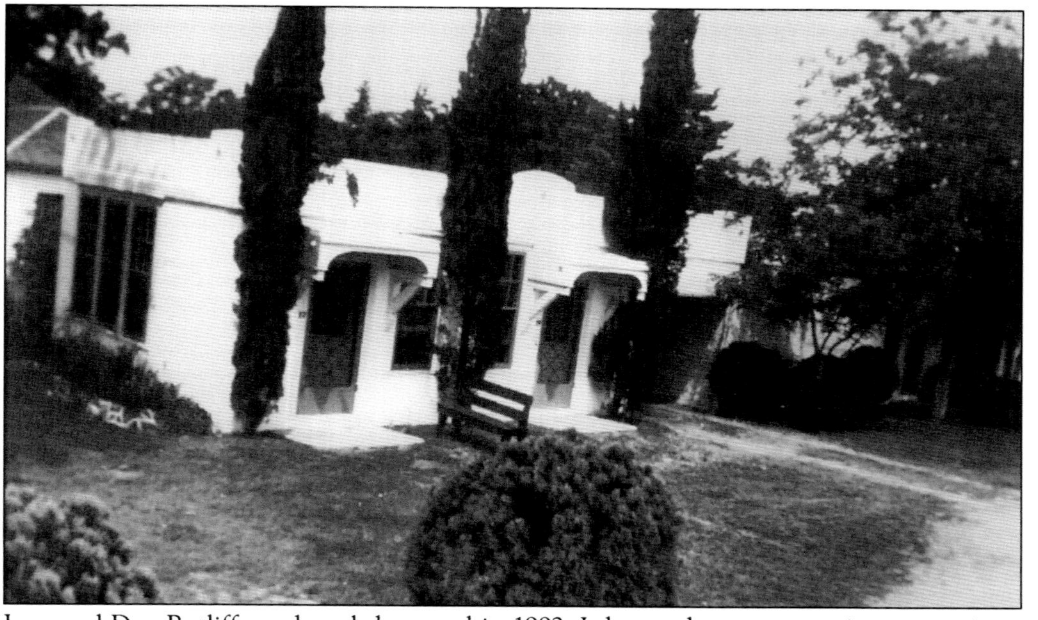

Joan and Dan Ratliff purchased the motel in 1992. It has undergone extensive renovations, but the motel retains its original look, adding to the charm of the lovely grounds and pleasing atmosphere. (Photograph courtesy of Joan and Dan Ratliff.)

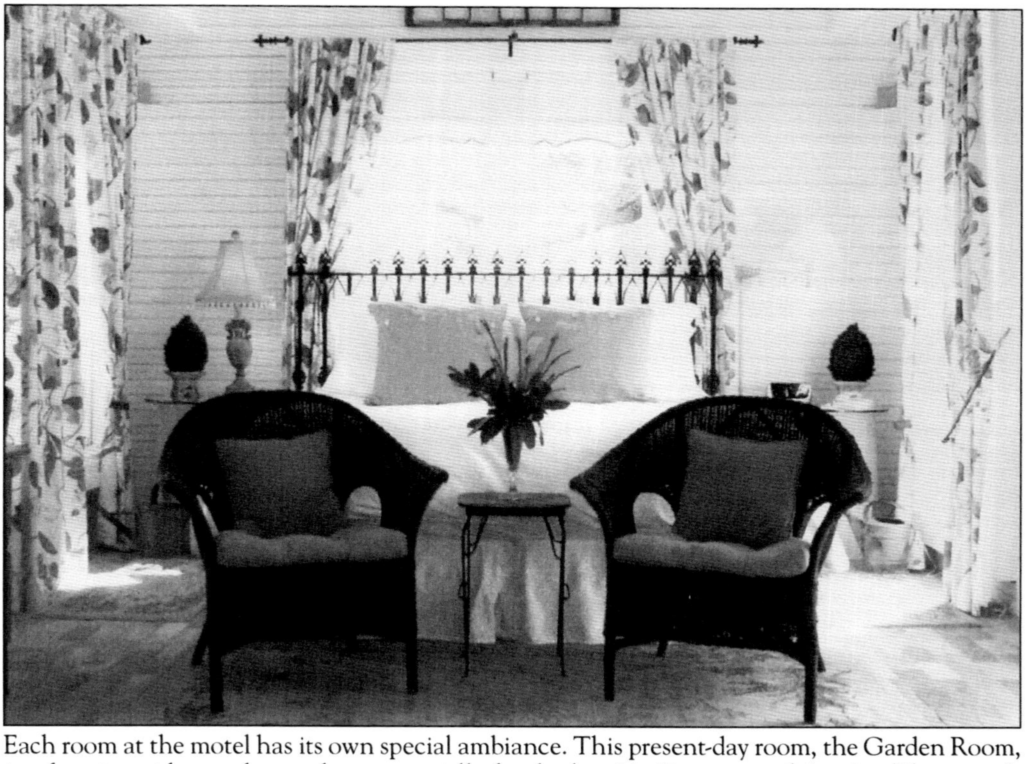

Each room at the motel has its own special ambiance. This present-day room, the Garden Room, is a favorite with travelers and was especially for the late Liz Carpenter of Austin. (Photograph courtesy of Joan and Dan Ratliff.)

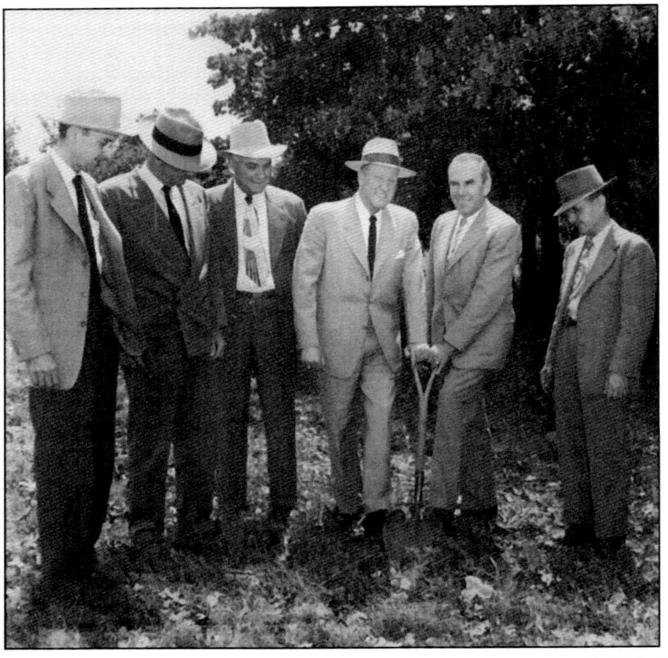

The ground-breaking ceremony for the Alcoa facility in 1951 marked the beginning of a new era in Rockdale. I.B. Bullock is third from left in this image. (Photograph courtesy of Joan and Dan Ratliff.)

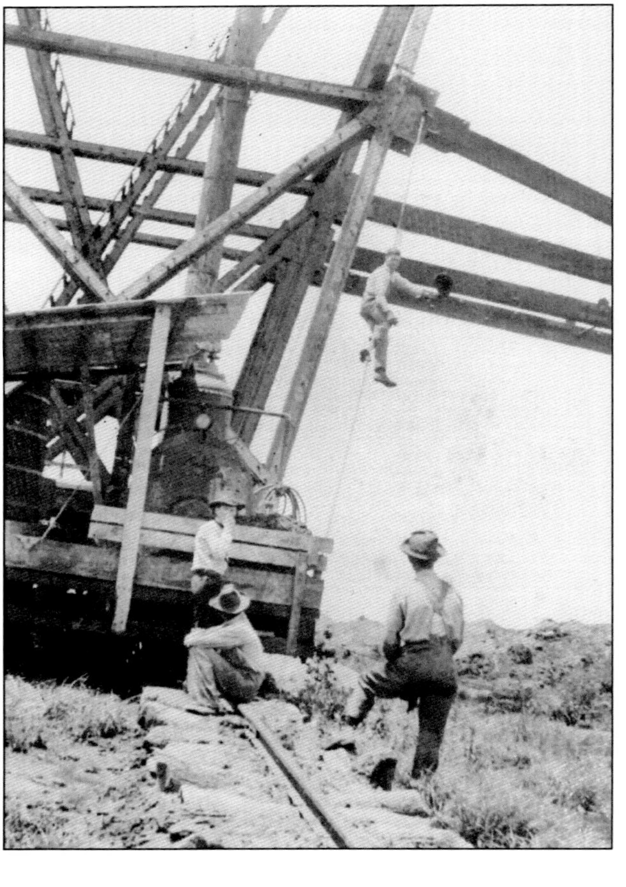

The Alcoa plant was assured in July 1951. Within three months, construction had begun on 78 new homes in Rockdale. In May 1952, there were 1,773 workers building the new plant. This steam shovel works on the early construction of the plant. (Photograph courtesy of Alcoa Inc.)

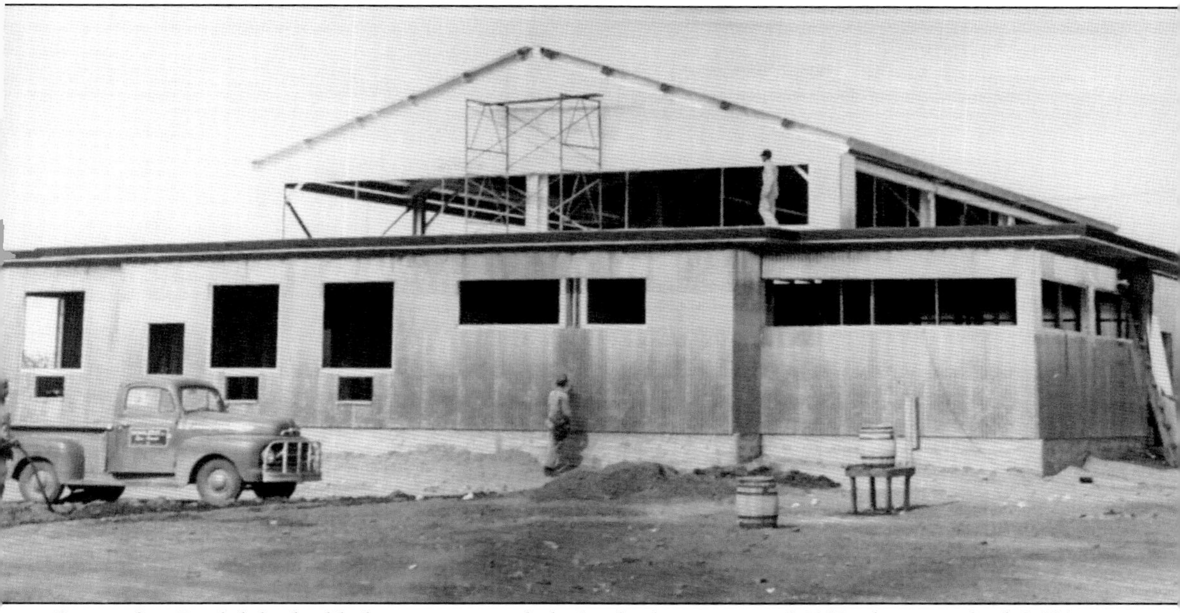

Soon after Rockdale doubled in size, it tripled. At the beginning of 1953, the town had 2,311 residents, and by the end of that year, the population was 4,950. By late 1955, some 6,027 people lived in Rockdale as construction continued at Alcoa. (Photograph courtesy of Alcoa Inc.)

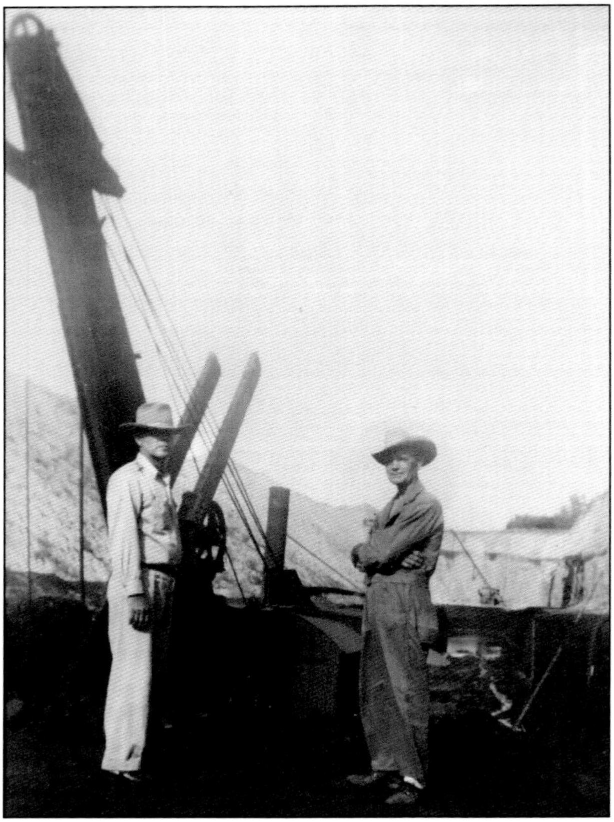

In March 1952, Alcoa set up a hiring office downtown above Prewitt Drug Store, and there were 50 contractors on-site by May. The Alcoa Carbon Plant, with the first nine employees, went on line in August. This photograph shows more of the early construction at Alcoa. (Photograph courtesy of Alcoa Inc.)

On November 4, 1952, power from the Texas Power & Light (TP&L) grid went to the first unit. In 20 days, Alcoa was making metal. This photograph shows the shovel and pit at the site. (Photograph courtesy of Alcoa Inc.)

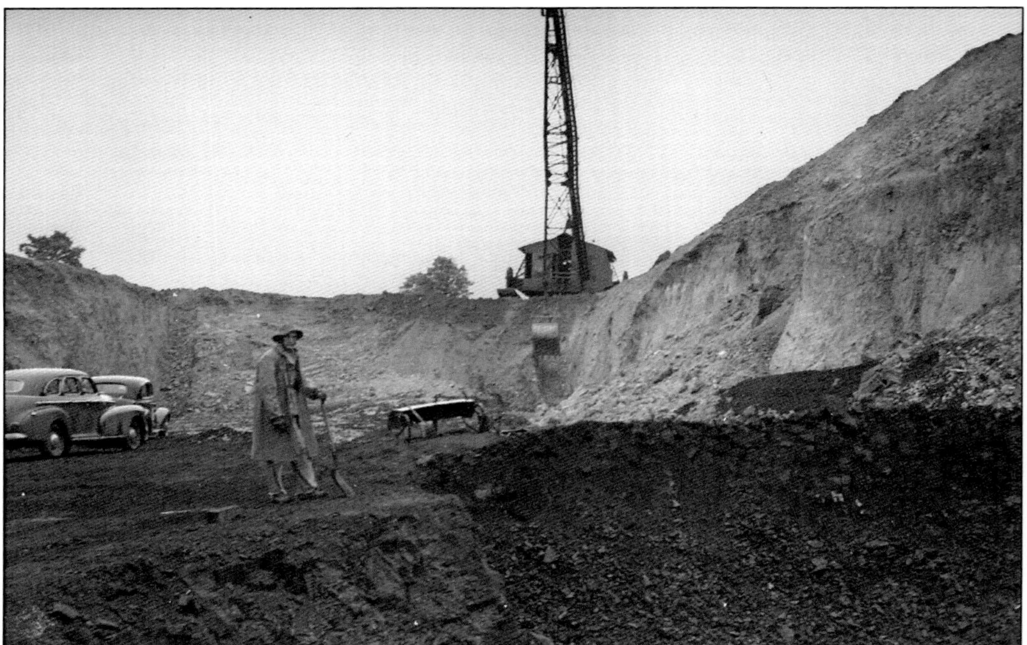

The grand opening for the plant was held on April 24–25, 1954. According to the records, 19,471 people toured the plant that weekend. An estimated 15,220 were present for Sunday's grand opening. (Photograph courtesy of Alcoa Inc.)

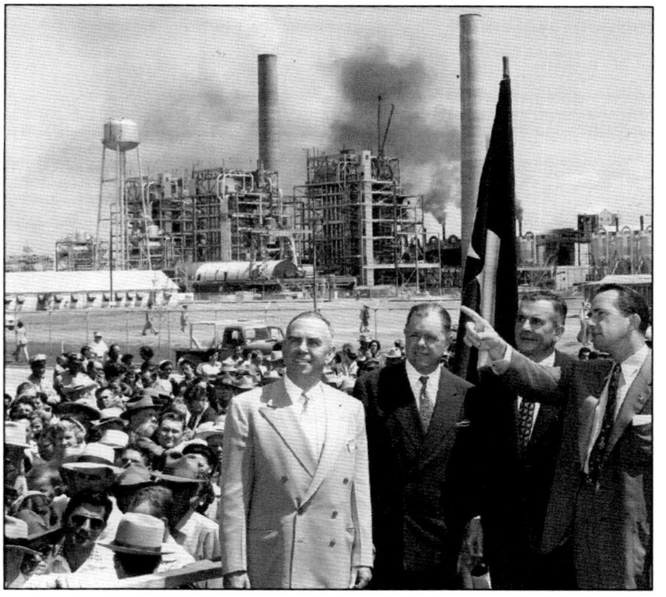

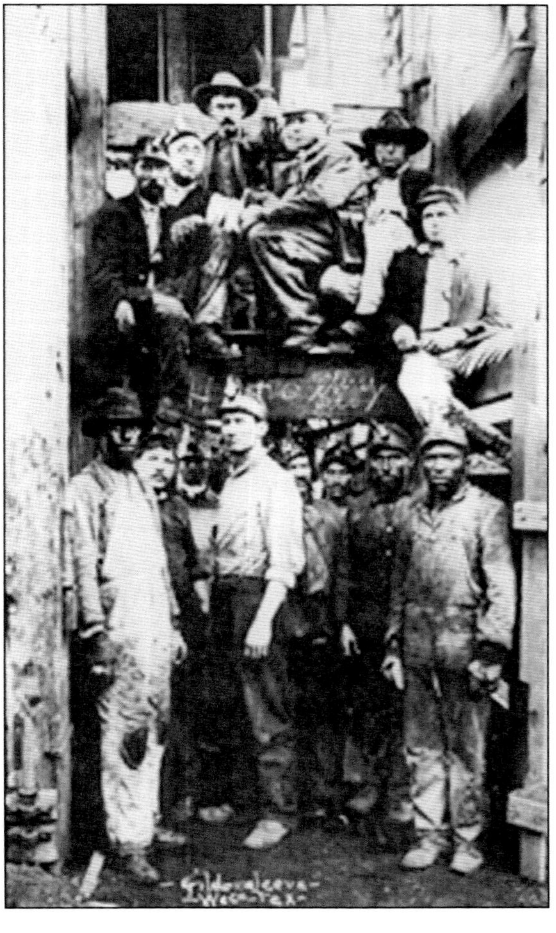

On December 27, 1952, Rockdale author George Sessions Perry wrote an article for the *Saturday Evening Post* titled "The Town Where it Rains Money," and Rockdale became known nationwide. Here, early miners work at the Sandow mines. (Photograph courtesy of Alcoa Inc.)

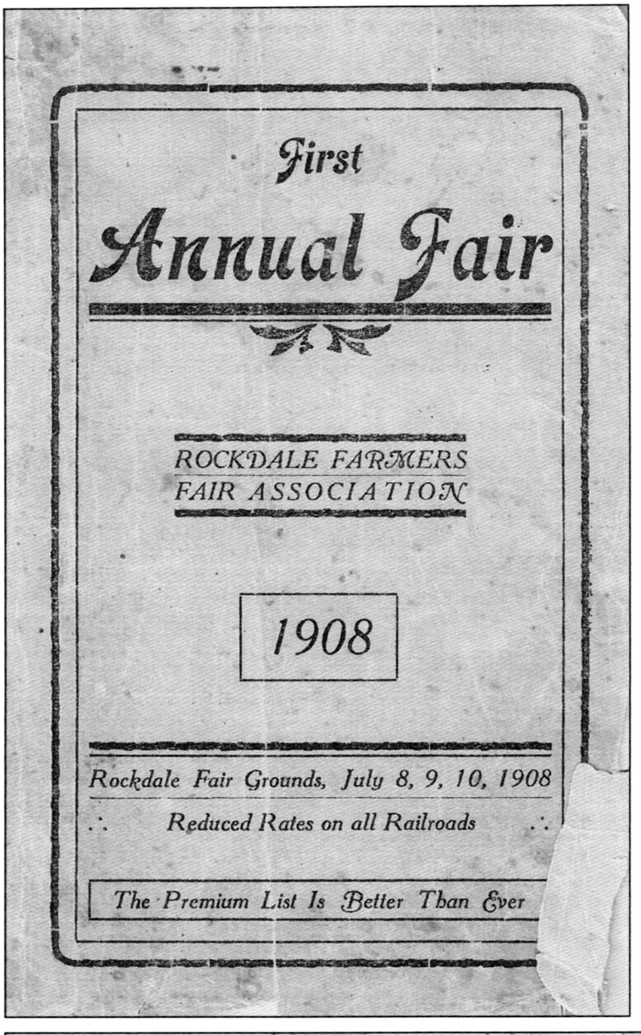

First

Annual Fair

ROCKDALE FARMERS
FAIR ASSOCIATION

1908

Rockdale Fair Grounds, July 8, 9, 10, 1908

Reduced Rates on all Railroads

The Premium List Is Better Than Ever

Rockdale hosted its first Farmers Union Fair on July 8–10, 1908. It was a roaring success, which *Rockdale Reporter* editor R.W.H. Kennon called "the biggest thing in our history." (Photograph courtesy of the author.)

Approximately 10,000 people attended the 1908 fair, with an estimated 6,000 lining the streets for the parade. (Photograph courtesy of the author.)

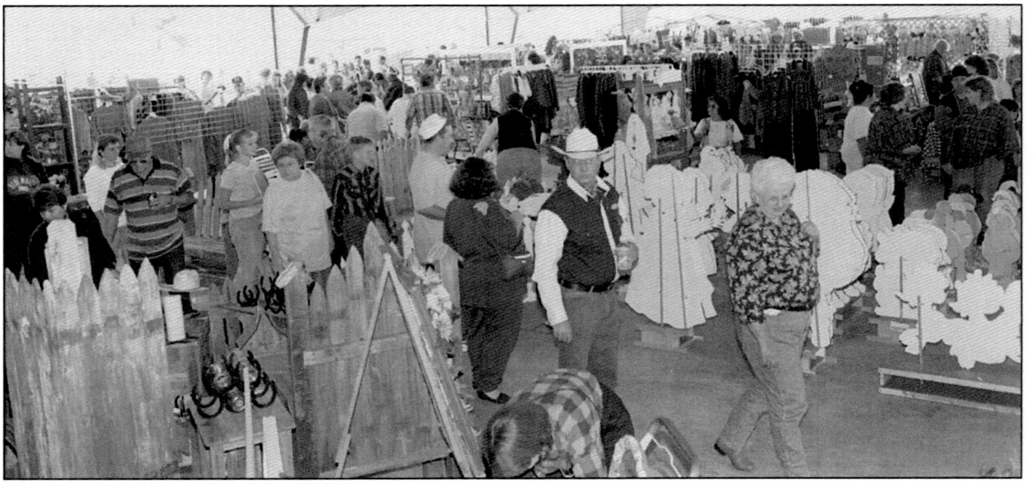

Exhibits at the fair were divided into 11 departments, each with a manager. Heads of these departments are indicated on page 14 of that year's fair booklet. (Photograph courtesy of the author.)

Division of Departments

Exhibits will be divided into departments and classes under direction of the following managers. Each manager will select assistance necessary to care for the different classes.

Department A.................... Horses and Mules
Jess Hillin, Manager.
Class 1—Horses. Class 2—Mules

Department B.............................. Cattle
Hill Marshall, Manager.
Class 1—Jerseys. Class 2—Red Polls
Class 3—Durhams.

Department C .... Hogs
W. D. Turner, Manager.
Class 1—Poland Chinas. Class 2—Berkshires
Class 3—Red Jerseys.

Department D............................. Poultry
N. J. Bagley, Manager.

Department E .... Goats and Sheep
E. G. Simms, Manager.

Department F............ Farm and Garden Products
Class 1—Farm Products.
Geo. Banzhaf and J. A. Touchstone, Managers.
Class 2—Garden Products,
Geo. Doss and W. W. Kyle, Managers.

Department G......... Canned Fruits and Vegetables
Mrs. A. H. Wilkens and O. K. Phillips, Managers.

Department H...Flowers, Ferns and Decorative Plants
Mrs. O. K. Phillips and Mrs. J. W. Clark, Managers.

Department I .... Fancy Needle Work
Mrs. A. B. Dickerson and Mrs. T. H. Paul, Managers.

Department J .... School Exhibits
Professors G. W. Gillis and J. W. Clark, Managers.

Department K .... Culinary
Mrs. Howard Willson and Mrs. A. P. Perry, Sr., Managers.

14

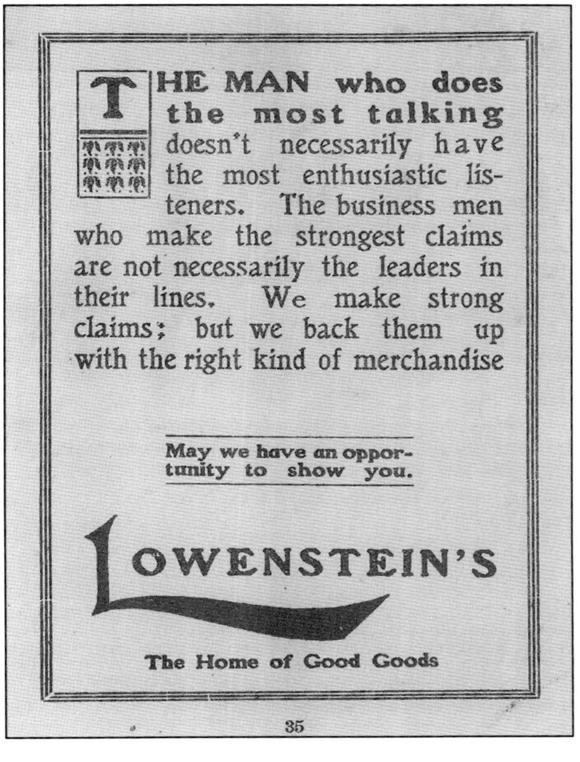

Loewenstein's took out a full-page ad in the booklet. (Photograph courtesy of the author.)

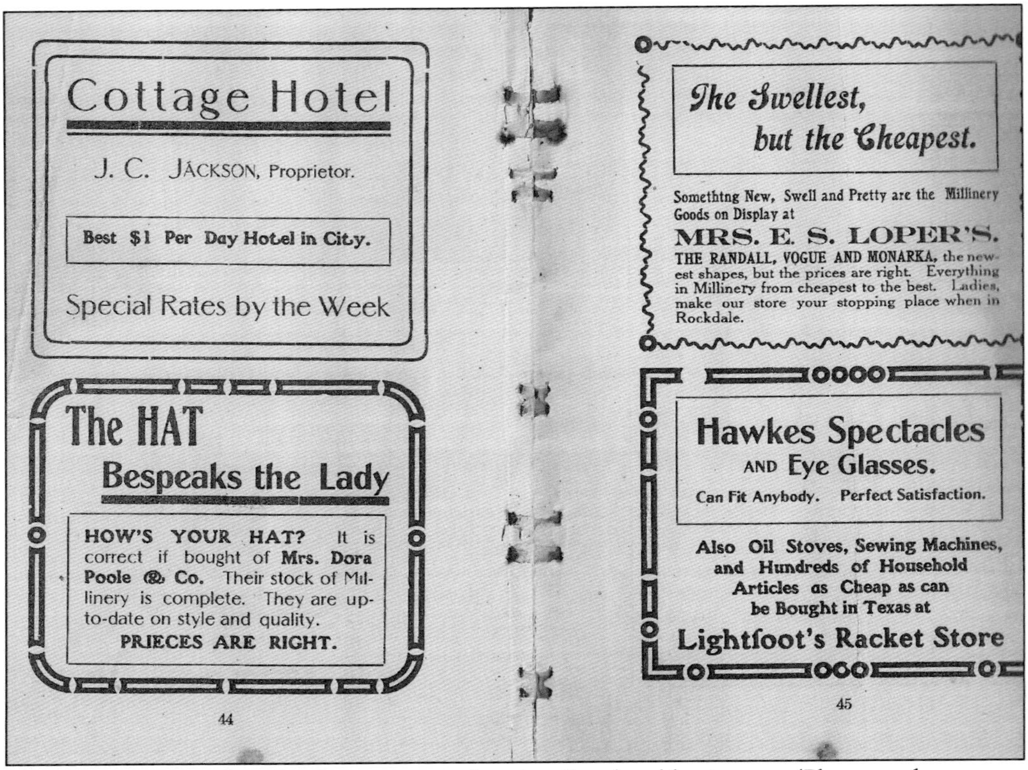

This two-page spread in the fair program advertises four local businesses. (Photograph courtesy of the author.)

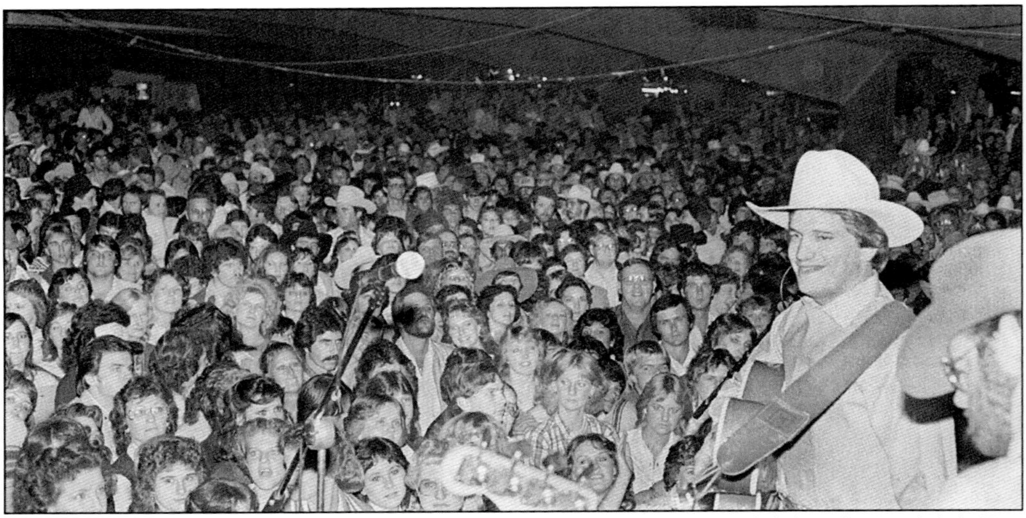

The October 22, 1983, fair probably saw the largest crowd ever in Rockdale. The Rockdale Fair Association had booked a little-known cowboy from San Marcos for its Saturday night dance, and two weeks before coming to Rockdale, George Strait won the two top Country Music Association awards. An estimated 13,000 people heard him in Fair Park. (Photograph courtesy of *Rockdale Reporter*.)

Inside Ashby's Confectionery and Grover York's Chili Joint are, from left to right, Grover York, Claud Ashby, Charlie Gohman, and Helen Ashby. (Photograph courtesy of Judy York.)

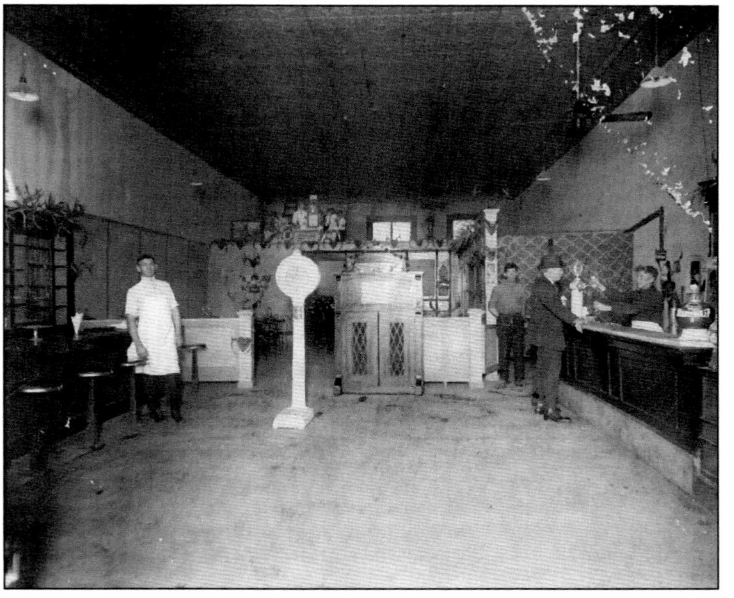

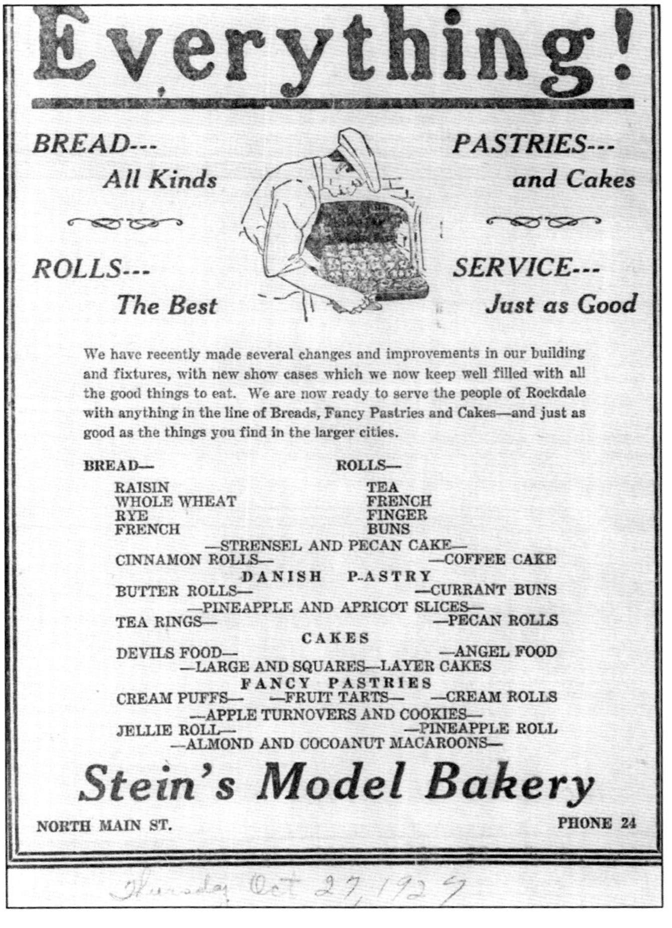

Everything!

BREAD--- *All Kinds*

PASTRIES--- *and Cakes*

ROLLS--- *The Best*

SERVICE--- *Just as Good*

We have recently made several changes and improvements in our building and fixtures, with new show cases which we now keep well filled with all the good things to eat. We are now ready to serve the people of Rockdale with anything in the line of Breads, Fancy Pastries and Cakes—and just as good as the things you find in the larger cities.

BREAD—
RAISIN
WHOLE WHEAT
RYE
FRENCH

ROLLS—
TEA
FRENCH
FINGER
BUNS

—STRENSEL AND PECAN CAKE—
CINNAMON ROLLS— —COFFEE CAKE
DANISH PASTRY
BUTTER ROLLS— —CURRANT BUNS
—PINEAPPLE AND APRICOT SLICES—
TEA RINGS— —PECAN ROLLS
CAKES
DEVILS FOOD— —ANGEL FOOD
—LARGE AND SQUARES—LAYER CAKES
FANCY PASTRIES
CREAM PUFFS— —FRUIT TARTS— —CREAM ROLLS
—APPLE TURNOVERS AND COOKIES—
JELLIE ROLL— —PINEAPPLE ROLL
—ALMOND AND COCOANUT MACAROONS—

Stein's Model Bakery

NORTH MAIN ST. PHONE 24

Thursday Oct 27, 1927

The Hobart Manufacturing Company of Akron, Ohio, sponsored a large advertisement stating that it had sold Stein Bakery a high-speed bread-and-cake-mixing machine and inviting patrons to go by and view it. (Courtesy of Judy York.)

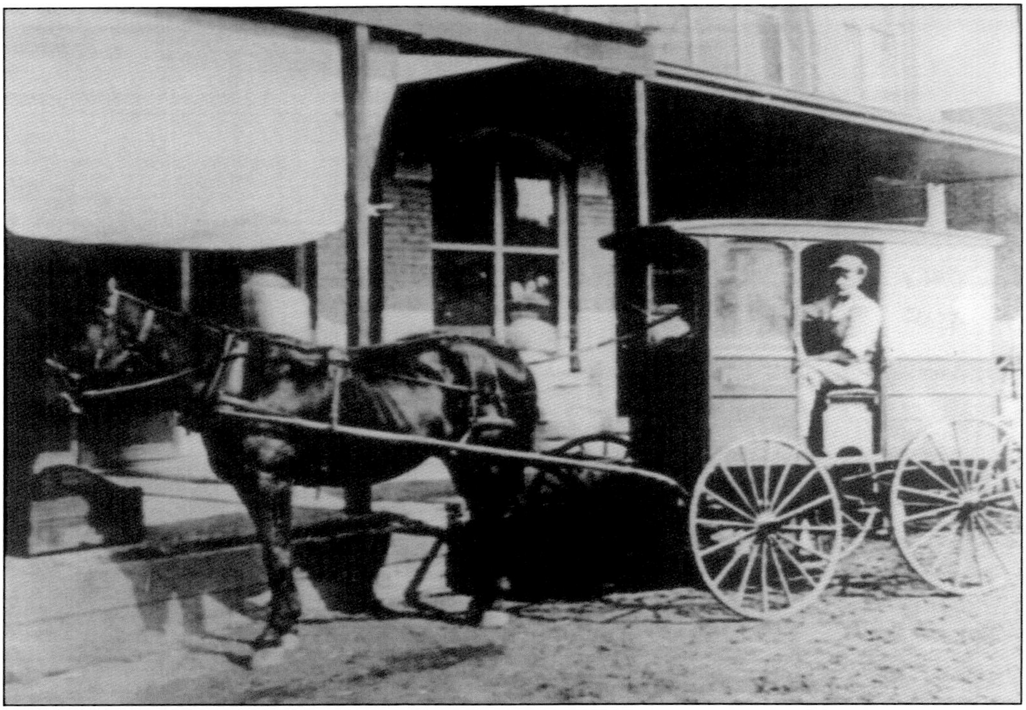

14-year-old Otto Stein delivers bread in Rockdale. (Photograph courtesy of Judy York.)

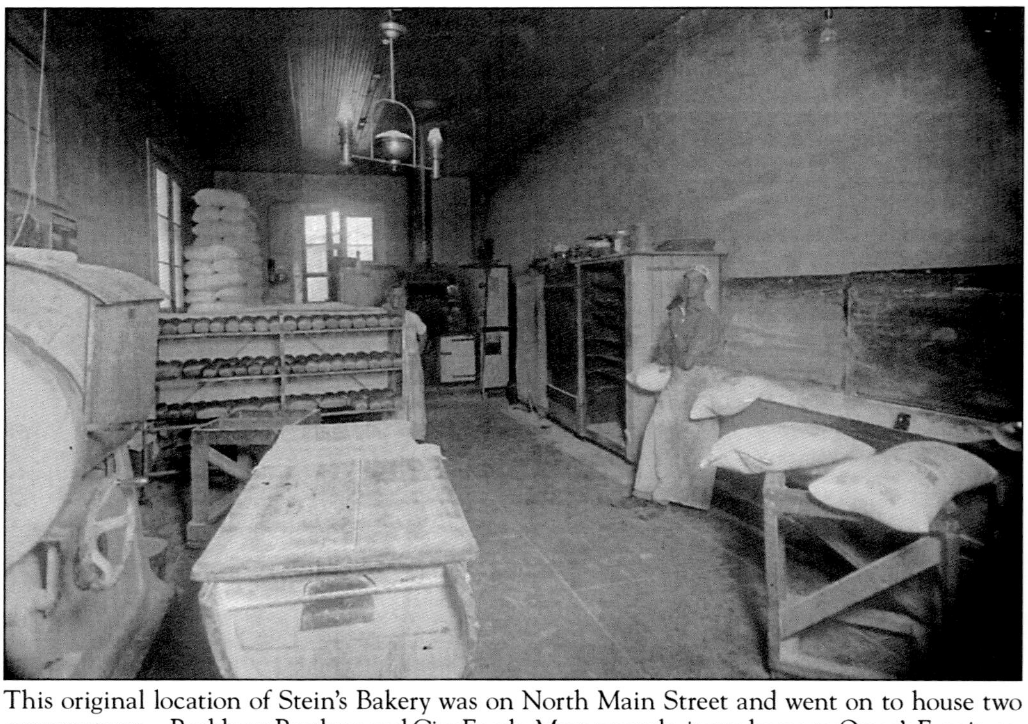

This original location of Stein's Bakery was on North Main Street and went on to house two grocery stores—Backhaus Brothers and City Foods. Most recently, it was home to Orsag's Furniture. The building is currently unoccupied. (Photograph courtesy of Judy York.)

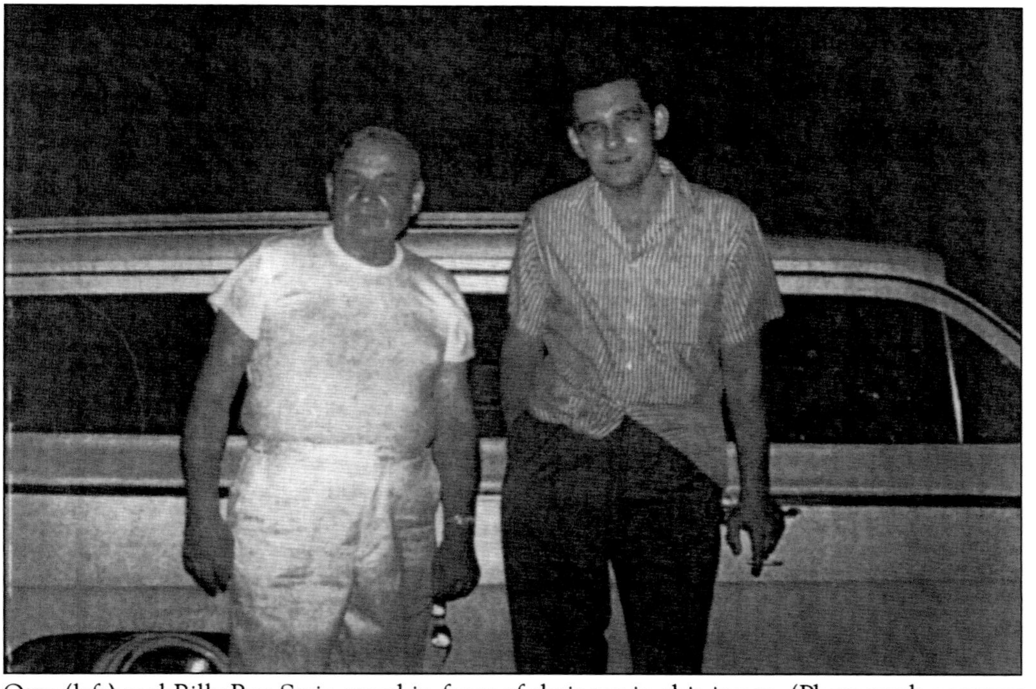

Otto (left) and Billy Ray Stein stand in front of their car in this image. (Photograph courtesy of Judy York.)

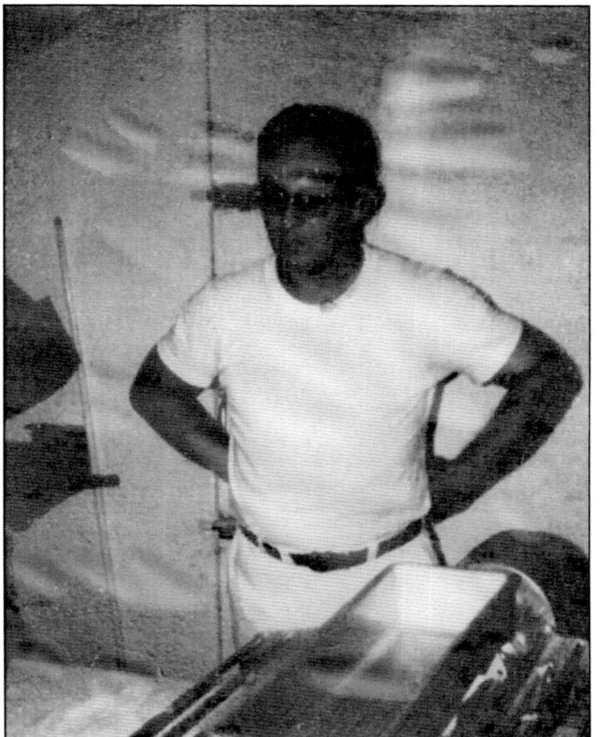

Judy and Pete York were the next owners of the bakery, located at 237 North Main Street, from 1976 to 1980. Here, Pete York takes a break from baking duties. (Photograph courtesy of Judy York.)

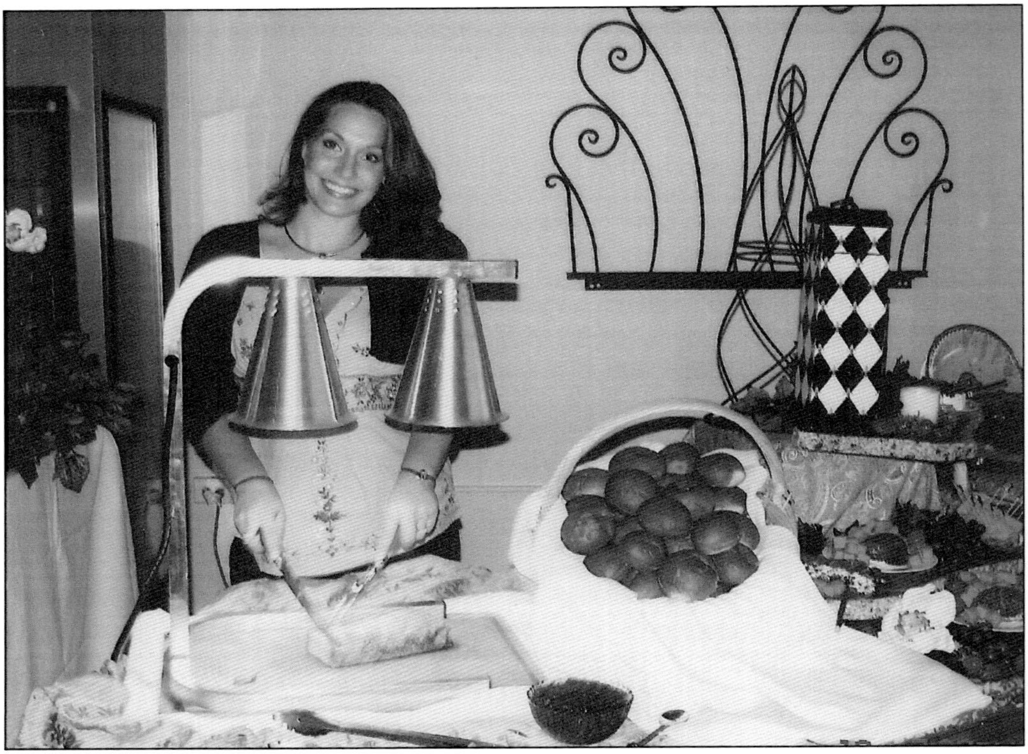

Stein's Bakery is still alive and well in Rockdale in the form of Terri's Sweet Shop – A Touch of Elegance, owned and operated by Terri York Sandoval, the daughter of Judy and Pete York. Sandoval continues the Steins' tradition with her widely admired cakes and special touch in catering. (Photograph courtesy of Judy York.)

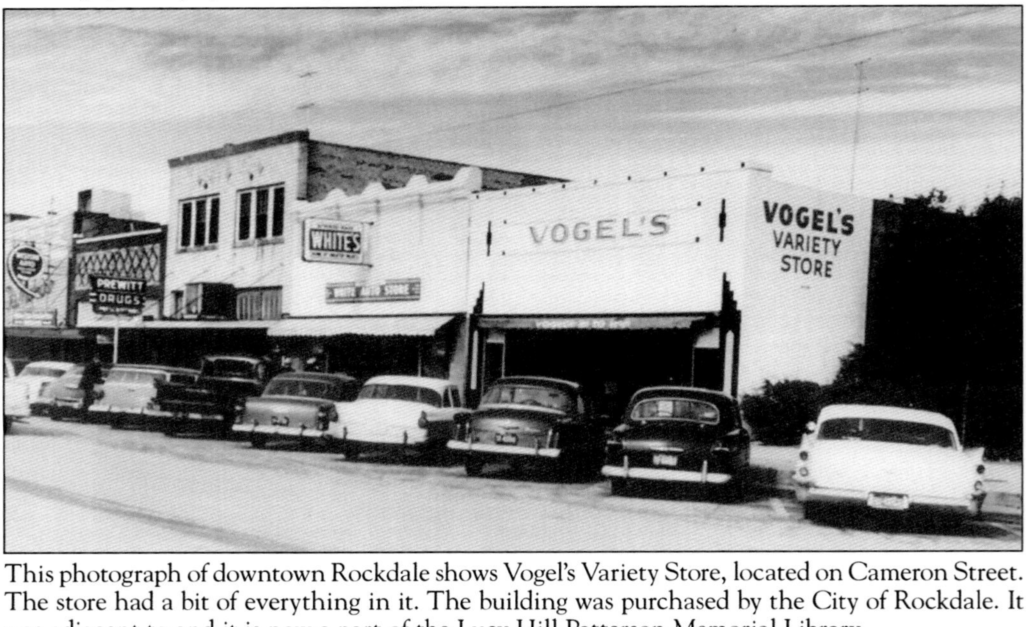

This photograph of downtown Rockdale shows Vogel's Variety Store, located on Cameron Street. The store had a bit of everything in it. The building was purchased by the City of Rockdale. It was adjacent to and it is now a part of the Lucy Hill Patterson Memorial Library.

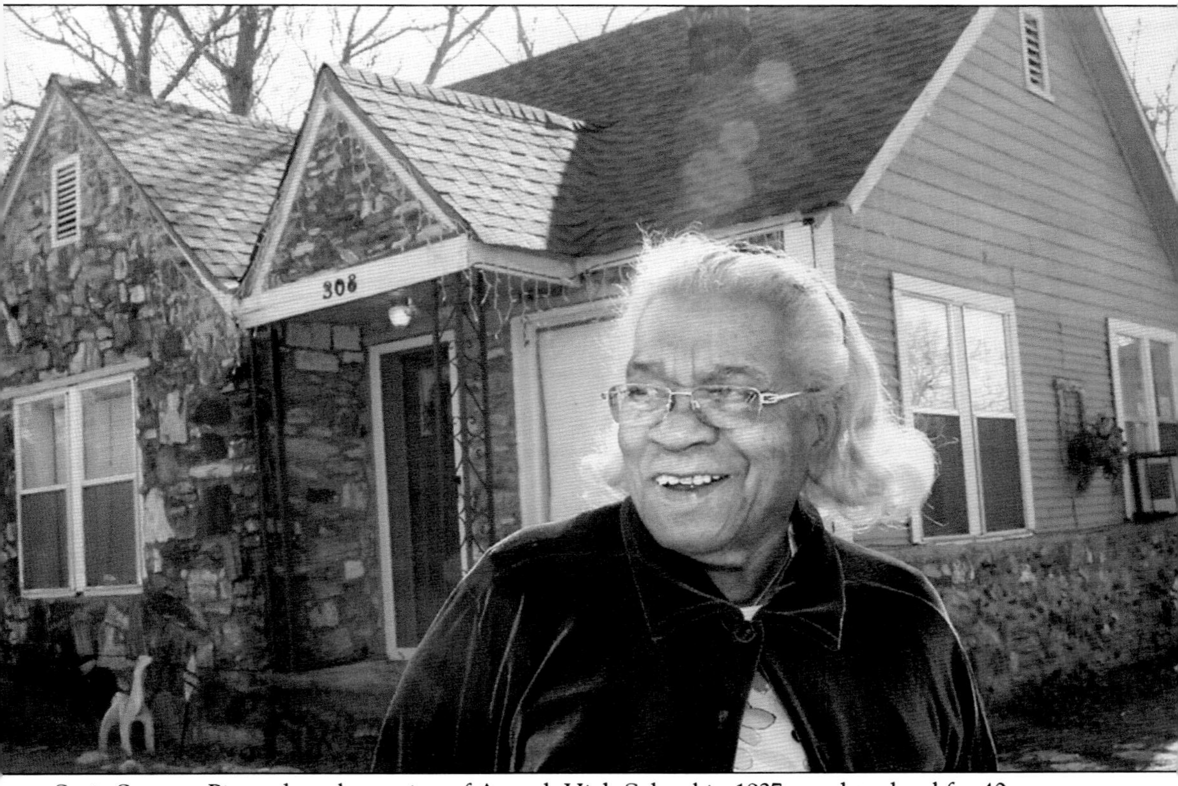

Susie Sansom Piper, the salutatorian of Aycock High School in 1937, taught school for 40 years, including 23 and a half years at Aycock, where she was the last principal before desegregation closed the school in 1966. Piper has chronicled much of the history of Rockdale in her *Rockdale Reporter* column Ebony Etchings. Especially memorable column titles have included "The Other Side of the Tracks," "Way Back When," "Aycock Nostaglia," and "A'Tied to Mama's Apron Strings." (Photograph courtesy of *Rockdale Reporter.*)

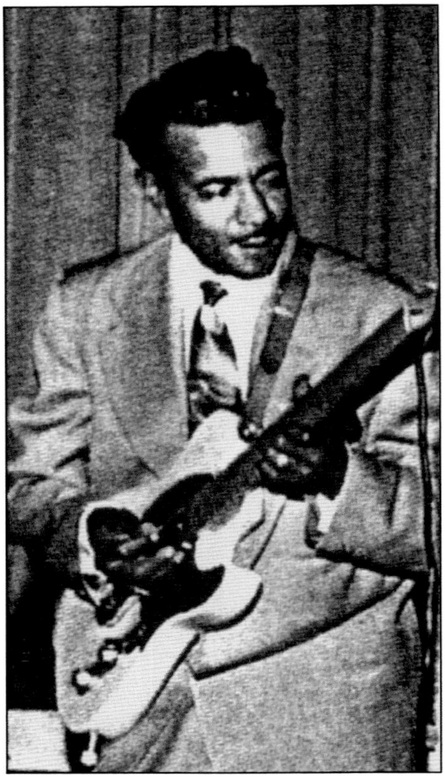

Susie Sansom Piper also wrote about well-known area musicians. In the late 1920s and early 1930s, four Moultry brothers, four Kennedy brothers, and two Shields brothers formed the first 10-piece jazz band in this area. Pee Wee Crayton, seen here, was another well-known musician. (Photograph courtesy of *Rockdale Reporter.*)

Susie Sansom Piper's parents, Eula Bell Crayton, of Liberty Hill, and Julium "Bose" Moultry, were married in 1920. Her mother was a respected nurse, medical advisor, and dentist; and her father operated a blacksmith shop. (Photograph courtesy of *Rockdale Reporter.*)

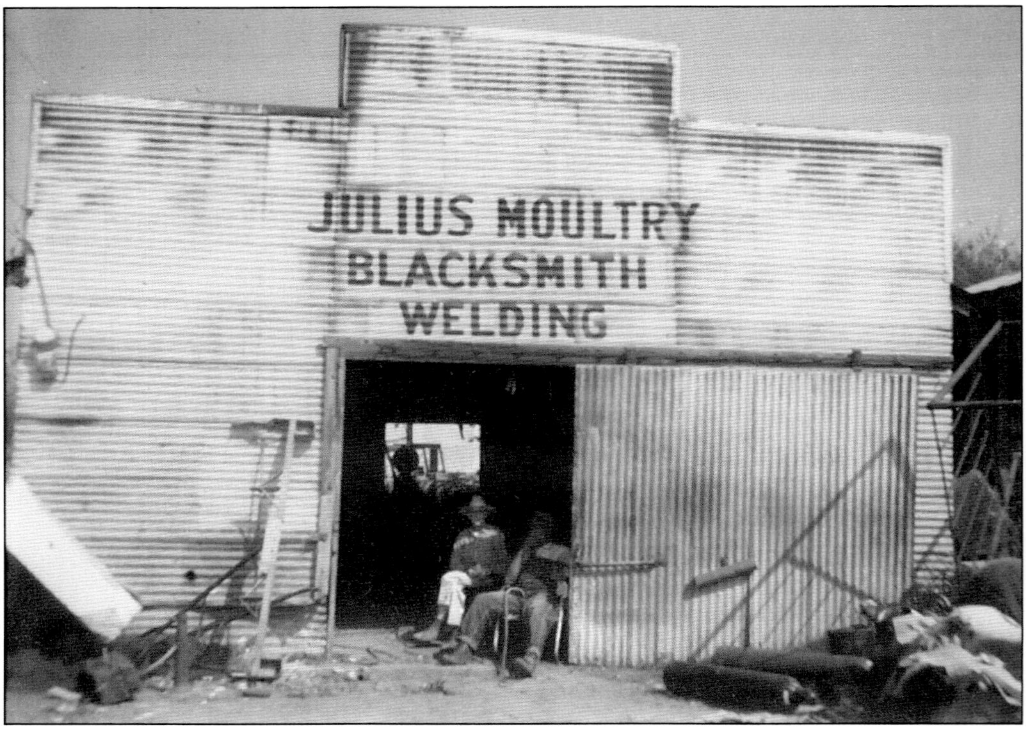

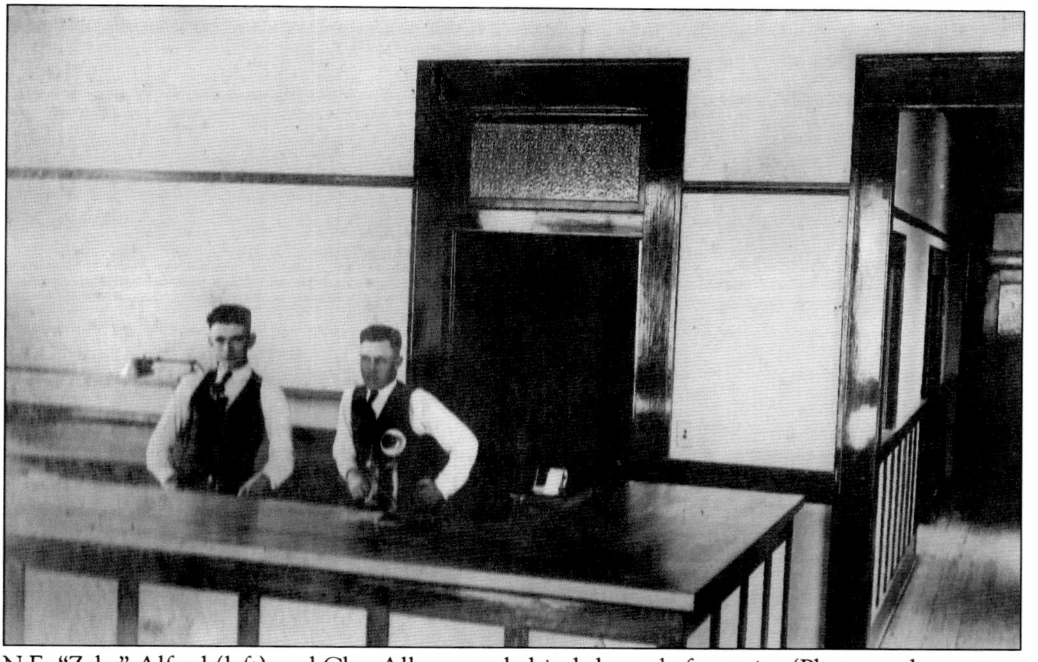

N.E. "Zeke" Alford (left) and Clay Allen pose behind the soda fountain. (Photograph courtesy of Eugenia Wolf Newton.)

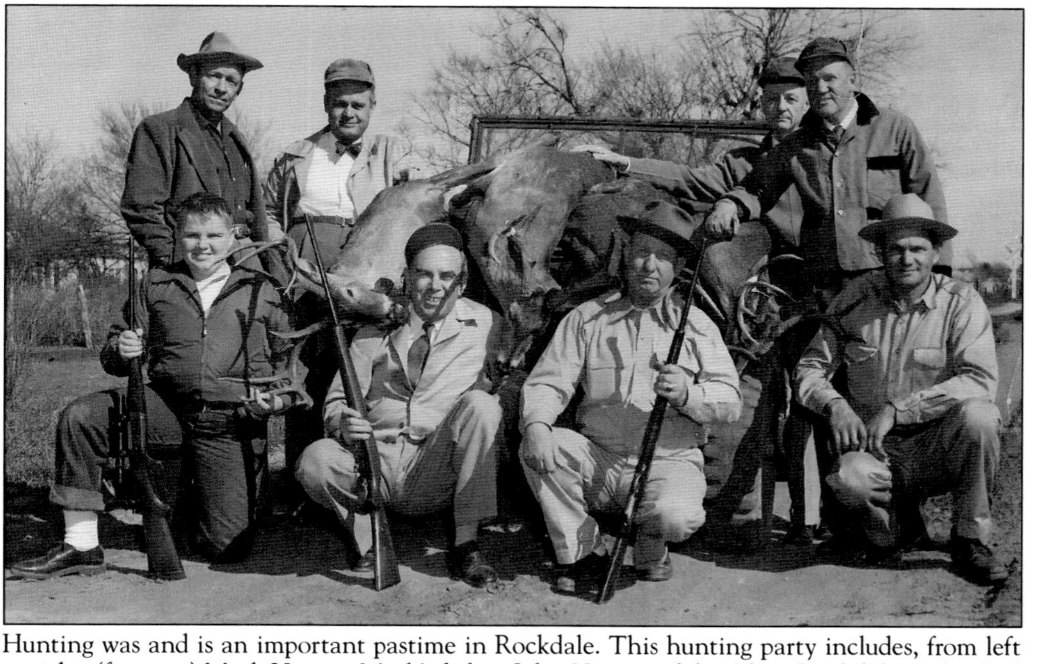

Hunting was and is an important pastime in Rockdale. This hunting party includes, from left to right, (first row) Mack Harper; Mack's father, John Harper, of the Alcoa Rockdale works; Earl Leech, shop foreman for Rockdale Pipe Yard; and Harry Timmerman, employee of H.H. Coffield of Rockdale; (second row) Murrell Camp, board of directors, Rockdale State Bank; Dr. John Richards, of the Richards Clinic; Ted Ryan, president of Rockdale State Bank; and W.P. "Red" Hogan, of Gaither Motor Company.

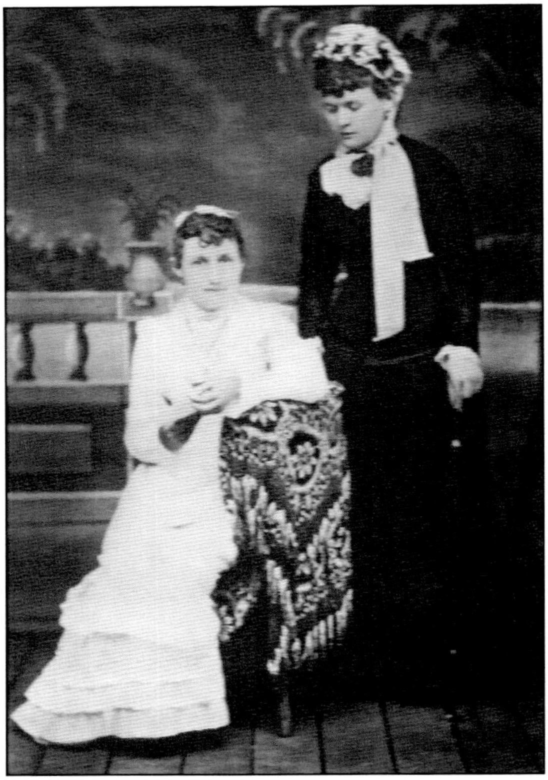

Mattie Orr Clark (seated) and Dora Orr Poole were pioneer educators in Milam County. Riding a pony to school each day, Poole taught in Bushdale. She told of being chased by wolves. (Photograph courtesy of the author.)

Rockdale had a softball team at one time. The mascot for this team is Rufus Graves (first row, center) of Sharp. (Photograph courtesy of Eugenia Wolf Newton.)

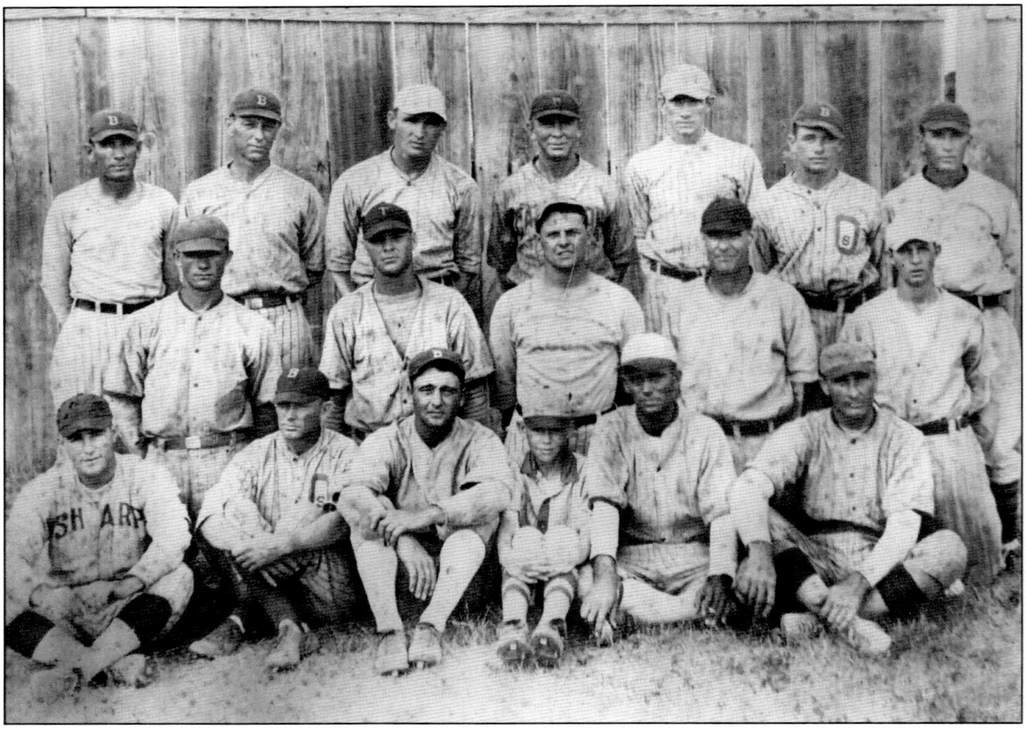

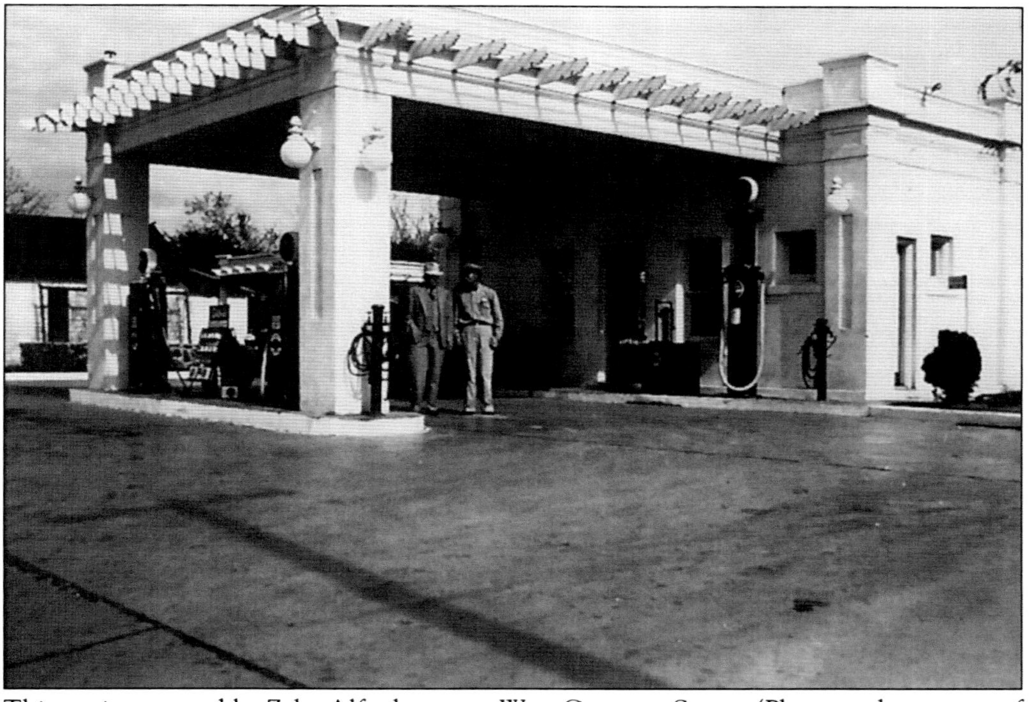

This station, owned by Zeke Alford, was on West Cameron Street. (Photograph courtesy of Eugenia Wolf Newton.)

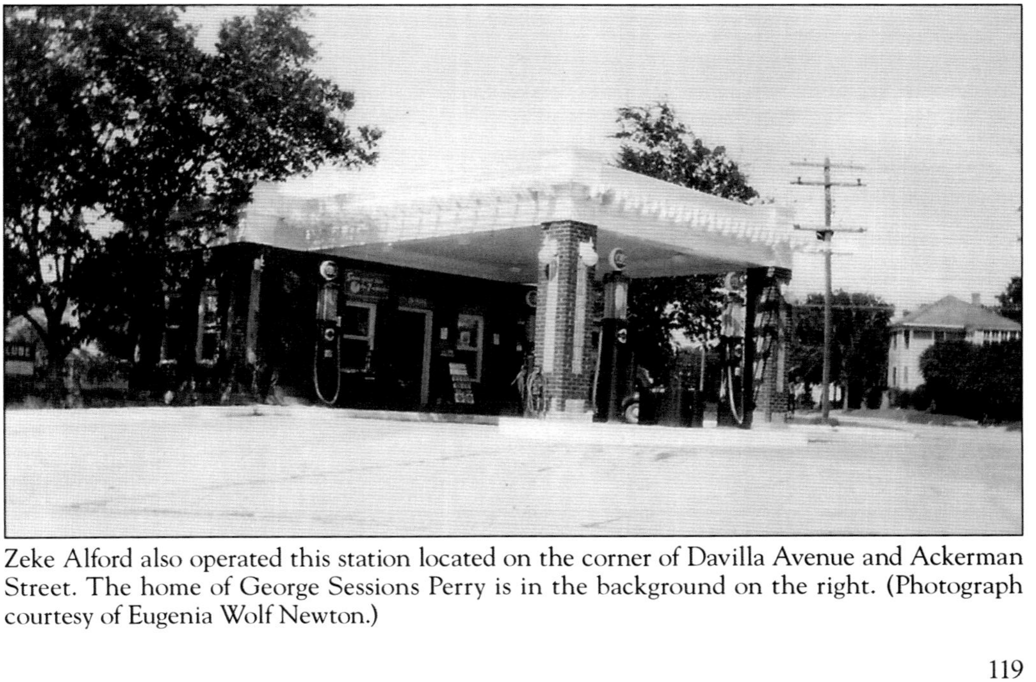

Zeke Alford also operated this station located on the corner of Davilla Avenue and Ackerman Street. The home of George Sessions Perry is in the background on the right. (Photograph courtesy of Eugenia Wolf Newton.)

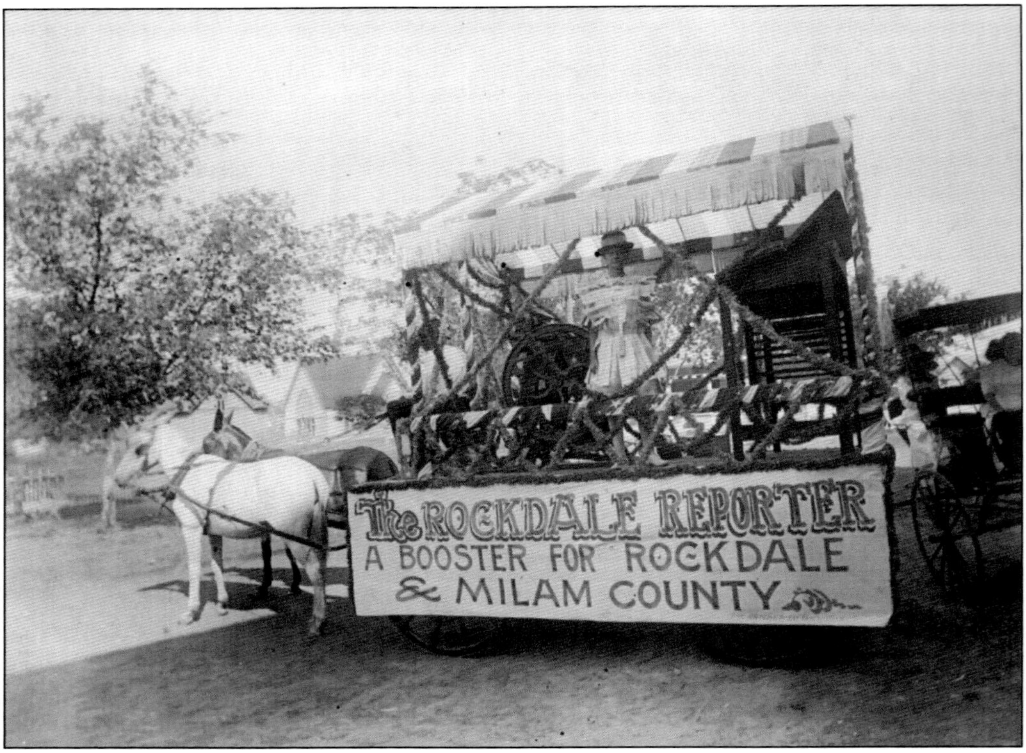

This float was entered into the fair parade by the *Reporter* when it was owned by John Esten Cooke. Agnes Cooke, daughter of Mr. and Mrs. John Esten Cooke, was the queen. Her dress was made of newspapers. (Photograph courtesy of *Rockdale Reporter.*)

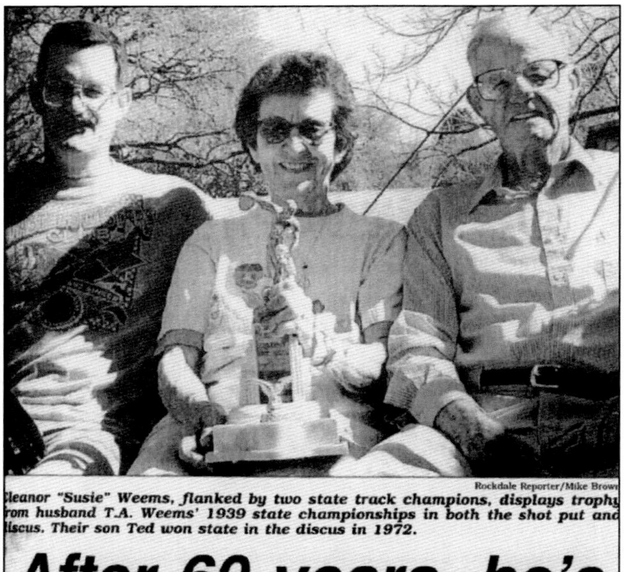

Rockdale Reporter/Mike Brow

leanor "Susie" Weems, flanked by two state track champions, displays troph rom husband T.A. Weems' 1939 state championships in both the shot put an iscus. Their son Ted won state in the discus in 1972.

After 60 years, he's still the No. 1 Tiger

Y MIKE BROWN
porter Editor

It's been more than 50 years since T. A. eems has picked up a football competitively

letic career at the 1939 state track meet in Austin by winning the shot put and discus and plac- ing fourth in the javelin. "Rockdale" finished second in the state meet's team competition.

Eleanor Weems sits between her son Ted (left) and her husband, T.A., as they celebrate the 60th anniversary of T.A. Weems's high school graduation. Weems was a noted athlete at Rockdale High School. (Photograph courtesy of Eleanor Weems.)

Thomas Barkley, MD, practiced medicine in Rockdale for many years, beginning his practice in 1912. He was a 32nd Degree Mason and died in 1965. (Photograph courtesy of *Rockdale Reporter.*)

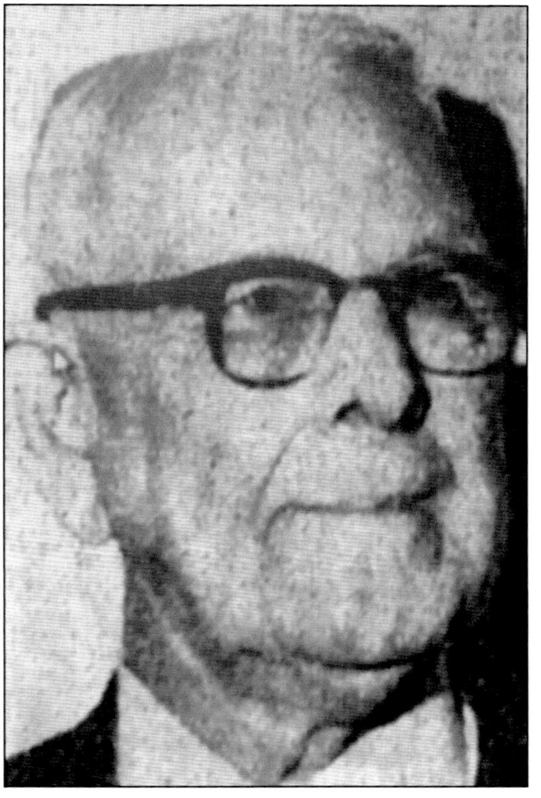

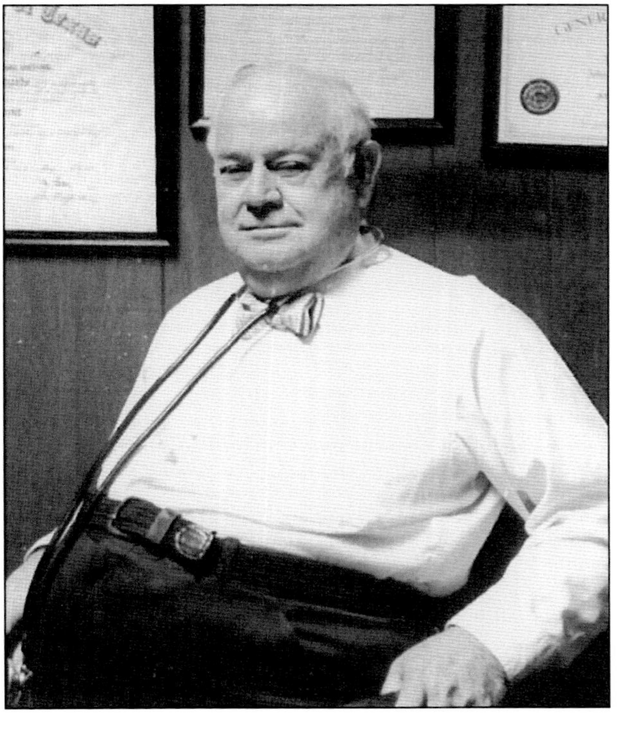

John Richards, MD, a Rockdale native, practiced medicine here for many years. Richards Memorial Hospital is named in his honor. (Photograph courtesy of *Rockdale Reporter.*)

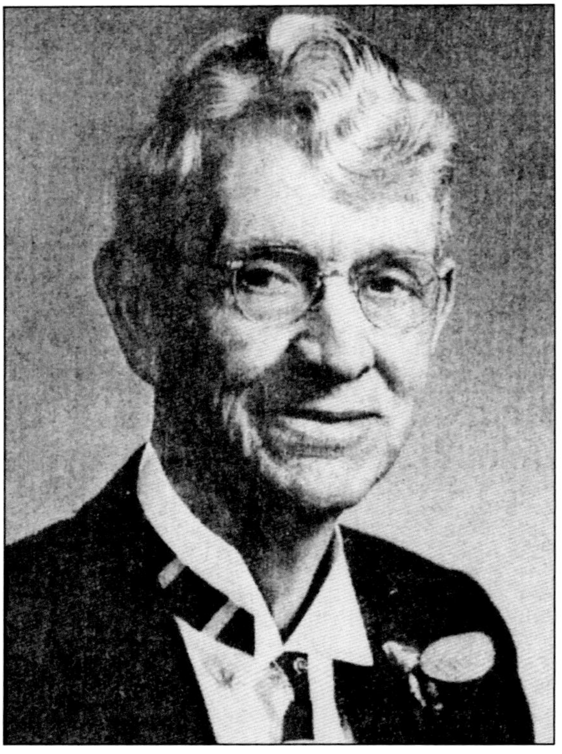

E.A. Camp had every reason to be called "Mr. Rockdale." He practiced law for 58 years and was a friend and father figure to many people in town. Once, he was elected mayor despite the fact that he did not run and his name was not on the ballot. Camp was a legend in his town because of the deep compassion he had for his neighbors. (Photograph courtesy of *Rockdale Reporter.*)

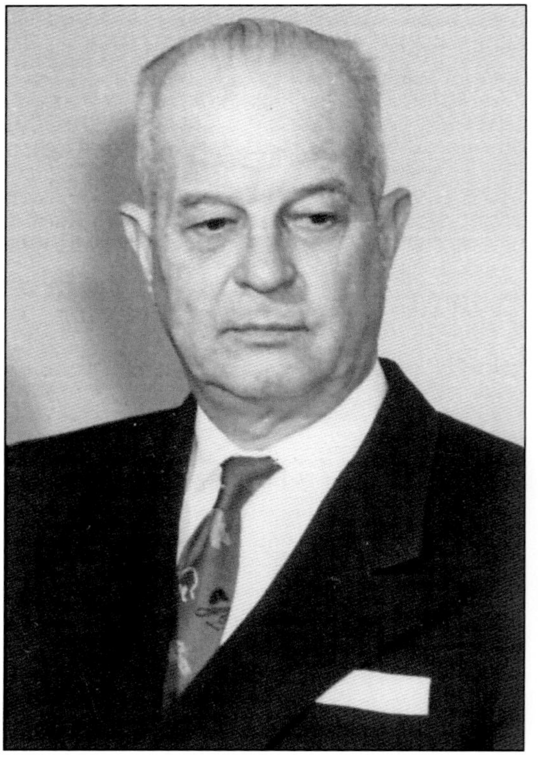

H.H. Coffield was a native of Rockdale. He was a poor boy from a small town, but his wise investments in real estate and mineral rights made him a rich man. At the time of his death in 1979, his estate was estimated to be worth $100 million. He was also the longtime chairman of the prison board. (Photograph courtesy of *Rockdale Reporter.*)

This photograph is from a postcard that shows both the Methodist and Baptist churches in Rockdale. Not many people saw the Baptist church like this, as this steeple was later removed and the building was painted white. The Methodist church is not shown in this image. (Photograph courtesy of Joy Graham.)

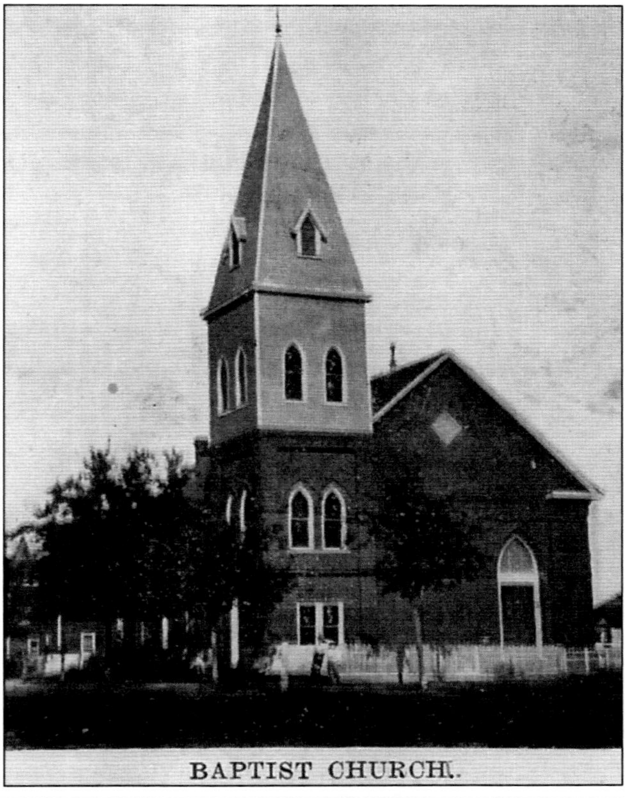

Dan Kubiak, pictured here with future president George W. Bush when Bush was governor of Texas, was an educator and businessman who served as a Democratic member of the Texas House of Representatives from 1969 to 1983 and from 1991 until his death in 1998. (Photograph courtesy of Milam County Historical Museum.)

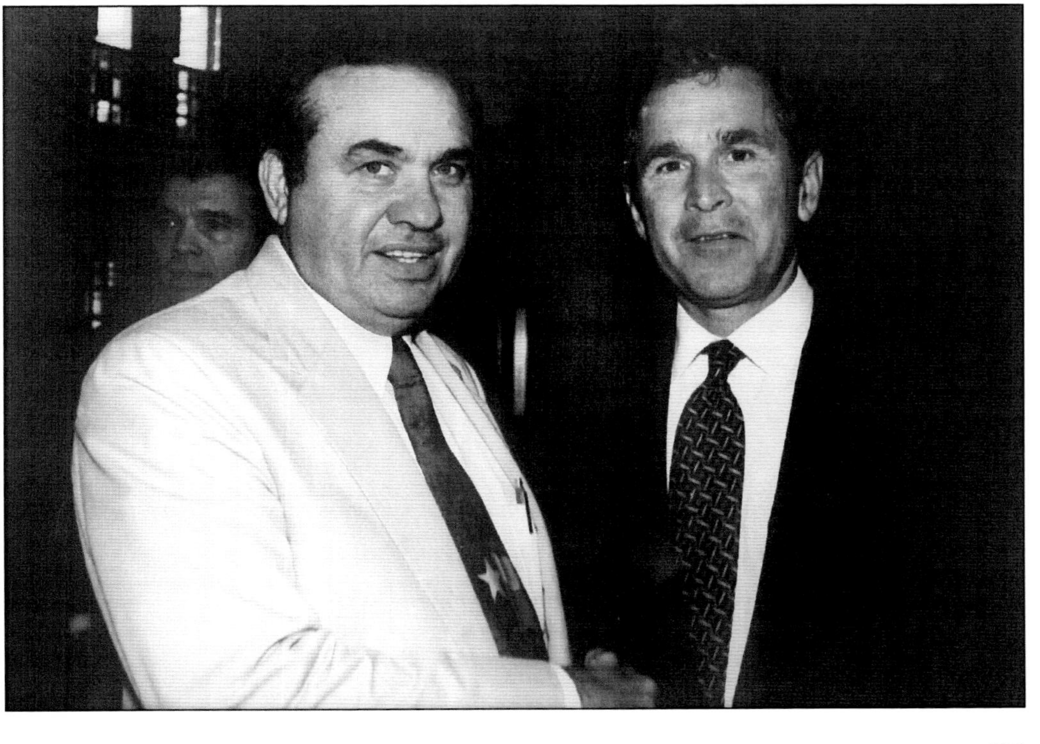

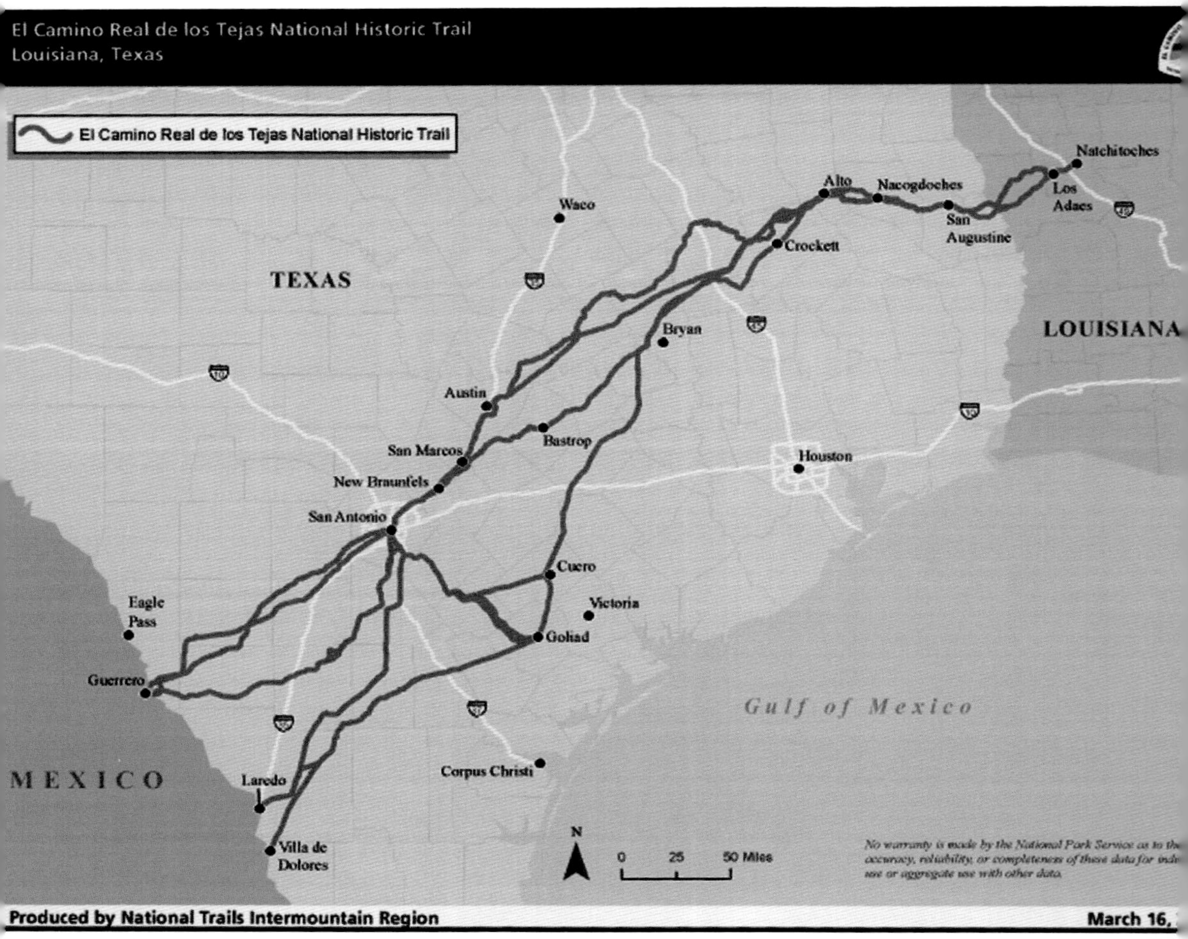

This is a map of El Camino Real de los Tejas, the first national trail designated in Texas by the US Congress. The trail is a long one, moving across Texas from Mexico to Louisiana. Woven into the history of this trail is the history of the men, women, and children who traveled it as Texas expanded. (Map courtesy of National Park Service.)

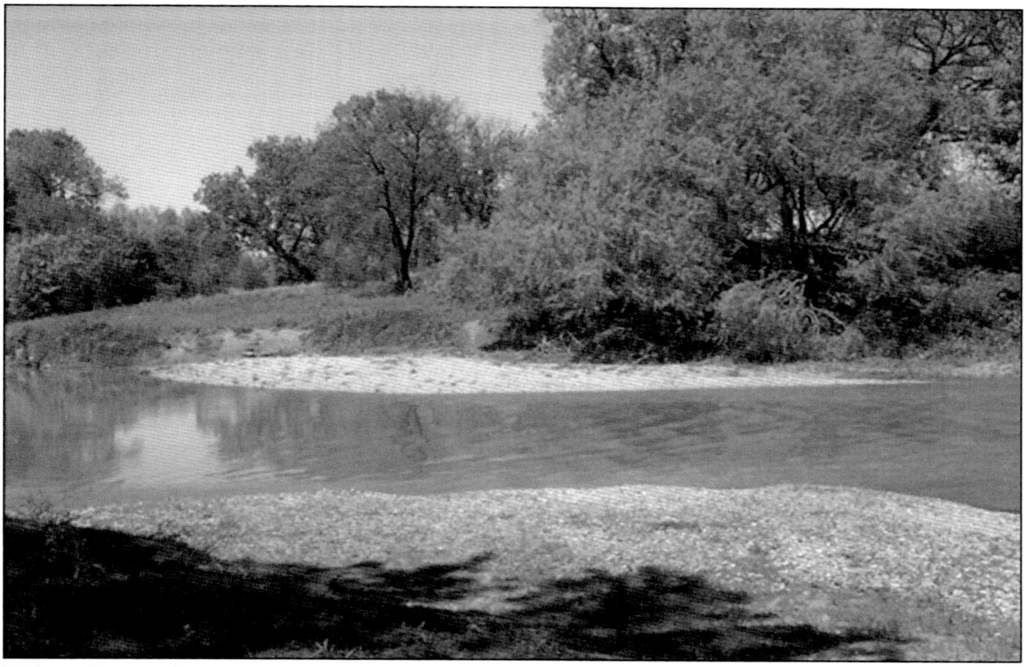

Milam County has six sites of significance on the trail. Shown here is the Apache Pass river crossing, which has been in use for many years. Apaches used this crossing long before white settlers did. This river crossing and the land surrounding it now belongs to the Kit Worley family. (Photograph courtesy of the author.)

The land around Apache Pass is owned by the Kit Worley family today, but for many years, it was the home of the Lipan Apaches and other Indian tribes. When Apache Pass was designated as a recreational facility, Apache chief Standing Bear came to bless the land. Three missions and a presidio were built on land around Apache Pass. (Photograph courtesy of the author.)

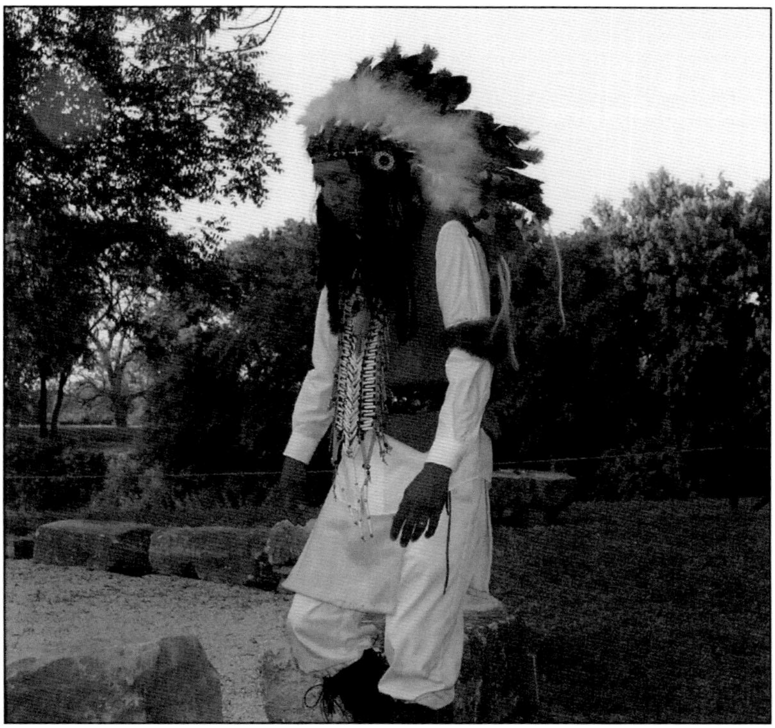

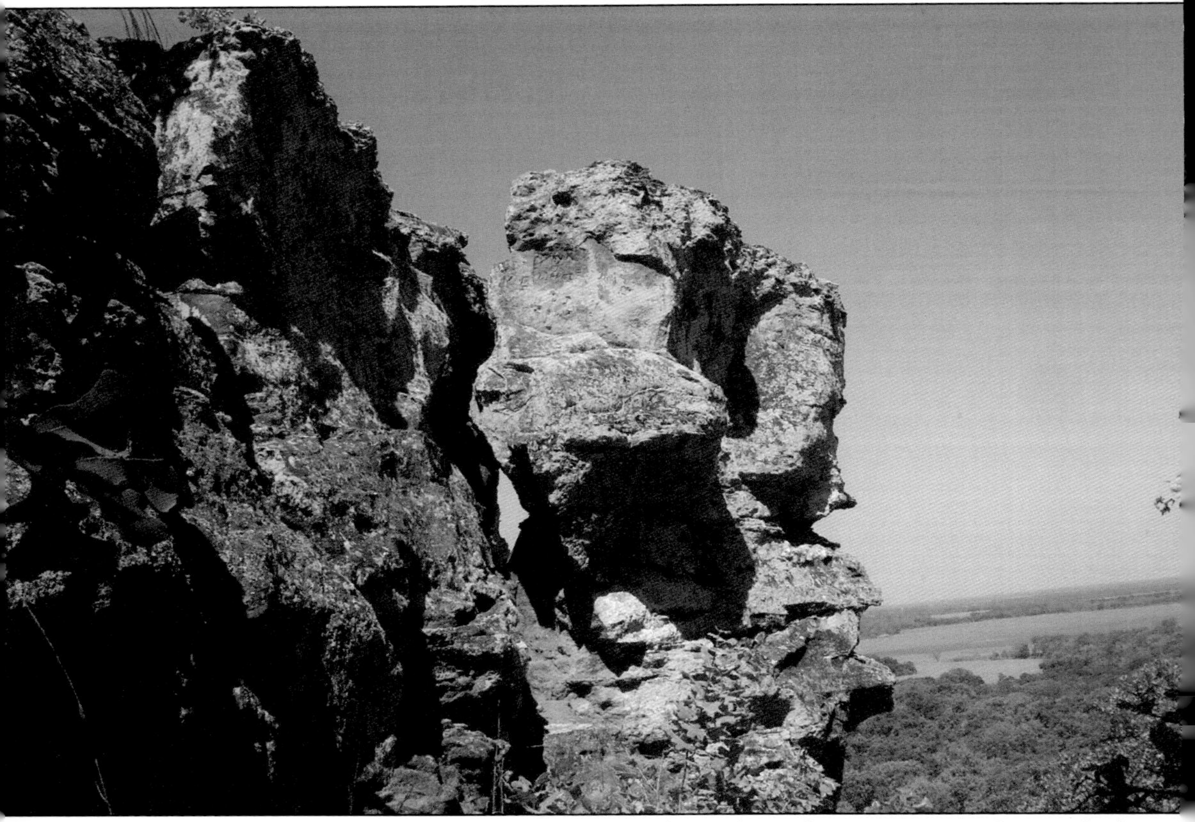

Another area of significance is Sugarloaf Mountain, located in Milam County near Gause, which is the ancestral home of the Tonkawa Indians and is of great importance to them. Today, it is privately owned. (Photograph courtesy of the author.)

Bibliography

Batte, Lelia M. *History of Milam County, Texas*. San Antonio: The Naylor Company, 1956.
Brown, Mike. Decade to the 20th Century. Various articles. *Rockdale Reporter*, 1990–2000.
Lengert, Margaret. *History of Milam County, Texas*. Master's thesis, University of Texas at Austin, 1949.
Marshall, Ida Jo, ed. *Rockdale Centennial*. Rockdale, TX: *Rockdale Reporter*, 1974.
Rinn, Pearl Harris. Unpublished historical notes on Rockdale, Texas. Private collection.